WILLIAM SHAKESPEARE wa____ _____ Stratford-upon-Avon in April, 156_ ____ _____ _____onally celebrated on April 23. T___ ____ ____ ____ __om surviving documents, _ ____ ____ ____. children born to John Sha___. ____ ____ __n _f __me standing in his community. William probably went to the King's New School in Stratford, but he had no university education. In November 1582, at the age of eighteen, he married Anne Hathaway, eight years his senior, who was pregnant with their first child, Susanna. She was born on May 26, 1583. Twins, a boy, Hamnet (who would die at age eleven), and a girl, Judith, were born in 1585. By 1592 Shakespeare had gone to London, working as an actor and already known as a playwright. A rival dramatist, Robert Greene, referred to him as "an upstart crow, beautified with our feathers." Shakespeare became a principal shareholder and playwright of the successful acting troupe the Lord Chamberlain's men (later, under James I, called the King's men). In 1599 the Lord Chamberlain's men built and occupied the Globe Theatre in Southwark near the Thames River. Here many of Shakespeare's plays were performed by the most famous actors of his time, including Richard Burbage, Will Kempe, and Robert Armin. In addition to his 37 plays, Shakespeare had a hand in others, including *Sir Thomas More* and *The Two Noble Kinsmen*, and he wrote poems, including *Venus and Adonis* and *The Rape of Lucrece*. His 154 sonnets were published, probably without his authorization, in 1609. In 1611 or 1612 he gave up his lodgings in London and devoted more and more of his time to retirement in Stratford, though he continued writing such plays as *The Tempest* and *Henry VIII* until about 1613. He died on April 23, 1616, and was buried in Holy Trinity Church, Stratford. No collected edition of his plays was published during his lifetime, but in 1623 two members of his acting company, John Heminges and Henry Condell, published the great collection now called the First Folio.

**Bantam Shakespeare
The Complete Works—29 Volumes
Edited by David Bevington
With forewords by Joseph Papp on the plays**

The Poems: Venus and Adonis, The Rape of Lucrece, The
Phoenix and Turtle, A Lover's Complaint,
the Sonnets

Antony and Cleopatra	*The Merchant of Venice*
As You Like It	*A Midsummer Night's Dream*
The Comedy of Errors	*Much Ado about Nothing*
Hamlet	*Othello*
Henry IV, Part One	*Richard II*
Henry IV, Part Two	*Richard III*
Henry V	*Romeo and Juliet*
Julius Caesar	*The Taming of the Shrew*
King Lear	*The Tempest*
Macbeth	*Twelfth Night*

Together in one volume:

Henry VI, Parts One, Two, and Three
King John and Henry VIII
*Measure for Measure, All's Well that Ends Well, and
Troilus and Cressida*
Three Early Comedies: Love's Labor's Lost, The Two
Gentlemen of Verona, The Merry
Wives of Windsor
Three Classical Tragedies: Titus Andronicus, Timon
of Athens, Coriolanus
The Late Romances: Pericles, Cymbeline, The Winter's
Tale, The Tempest

Two collections:

Four Comedies: The Taming of the Shrew, A Midsummer
Night's Dream, The Merchant of Venice,
Twelfth Night
Four Tragedies: Hamlet, Othello, King Lear, Macbeth

William Shakespeare

RICHARD III

Edited by
David Bevington

**David Scott Kastan,
James Hammersmith,
and Robert Kean Turner,
Associate Editors**

**With a Foreword by
Joseph Papp**

BANTAM BOOKS
TORONTO / NEW YORK / LONDON / SYDNEY / AUCKLAND

RICHARD III

*A Bantam Book / published by arrangement
with Scott, Foresman and Company*

PRINTING HISTORY
Scott, Foresman edition published / January 1980
*Bantam edition, with newly edited text and substantially revised,
edited, and amplified notes, introductions, and other
materials, published / February 1988*
*Valuable advice on staging matters has been
provided by Richard Hosley.*
Collations checked by Eric Rasmussen.
Additional editorial assistance by Claire McEachern.

Library of Congress Cataloging-in-Publication Data

Shakespeare, William, 1564–1616.
  [King Richard III]
    Richard III / William Shakespeare; edited by David Bevington;
  David Scott Kastan, James Hammersmith, and Robert Kean Turner,
  associate editors; with a foreword by Joseph Papp.
      p.   cm.—(A Bantam classic)
    Bibliography: p.
    ISBN 0-553-21304-0 (pbk.)
    1. Richard III, King of England, 1452–1485—Drama.   I. Bevington,
  David M.   II. Title.   III. Title: Richard the Third.
  PR2821.A2B48   1988
  822.3'3—dc19   87–23197
                                                              CIP

Published simultaneously in the United States and Canada

PRINTED IN THE UNITED STATES OF AMERICA

O   0 9 8 7 6 5 4 3 2 1

Contents

Foreword   xi

Introduction   xxi

Richard III
   in Performance   xxix

The Playhouse   xxxviii

RICHARD III   1

Date and Text   147

Textual Notes   149

Shakespeare's Sources   153

Further Reading   185

Memorable Lines   189

Foreword

It's hard to imagine, but Shakespeare wrote all of his plays with a quill pen, a goose feather whose hard end had to be sharpened frequently. How many times did he scrape the dull end to a point with his knife, dip it into the inkwell, and bring up, dripping wet, those wonderful words and ideas that are known all over the world?

In the age of word processors, typewriters, and ballpoint pens, we have almost forgotten the meaning of the word "blot." Yet when I went to school, in the 1930s, my classmates and I knew all too well what an inkblot from the metal-tipped pens we used would do to a nice clean page of a test paper, and we groaned whenever a splotch fell across the sheet. Most of us finished the school day with ink-stained fingers; those who were less careful also went home with ink-stained shirts, which were almost impossible to get clean.

When I think about how long it took me to write the simplest composition with a metal-tipped pen and ink, I can only marvel at how many plays Shakespeare scratched out with his goose-feather quill pen, year after year. Imagine him walking down one of the narrow cobblestoned streets of London, or perhaps drinking a pint of beer in his local alehouse. Suddenly his mind catches fire with an idea, or a sentence, or a previously elusive phrase. He is burning with impatience to write it down—but because he doesn't have a ballpoint pen or even a pencil in his pocket, he has to keep the idea in his head until he can get to his quill and parchment.

He rushes back to his lodgings on Silver Street, ignoring the vendors hawking brooms, the coaches clattering by, the piteous wails of beggars and prisoners. Bounding up the stairs, he snatches his quill and starts to write furiously, not even bothering to light a candle against the dusk. "To be, or not to be," he scrawls, "that is the—." But the quill point has gone dull, the letters have fattened out illegibly, and in the middle of writing one of the most famous passages in the history of dramatic literature, Shakespeare has to stop to sharpen his pen:

Taking a deep breath, he lights a candle now that it' dark, sits down, and begins again. By the time the candl has burned out and the noisy apprentices of his Frenc Huguenot landlord have quieted down, Shakespeare ha finished Act 3 of *Hamlet* with scarcely a blot.

Early the next morning, he hurries through the fog of London summer morning to the rooms of his colleagu Richard Burbage, the actor for whom the role of Hamlet i being written. He finds Burbage asleep and snoring loudly sprawled across his straw mattress. Not only had the acto performed in *Henry V* the previous afternoon, but he had then gone out carousing all night with some friends wh had come to the performance.

Shakespeare shakes his friend awake, until, bleary-eyed Burbage sits up in his bed. "Dammit, Will," he grumbles "can't you let an honest man sleep?" But the playwright his eyes shining and the words tumbling out of his mouth says, "Shut up and listen—tell me what you think of *this*!

He begins to read to the still half-asleep Burbage, pacing around the room as he speaks. ". . . Whether 'tis nobler in the mind to suffer the slings and arrows of outrageous fortune—"

Burbage interrupts, suddenly wide awake, "That's excel lent, very good, 'the slings and arrows of outrageous for tune,' yes, I think it will work quite well. . . ." He takes the parchment from Shakespeare and murmurs the lines to himself, slowly at first but with growing excitement.

The sun is just coming up, and the words of one of Shake speare's most famous soliloquies are being uttered for the first time by the first actor ever to bring Hamlet to life. I must have been an exhilarating moment.

Shakespeare wrote most of his plays to be performed live by the actor Richard Burbage and the rest of the Lord Chamberlain's men (later the King's men). Today, however, our first encounter with the plays is usually in the form of the printed word. And there is no question that reading Shakespeare for the first time isn't easy. His plays aren't comic books or magazines or the dime-store detective nov els I read when I was young. A lot of his sentences are com plex. Many of his words are no longer used in our everyday speech. His profound thoughts are often condensed into poetry, which is not as straightforward as prose.

Yet when you hear the words spoken aloud, a lot of the language may strike you as unexpectedly modern. For Shakespeare's plays, like any dramatic work, weren't really meant to be read; they were meant to be spoken, seen, and performed. It's amazing how lines that are so troublesome in print can flow so naturally and easily when spoken.

I think it is precisely this music that first fascinated me. When I was growing up, Shakespeare was a stranger to me. I had no particular interest in him, for I was from a different cultural tradition. It never occurred to me that his plays might be more than just something to "get through" in school, like science or math or the physical education requirement we had to fulfill. My passions then were movies, radio, and vaudeville—certainly not Elizabethan drama.

I was, however, fascinated by words and language. Because I grew up in a home where Yiddish was spoken, and English was only a second language, I was acutely sensitive to the musical sounds of different languages and had an ear for lilt and cadence and rhythm in the spoken word. And so I loved reciting poems and speeches even as a very young child. In first grade I learned lots of short nature verses— "Who has seen the wind?," one of them began. My first foray into drama was playing the role of Scrooge in Charles Dickens's *A Christmas Carol* when I was eight years old. I liked summoning all the scorn and coldness I possessed and putting them into the words, "Bah, humbug!"

From there I moved on to longer and more famous poems and other works by writers of the 1930s. Then, in junior high school, I made my first acquaintance with Shakespeare through his play *Julius Caesar*. Our teacher, Miss McKay, assigned the class a passage to memorize from the opening scene of the play, the one that begins "Wherefore rejoice? What conquest brings he home?" The passage seemed so wonderfully theatrical and alive to me, and the experience of memorizing and reciting it was so much fun, that I went on to memorize another speech from the play on my own.

I chose Mark Antony's address to the crowd in Act 3,

scene 2, which struck me then as incredibly high drama. Even today, when I speak the words, I feel the same thrill I did that first time. There is the strong and athletic Antony descending from the raised pulpit where he has been speaking, right into the midst of a crowded Roman square. Holding the torn and bloody cloak of the murdered Julius Caesar in his hand, he begins to speak to the people of Rome:

> If you have tears, prepare to shed them now.
> You all do know this mantle. I remember
> The first time ever Caesar put it on;
> 'Twas on a summer's evening in his tent,
> That day he overcame the Nervii.
> Look, in this place ran Cassius' dagger through.
> See what a rent the envious Casca made.
> Through this the well-belovèd Brutus stabbed,
> And as he plucked his cursèd steel away,
> Mark how the blood of Caesar followed it,
> As rushing out of doors to be resolved
> If Brutus so unkindly knocked or no;
> For Brutus, as you know, was Caesar's angel.
> Judge, O you gods, how dearly Caesar loved him!
> This was the most unkindest cut of all . . .

I'm not sure now that I even knew Shakespeare had written a lot of other plays, or that he was considered "timeless," "universal," or "classic"—but I knew a good speech when I heard one, and I found the splendid rhythms of Antony's rhetoric as exciting as anything I'd ever come across.

Fifty years later, I still feel that way. Hearing good actors speak Shakespeare gracefully and naturally is a wonderful experience, unlike any other I know. There's a satisfying fullness to the spoken word that the printed page just can't convey. This is why seeing the plays of Shakespeare performed live in a theater is the best way to appreciate them. If you can't do that, listening to sound recordings or watching film versions of the plays is the next best thing.

But if you do start with the printed word, use the play as a script. Be an actor yourself and say the lines out loud. Don't worry too much at first about words you don't immediately understand. Look them up in the footnotes or a dictionary, but don't spend too much time on this. It is more profitable (and fun) to get the sense of a passage and sing it out. Speak naturally, almost as if you were talking to a friend, but be sure to enunciate the words properly. You'll be surprised at how much you understand simply by speaking the speech "trippingly on the tongue," as Hamlet advises the Players.

You might start, as I once did, with a speech from *Julius Caesar*, in which the tribune (city official) Marullus scolds the commoners for transferring their loyalties so quickly from the defeated and murdered general Pompey to the newly victorious Julius Caesar:

> Wherefore rejoice? What conquest brings he home?
> What tributaries follow him to Rome
> To grace in captive bonds his chariot wheels?
> You blocks, you stones, you worse than senseless things!
> O you hard hearts, you cruel men of Rome,
> Knew you not Pompey? Many a time and oft
> Have you climbed up to walls and battlements,
> To towers and windows, yea, to chimney tops,
> Your infants in your arms, and there have sat
> The livelong day, with patient expectation,
> To see great Pompey pass the streets of Rome.

With the exception of one or two words like "wherefore" (which means "why," not "where"), "tributaries" (which means "captives"), and "patient expectation" (which means patient waiting), the meaning and emotions of this speech can be easily understood.

From here you can go on to dialogues or other more challenging scenes. Although you may stumble over unaccustomed phrases or unfamiliar words at first, and even fall flat when you're crossing some particularly rocky passages, pick yourself up and stay with it. Remember that it takes time to feel at home with anything new. Soon you'll come to recognize Shakespeare's unique sense of humor and way of saying things as easily as you recognize a friend's laughter.

And then it will just be a matter of choosing which one of Shakespeare's plays you want to tackle next. As a true fan of his, you'll find that you're constantly learning from his plays. It's a journey of discovery that you can continue for the rest of your life. For no matter how many times you read or see a particular play, there will always be something new there that you won't have noticed before.

Why do so many thousands of people get hooked on Shakespeare and develop a habit that lasts a lifetime? What can he really say to us today, in a world filled with inventions and problems he never could have imagined? And how do you get past his special language and difficult sentence structure to understand him?

The best way to answer these questions is to go see a live production. You might not know much about Shakespeare, or much about the theater, but when you watch actors performing one of his plays on the stage, it will soon become clear to you why people get so excited about a playwright who lived hundreds of years ago.

For the story—what's happening in the play—is the most accessible part of Shakespeare. In *A Midsummer Night's Dream*, for example, you can immediately understand the situation: a girl is chasing a guy who's chasing a girl who's chasing another guy. No wonder *A Midsummer Night's Dream* is one of the most popular of Shakespeare's plays: it's about one of the world's most popular pastimes—falling in love.

But the course of true love never did run smooth, as the young suitor Lysander says. Often in Shakespeare's comedies the girl whom the guy loves doesn't love him back, or she loves him but he loves someone else. In *The Two Gentlemen of Verona*, Julia loves Proteus, Proteus loves Sylvia, and Sylvia loves Valentine, who is Proteus's best friend. In the end, of course, true love prevails, but not without lots of complications along the way.

For in all of his plays—comedies, histories, and tragedies—Shakespeare is showing you human nature. His characters act and react in the most extraordinary ways—and sometimes in the most incomprehensible ways. People are always trying to find motivations for what a character does. They ask, "Why does Iago want to destroy Othello?"

The answer, to me, is very simple—because that's the way Iago is. That's just his nature. Shakespeare doesn't explain his characters; he sets them in motion—and away they go. He doesn't worry about whether they're likable or not. He's interested in interesting people, and his most fascinating characters are those who are unpredictable. If you lean back in your chair early on in one of his plays, thinking you've figured out what Iago or Shylock (in *The Merchant of Venice*) is up to, don't be too sure—because that great judge of human nature, Shakespeare, will surprise you every time.

He is just as wily in the way he structures a play. In *Macbeth*, a comic scene is suddenly introduced just after the bloodiest and most treacherous slaughter imaginable, of a guest and king by his host and subject, when in comes a drunk porter who has to go to the bathroom. Shakespeare is tickling your emotions by bringing a stand-up comic on-stage right on the heels of a savage murder.

It has taken me thirty years to understand even some of these things, and so I'm not suggesting that Shakespeare is immediately understandable. I've gotten to know him not through theory but through practice, the practice of the *living* Shakespeare—the playwright of the theater.

Of course the plays are a great achievement of dramatic literature, and they should be studied and analyzed in schools and universities. But you must always remember, when reading all the words *about* the playwright and his plays, that *Shakespeare's* words came first and that in the end there is nothing greater than a single actor on the stage speaking the lines of Shakespeare.

Everything important that I know about Shakespeare comes from the practical business of producing and directing his plays in the theater. The task of classifying, criticizing, and editing Shakespeare's printed works I happily leave to others. For me, his plays really do live on the stage, not on the page. That is what he wrote them for and that is how they are best appreciated.

Although Shakespeare lived and wrote hundreds of years ago, his name rolls off my tongue as if he were my brother. As a producer and director, I feel that there is a professional relationship between us that spans the centuries. As a human being, I feel that Shakespeare has enriched my understanding of life immeasurably. I hope you'll let him do the same for you.

❧

Richard III is the best advertisement I know of for a life devoted to villainy. Of course, villains are always attractive—witness the popularity of gangster movies in this country for so many years. We want to see them done in, but we also love watching them along the way as they plan and execute their dastardly crimes. This is what's so much fun about Richard III—he is so full of action and energy, as he darts from one scheme to another with diabolical glee, that it's impossible not to enjoy him.

There are two scenes in particular where Richard establishes himself as one of the greatest stage personalities of all time. The first is that incredible scene in Act 1 where he woos Anne (whose husband, the Prince of Wales, was killed by Richard) as she mourns her dead father-in-law, Henry VI, also slain by Richard. It's a powerfully dramatic scene, one which can easily be read aloud by two people. The cross fire of Richard's and Anne's language is fast and furious, as they play off one another's words:

> ANNE
> O, wonderful, when devils tell the truth!
>
> RICHARD
> More wonderful, when angels are so angry.
> Vouchsafe, divine perfection of a woman.
> Of these supposèd crimes to give me leave
> By circumstance but to acquit myself.
>
> ANNE
> Vouchsafe, defused infection of a man,
> Of these known evils but to give me leave
> By circumstance t' accuse thy cursèd self.

Though Anne is bitter and unyielding at first, by the end of the scene Richard has out-talked her, and he gets what he wants—her favor. We watch, spellbound and amazed as his glib tongue and smooth persuasiveness completely turn this woman around until she promises him her love, even as she stands in front of the corpse of the father-in-law whom Richard has recently killed. He is a lover indeed.

If you think that *this* is enough to establish Richard as a master of manipulation, wait until you get to the scene where he approaches Queen Elizabeth, immediately after he has had her two young sons, the innocent little princes, murdered in the Tower—a deed that the murderer Tyrrel calls "the tyrannous and bloody act. . . . The most arch deed of piteous massacre / That ever yet this land was guilty of.''

Richard insinuates himself right into the midst of their mother's grief and mourning, hellbent on gaining a political objective he considers absolutely essential to his retention of the crown—namely, the hand of her daughter in marriage. The long scene between the embittered, grief-stricken mother and the fiendishly logical King makes Richard's previous debate with Anne look like the first effort of an amateur.

His inexorable and terrifying logic becomes perfectly normal within the context of the world he has created, a world where murder is the most effective—and acceptable—means of dealing with a political problem:

> Look what is done cannot be now amended.
> Men shall deal unadvisedly sometimes,
> Which after-hours gives leisure to repent.
> If I did take the kingdom from your sons,
> To make amends I'll give it to your daughter.

In the psychologically charged atmosphere in which their encounter takes place, Richard's appeal to Elizabeth appears less irrational than it would in another setting.

This scene reveals the power of Richard's mind and the formidable intellect that endows him with the extraordinary ability to be clear and decisive; he zeroes in on the immediate problem, decides what has to be done, and then does it. Morality aside, these skills would propel him to the top of the modern corporate world today; he has raised acuity to the level of an art. If it weren't for his utter wickedness, one might almost be tempted to eulogize him at this death with the words Ophelia speaks about Hamlet: "O, what a noble mind is here o'erthrown!"

But in the end we can't really set those questions of morality aside. For Elizabeth sees past all of his well-argued rationales for this outrageous alliance to the blood-stained dagger grasped in Richard's hand. And that changes everything.

As Shakespeare pays homage to Richard's mental prowess and potential for great leadership in parts of this scene, he's also telling us to remember that Richard *is* evil. This is important because as a stage character, Richard is so attractive, so delightfully mischievous in his wicked revelry, so irrepressibly and irresistibly murderous, that we in the audience are inclined not to take his actions seriously. And unless we take him seriously, we will miss the complexity of Shakespeare's treatment of the man and the milieu in which he operated.

Richard is such an amazing, vital character—no wonder he is a coveted role for actors. He is a superbly theatrical being, really playing the stage for all it's worth, from the moment he opens the play with, "Now is the winter of our discontent / Made glorious summer by this sun of York," to his final dramatic cry, "A horse! A horse! My kingdom for a horse!" In the midst of wiping out people as if they were mere dolls, Richard is in charge—controlling the action, directing the plot, and upstaging every other character in the play with his unforgettable theatrics.

JOSEPH PAPP

JOSEPH PAPP GRATEFULLY ACKNOWLEDGES THE HELP OF ELIZABETH KIRKLAND IN PREPARING THIS FOREWORD.

RICHARD III

Introduction

Richard III begins where *3 Henry VI* left off, and completes the action of the four-play series begun with *1 Henry VI*. On the basis of its Senecan style, the play appears to have been written soon after its predecessors, some time between 1591 and 1594. Richard's evil character, which had already begun to emerge in the last of the *Henry VI* plays, now stands fully revealed. His opening soliloquy depends for its ironically mocking effect on our familiarity with recent events. An end to the Yorkist-Lancastrian hostilities has come at last; but with his genius for evil, Richard looks upon a time of peace with only envy and contempt. His intense self-assertion and his aggressive energy must find new employment. No peace can withstand the machinations of this consummate deceiver, who gave his nephew Edward the kiss of Judas during the Yorkist triumph concluding *3 Henry VI*.

Richard dominates the play of *Richard III* to an extraordinary extent. He is the central character that the earlier plays, especially *3 Henry VI*, lacked. He is onstage almost continuously and, until the end, completely manipulates the actions of others. As chief actor and stage manager in his own drama, Richard chortlingly takes the audience into his confidence. His revelation of his plotting serves as a structural device for the play even as it manipulates and directs the audience's attention; we know in advance that Clarence's turn is next, that Richard will then attempt to woo the Lady Anne, and so forth. The dramatic excitement we experience in watching the action is not that of wondering what will happen next but that of seeing how cleverly the preannounced plans will be executed. Not until the rise of Richmond near the end of the play does Richard meet effective opposition, though quite early the voice of the deposed Queen Margaret is raised against him (1.3.117–143, 215–293). Margaret's curses upon the enemies of the Lancastrian House and her warning to Buckingham also serve as a structural device preparing us for what will happen, and they complement Richard's gloating and sardonic tone by striking a bitter and ominous note. Again the dramatic interest lies in the way the fates of the characters come upon them; these persons fall victim to Richard's machinations, and yet their downfalls also fulfill a larger, seemingly providential scheme of retribution for injustice and wickedness.

Richard's ability as an actor is seemingly limitless. He has already boasted, in *3 Henry VI*, that he can deceive more slyly than Ulysses, Sinon, or Machiavelli, and put on more false shapes than Proteus. To us as audience he is cynically candid and boastful, setting us up in advance to watch his unbelievable performances. In an instant, before our eyes, he is the concerned younger brother of Clarence, sharing a hatred of Queen Elizabeth and her kindred; or he is the jocular uncle of the little princes; or he is the pious recluse studying divinity with his clerical teachers, reluctant to accept the responsibilities of state that are thrust upon him by his importunate subjects (that is to say, by Catesby and Buckingham, who are also actors in this staged scene). Yet none of these bravura performances can match the wooing of the Lady Anne.

Is the wooing of the Lady Anne credible? One key to credibility must lie in superb acting. The actor who plays Richard must transform himself from the gloating villain we know in soliloquy to the grief-stricken lover. Richard's argument is, after all, speciously plausible: that he has killed Anne's husband and father-in-law out of desperate love for her. The argument appeals to vanity, that most fatal of human weaknesses. What power Anne suddenly appears to have over Richard! She can spare his life, or kill him. Richard shrewdly judges her as one not able to kill, and so risks offering her his sword. As stage manager, he has altered her role from that of sincere mourner to the stereotype of the proud woman worshiped by her groveling servant in love. With superb irony, Richard has inverted the appearance and the reality of control in this struggle between man and woman. He wins mastery by flattering her that only she can spare his miserable life. The implausibility of what Richard has achieved merely illustrates his thesis that ordinary men and women can be made to believe anything, and betray their own best instincts, by "the plain devil and dissembling looks" (1.2.239). Richard is of course devillike; his role as actor stems from that of the Vice in the morality play, brilliantly comic and sinister. Yet even the devil can prevail over his victims only when they acquiesce in evil. The devil can deceive the senses, but acceptance of evil is still an act of the perverted will. Anne is guilty, however much we can appreciate the mesmerizing power of Richard's personality. By the end of the scene she has violated everything she had held sacred.

The image of Richard as devil or Vice raises questions of motivation and of symbolic meaning. Is Richard a human character propelled toward the throne by his insatiable ambition, like Macbeth? Is there a clue to his behavior in his ugliness and misanthropy? Modern psychological criticism might well be tempted to examine Richard's childhood: by his own admission, he was born feet forward, hunchbacked, withered in one arm, and already toothed ("which plainly signified / That I should snarl and bite and play the dog," *3 Henry VI*, 5.6.76–77). One might argue that he compensates for his ugliness and unlovability by resolving to domineer. Feeling unwanted, he despises all men and undertakes to prove them weak and corrupt. This reading is not without merit; indeed, no matter how extraordinary Richard's behavior, he does seem plausible. He expresses a universal human penchant for cruelty and senseless domination. Yet the proposition that Richard is evil *because* he was born ugly can be logically reversed as well: he was born ugly *because* he is evil.

This concept, owing much to Renaissance notions of Platonic correspondence between outer appearances and inner qualities, is grounded on the idea of a vast struggle in the cosmos between the forces of absolute good and the forces of absolute evil, one in which every event in human life has divine meaning and cause. Richard's birth is a physical manifestation of that divine meaning. Providential destiny, having determined the need for a genius of evil at this point in English history, decrees that Richard shall be born. The teeth and hunched back merely give evidence of what is already predetermined. In the apt words of the choric Queen Margaret, Richard was "sealed in thy nativity / The slave of nature and the son of hell" (1.3.228–229). Although Richard is also plausible as a man, he is in part an emissary of the devil, and ultimately serves the righteous purpose of divine Providence in human affairs. Such a symbolic reading clarifies our impression that Richard is fundamentally unlike many of Shakespeare's human villains, such as Macbeth or King Claudius. Richard belongs instead to a special group of villains including Iago in *Othello* and Edmund in *King Lear*. Like them, Richard is driven both by human motivation and by his preexistent evil genius; he displays the "motiveless malignity" ascribed by Coleridge to Iago.

Such a reading helps explain not only Richard's delight in evil but also the necessity for so much evil and suffering in England's civil wars. This theory of history owes much to Edward Hall's *Union of the Two Noble and Illustre Families of Lancaster and York* (1542), Shakespeare's immediate source, along with Raphael Holinshed's *Chronicles* (1578), for his *Henry VI* plays. Shakespeare's treatment of Richard is ultimately indebted to Polydore Vergil's *Anglica Historia* (1534) and especially to *The History of King Richard the Third* attributed to Sir Thomas More (published 1557). This latter work, adopted in turn by Edward Hall, Richard Grafton, and Raphael Holinshed, purposefully blackens Richard's character. He becomes a study in the nature of tyranny, an object lesson to future rulers and their subjects. He is, moreover, a result of the curse placed by God on the English people for their sinful disobedience. Richard III functions as the scourge of God, destroying God's enemies until he too is destroyed for his own colossal evil.

Henry VII, in this Tudor explanation, becomes God's minister chosen to destroy the scourge and thereafter to fulfill a new and happy covenant between God and man. Although modern historians more impartially regard the defeat of Richard III at Bosworth Field in 1485 as a political overthrow not unlike Henry IV's overthrow of Richard II, and stress that Richard III was a talented administrator guilty of no worse political crimes than those of his more fortunate successor, Tudor Englishmen could not have found meaning in such a neutral interpretation. History had to reveal God's intention. Henry VII's accession could not be viewed as parallel to the rebellion of Henry IV against Richard II, but was seen as a divinely sanctioned deliverance of the English nation, a blessing continued in the reign of Elizabeth I. Accordingly, the Tudor myth stressed the tyrannical nature of Richard III's seizure of power and conversely minimized the political element in

Henry VII's takeover. Bosworth Field was seen as an act of God, a rising up of some irresistible force, and under no circumstances as a precedent for future rebellion.

In the *Henry VI* plays, Shakespeare puts considerable distance between himself and the Tudor orthodox reading of history, allowing the grim realities of civil war to speak for themselves. In *Richard III*, however, the pattern shown in the chronicles provides Shakespeare with an essential structural device. Viewing the civil wars in retrospect, *Richard III* perhaps discovers a cohesive sense in which England's suffering has fulfilled a necessary plan of fall from innocence leading through sin and penitence to regeneration. Evil is seen at last as something through which good triumphs, in English history as in the story of man's fall from grace.

This providential scheme imposes a double irony on *Richard III*. In the short run, Richard appears to be complete master over his victims. "Your imprisonment shall not be long," Richard assures his brother Clarence. "I will deliver you, or else lie for you" (1.1.114–115). The audience, already let in on the secret, can shiver at the grisly humor of these double entendres. Clarence will indeed soon be delivered—to his death. Richard's henchmen are fond of such jokes too. When Lord Hastings is on his way to the Tower, from which he will never return, and announces his intention of staying for dinner in the Tower, Buckingham observes aside, "And supper too, although thou know'st it not" (3.2.122). Shortly before, Catesby has assured Hastings of Richard's and Buckingham's favor toward him: "The princes both make high account of you— / [*Aside*.] For they account his head upon the Bridge" (3.2.69–70). Richard has a phrase for such wit: "Thus, like the formal Vice, Iniquity, / I moralize two meanings in one word" (3.1.82–83). The point of such ironies is always the same: the devil is cleverer than his victims, deceiving them through equivocation, triumphing in their spiritual blindness.

The delayed irony of the play, however, ultimately offers another possible explanation for the seemingly nihilistic conclusions of the early scenes. That is, there may be a larger plan at work, one of which Richard is unconscious and in which he plays a role quite unlike the one he creates for himself. Perhaps Shakespeare's Richard is, as he was regarded in the chronicles of Edward Hall and others, the scourge of God, fulfilling a divine plan even in the process of what he gloatingly regards as his own self-aggrandizement. Divine plans are always complex, inscrutable to the minds of mortals, understood least by those who unwittingly execute them. In attempting to prove his own contention that human nature is bestial and that a Machiavellian man of utter self-confidence can force his way to the top, flouting all conventions of morality, Richard may have succeeded in demonstrating exactly the opposite. His role in this case becomes sardonically comic: that of the proverbial beguiler beguiled.

Certainly the play offers for our consideration a theory of divine causality in which virtually all of Richard's victims deserve their fate because they have offended God. Prophecies and dreams give structure to the sequence of retributive actions and keep grim score. As the choric Margaret observes, a York must pay for a Lancaster, eye for an eye: Edward IV for Henry VI, young Edward V for Henry VI's son Edward. Thus the Yorkist princes, though guiltless, die for their family's sins. The Yorkist Queen Elizabeth, like the Lancastrian Margaret, must outlive her husband into impotent old age, bewailing her children's cruel deaths. Clarence sees his death as punishment for breaking his oath at the battle of Tewkesbury and for his part in murdering Henry VI's son, Prince Edward. The Queen's kindred have been guilty of ambition, and Lord Hastings in turn is vulnerable because he has been willing to plot with Richard against the Queen's kindred. Margaret's curses serve both to warn the characters of their fates (a warning they blindly ignore) and to invite each person to curse himself unwittingly but with ironic appropriateness. The Lady Anne wishes unhappiness on any woman so insane as to marry Richard. Buckingham protests in a most sacred oath that whenever he turns again on the Queen's kindred, he will deserve to be punished by the treachery of his dearest friend (i.e., Richard). Dreams serve the same purpose of divine warning, giving Clarence a grotesque intimation of his death by drowning (in a butt of malmsey wine), and warning Hastings (through Stanley's dream) that the boar, Richard, will cut off his head. Thus the English court punishes itself through Richard. He is the essence of the courtiers' factionalism, able to succeed as he does only because they forswear their most holy vows and conspire to destroy one another. They deserve to be outwitted at their own dismal game. Yet their falls are curative as well; again and again, Richard's victims acknowledge the justice of their undoings and penitently implore divine forgiveness. Richard alone finds conscience a torment rather than a voice of comfort and wisdom.

Richard III is not without its ironies and historical anxieties. Richard's own successful career of evil through much of the play demonstrates how rhetoric and theater itself can be used to dupe and corrupt. The political process seems endlessly prone to cynical manipulation, and triumph comes chiefly to those who know how to use rhetoric to calculated effect. The Lord Mayor and his London associates are as pliable as the aristocracy. For all the belated assurances of providential meaning in Richard's rise to power and overthrow, we are allowed to speculate uncomfortably about the pragmatic action of history and its seeming ability to thrust forward into prominence an evil king or a good one as individual temperament happens to dictate. Finally, there is the question of how Richard is supplanted. Whatever the reasons for Richard's baleful emergence, the process of his overthrow requires human agency and a rebellion against established (even if tyrannical) royal authority. To thoughtful observers in the sixteenth century, including Queen Elizabeth, any such rebellion, no matter how seemingly necessary, established a disturbing precedent and a threat to Tudor monarchical stability. If *Richard III* finds reassuring answers in a concept of providential design, it does so in the face of pressing and troublesome circumstances.

Still, providential wisdom is at last affirmed, if only because some Englishmen have the patience and common sense to endure a presumably deserved punishment and wait for deliverance. As in *3 Henry VI*, the common people have little to do with the action of the play. They are choric spokesmen and bystanders, virtuous in their attitude (except for the two suborned murderers of Clarence). In their plain folk wisdom they see the folly and evil their betters ignore: "O, full of danger is the Duke of Gloucester, / And the Queen's sons and brothers haught and proud" (2.3.28–29). And although they accept Richard as ruler, they do so most reluctantly; Buckingham's first attempt to persuade the people to this course meets with apathy and silence. Their wisdom is to "leave it all to God" (l. 46). In the fullness of time, this passive obedience brings its just reward.

Richard III
in Performance

Richard III provides a star role that few leading actors, given the choice, have been able to resist. In a long play with an unusually large cast, Richard has a remarkably large percentage of the lines (comparable in this to Hamlet) and is onstage almost continuously. Richard Burbage, the leading player of Shakespeare's acting company (perhaps a combined company of the Lord Admiral's and Lord Strange's men when this play was first performed, c. 1593–1594), became famous in the part. As the dominating figure in the play, Richard is also acutely aware of his own theatricality. He is, as the Introduction has pointed out, a versatile actor, able to change at a moment's notice from gloating schemer (taking the audience into his confidence), to staunch protector of his brother Clarence, and thence to passionate wooer of the Lady Anne.

Because of this protean shifting of roles, dramatic irony is an essential part of our response to Richard. We know that he is only "acting" when he woos the Lady Anne, but actors after all are supposed to be able to transform themselves into the part they play, and so we admire Richard's skill as we might admire a professional coolly accomplishing his task. The more impossible the assignment—in this case, undertaking to convince a widow to marry her husband's murderer—the more credit belongs to the actor capable of sounding truly persuasive. Richard steps before us in soliloquy after he has won the Lady Anne to his will, incredulous at his own success, amused, proud of his ability as an actor. If the player in the theater has managed meantime to convince us for a moment that Richard really is in love with Anne after all, our admiration will be all the greater and our complicity in his role-playing will perhaps trouble us. Richard's triumphs as an actor subvert the moral claims of the theater, demonstrating with devastating effect that acting can be used to promote evil. The more believable the actor, the greater his potential for doing harm.

Richard not only acts in but directs and stage manages

his play. He disposes of his characters one after the other,
ordering the execution of Clarence and the Queen's kindred, sending his nephews to the Tower, discarding Anne
so that he can make a still more politically advantageous
marriage. He presides over scenes and arranges them to
suit his own penchant for highly theatrical entrances and
exits, as when he bursts in upon the Council meeting in the
Tower and angrily bares his arm, exclaiming, "Look how
I am bewitched!" (3.4.68), in order to accuse Hastings
of conspiring with Queen Elizabeth and Jane Shore. He
is a master of costuming effects, as when he enters
with Buckingham *in rotten armor, marvelous ill-favored*
(3.5.0). His conversation makes extensive use of theatrical
metaphor, as when he queries Buckingham about his skill
in deceiving appearances: "Come, cousin, canst thou quake
and change thy color, / Murder thy breath in middle of a
word, / And then again begin, and stop again, / As if thou
wert distraught and mad with terror?" Buckingham is
ready with a reply in kind: "Tut, I can counterfeit the deep
tragedian, / Speak and look back, and pry on every side, /
Tremble and start at wagging of a straw; / Intending deep
suspicion, ghastly looks / Are at my service, like enforcèd
smiles" (3.5.1–9).

Together, as an acting team, Richard and Buckingham exploit the Elizabethan theater with the practiced versatility
of their trade. When the Mayor and citizens arrive at Baynard's Castle at Buckingham's invitation, Richard is
coached by his acting partner to pretend reluctance to accept the crown: "And look you get a prayer book in your
hand, / And stand between two churchmen, good my lord, /
For on that ground I'll make a holy descant; / And be not
easily won to our requests. / Play the maid's part: still answer nay and take it" (3.7.47–51). Buckingham and Catesby,
on the main stage, receive the Mayor's delegation and undertake to intercede with Richard, though pretending to
fear a refusal from so unworldly a man. His entrance thus
prepared for, Richard enters *"aloft,"* that is, on the gallery
at the rear of the stage, between two bishops, in a tableau
designed to be emblematic of piety. The bishops and the
book of prayer are his properties, the Lord Mayor's party
his audience. The Elizabethan theater, without scenery, has

been transformed into the courtyard of Richard's residence, with the Mayor and his followers staring up in wonder at an apparition of holiness speaking to them from an upper vantage point in the house.

For all the histrionic skill he displays in attaining the English throne, Richard is unable to carry off the role he has supremely coveted, that of king. Ceremonies of royal authority, when invested in him, become travesties of themselves, exposing Richard as no more than a poor player, woefully miscast. Attired in all the trappings of kingship, entering *"in pomp"* with seeming majesty, Richard ascends the throne with Buckingham at his side: "Thus high, by thy advice, / And thy assistance, is King Richard seated" (4.2.3–4). Yet the first acts of this usurping monarch are all secret and murderous. He consults privately about the killing of his nephews or about the spreading of a rumor that Anne is sick and likely to die. He threatens Lord Stanley with dire reprisals if Stanley is caught conspiring with Richmond. His courtiers stand apart, whispering among themselves, wondering what will happen next. Throne, crown, and ceremonial occasion all reinforce by contrast the unworthiness of the present king.

At Bosworth Field, too, the play's staging effects turn decisively against this erstwhile genius of theatrical illusion. Two tents, symmetrically balanced and opposite one another, represent the camps of the usurping king and his virtuous challenger. In the Elizabethan theater, these tents must have actually been pitched onstage. The ghosts of Richard's many victims enter presumably center stage between the tents to offer curses for Richard, on the one hand, and blessings for Richmond, on the other. The antithetically balanced staging contrasts Richard and Richmond at every turn: in their relations with their subordinates, as orators to their armies, as generals. Richard is still very much the protagonist of his play, but he can no longer control its stage action. He is instead cast in the role of the villain, the scourge, whose usurped crown is offered to Richmond in a final stage gesture of restoration.

Leading actors have coveted Richard's part to such an extent that they have often enlarged it while reducing other parts of the play. Colley Cibber, at the Theatre Royal, Drury

Lane, in 1700, incorporated the ending of *3 Henry VI* (in later revivals, his version of the play opened with Richard's murder of King Henry VI in the Tower), along with parts of *Richard II* and *2 Henry IV* and *Henry V*, while excising Clarence's dream and Margaret's curse along with other matters. The roles of Clarence, Edward IV, Margaret, and Hastings were, in fact, omitted entirely, and the play's overall length was reduced from the original total of 3887 (in the Folio through-line numbering system) to some 2050 lines. Cibber wrote into the play a scene in which Richard informs his queen—the Lady Anne—that he has grown tired of her and wishes to marry someone else, and another scene of tearful farewell between Queen Elizabeth and her sons. This version, with its vividly melodramatic portrayal of Richard as villain, has had extraordinary staying power in the theater. It was the acting version of *Richard III* into the nineteenth century, and even today, many admirers of Shakespeare are not likely to know that Cibber wrote the lines "Off with his head; so much for Buckingham" and "Richard's himself again."

Shakespeare's play was taken even further afield in Nicholas Rowe's popular tragedy, *Jane Shore* (1714), but it was Cibber's version that held the stage. David Garrick made his debut on the English stage in a production of Cibber's *Richard III* at Henry Giffard's theater in Goodman's Fields, London, on October 19, 1741. Garrick kept Cibber's version in repertory during most of his years at Drury Lane in the mid-eighteenth century and was considerably more successful in the role of Richard than Cibber himself. In spite of Cibber's disdain for Garrick's performance ("all fuss and bustle"), Garrick's Richard propelled him to immediate stardom. John Philip Kemble also kept Cibber's version (albeit with minor Shakespearean restorations) in his productions at Drury Lane beginning in 1783. Edmund Kean successfully acted the part in Kemble's text at the same theater in 1814, eliciting critic William Hazlitt's enthusiastic praise for his "smooth, smiling villainy." William Charles Macready, in 1821 at the Theatre Royal, Covent Garden, hesitantly cleared away more of Cibber's interpolations and reintroduced at least a truncated role for Margaret. The production, despite its clear conception of restoring "alacrity and mirth of mind" to the character of Richard, was not successful and was withdrawn after only two performances.

Samuel Phelps was the first, at the Sadler's Wells Theatre in 1845, to restore the play to something like its original text, and in his revival of 1849 he came even closer to Shakespeare's original. Both productions were critically praised and succeeded at the box office. Phelps acted Richard "with sort of jovial *abandon*," the *Athenaeum* reviewer said; and the restored text also received favorable comment, especially for the unity brought to the play by the reintroduction of the prophetic role of Margaret, though the loss of some of Cibber's familiar phrases was lamented. Nonetheless, Shakespeare's text posed problems for the producer, as a review in *Punch* (March 15, 1845) made clear: "as for the getting up, it's twenty times as expensive as the original piece—I mean Colley Cibber's." In part for that reason, but more because he had no actress capable of playing Margaret, Phelps revived the Cibber version in 1861, as did Charles Kean at the Princess's Theatre in 1854 in an elaborate production with a cast of 121.

In America, Edwin Booth had decided to abandon Cibber's *Richard* sometime around 1868, although he was unable to mount a production of the play before Henry Jarrett and Henry Palmer claimed the honor of the first American production of Shakespeare's text in 1871 at Niblo's Garden in New York. Booth did act Shakespeare's play for several seasons after 1878 before he was persuaded to return to Cibber's version in 1886. Shakespeare "*reads* well enough," one of Booth's contemporaries said; "but Cibber's Richard *acts*." In England, meanwhile, Shakespeare's play had reclaimed the stage, though not always in responsible texts. Henry Irving's productions at London's Lyceum Theatre, in 1877 and 1896, while free of Cibber's improvements, made draconian cuts curtailing both Clarence's and Margaret's roles. The *Athenaeum* approved neither of the cuts nor of Irving's acting, in which the reviewer lamented the absence of tragic power. Irving's Richard seemed trivial, merely amusing, no more than "what is conventionally called 'a character-part.'" Other reviewers, pleased to find Cibber banished and Shakespeare restored, were more kind. Clement Scott in the *Daily Telegraph* found his pleasure in the production heightened by "the unexpected discovery of a new source of dramatic delight."

Twentieth-century directors and audiences have generally insisted on a return to something close to Shakespeare's complete play. Frank Benson acted a virtually intact Shakespearean text in his various productions of the play between 1886 and 1915 at Stratford-upon-Avon. Benson was an energetic and athletic Richard, with the capacity to "frighten as well as fascinate," in Robert Speaight's words. It was at the Old Vic that *Richard III* fully came into its own, mainly because of a group of directors at the theater before World War II who were deeply committed to simple, fast-paced staging and fidelity to Shakespeare's text. Ben Greet directed the play in 1915 with Robert Atkins as Richard and Sybil Thorndike as Anne. A program note ingenuously remarked: "we have endeavoured to arrange thirteen scenes as simple settings to avoid as many delays as possible, but our appliances are 100 years old, and our friends are asked to be forbearing." Atkins himself directed a virtually uncut *Richard III* in a four-hour production at the Old Vic in 1921. In 1925 Andrew Leigh directed Baliol Holloway as Richard and Edith Evans as Margaret in a production that emphatically showed once and for all that the play could be performed successfully much as Shakespeare wrote it and with stagecraft closer to Shakespeare's own than the elaborate scenic display of the Victorian stage.

Yet the Old Vic company's greatest triumph with the play was one that made use of some older rearrangements of the text and thus established an important precedent for more recent years, that of respect for Shakespeare's whole play combined with a pragmatic view that the play is long and that Richard's role is, after all, primary. John Burrell's production at the New Theatre in 1944, starring Laurence Olivier as Richard, used a cut text that eliminated all but one scene of Sybil Thorndike's Margaret. On a brightly lit stage ringed with darkness, Olivier played a sinuous Richard, at once menacing and mocking—"the true double Gloucester," as critic J. C. Trewin has written, "thinker and doer, mind and mask." Everything centered around the inventive villain, and audiences were invited to share in his gloating conspiracy. Revived in 1949, with Vivien Leigh as Anne, the production again was a great success, even if to one critic the "irony and glitter" of Olivier's original performance now seemed "mannered."

Olivier's Richard influenced a generation of actors. One could imitate or react against his sardonic villainy, but one could hardly ignore it. George C. Scott as Richard, in Stuart Vaughan's production for the New York Shakespeare Festival in 1957, adopted a similar mix of calculation and improvisational brilliance. When, on the other hand, Robert Helpmann consciously chose to play against Olivier's Richard in Douglas Seale's version at the Old Vic that same year, the critics were generally unhappy. One critic did call it a "fine and louring production," and audiences came in large numbers, but other reviewers missed the Olivier magic. Helpmann was no engaging villain but a nasty, brutish monster. In 1961 at Stratford-upon-Avon, Christopher Plummer's Richard was a cool, dispassionate villain, as one critic wrote, "the more frightening for his matter-of-fact, almost reasonable evil." Donald Madden's Richard at New York's Delacorte Theater in 1970 returned to something more like Olivier's Richard's grisly pleasure in his wickedness.

Terry Hands's *Richard III* in 1970 at Stratford-upon-Avon was perhaps the first significant production of the play since Olivier's triumph to focus on something other than the psychology of its fascinating hero. Successful at the box office, though not always with the critics, this often symbolic production, in which Norman Rodway's Richard was killed by Death, used other fine actors (including Ian Richardson as Buckingham and Patrick Stewart as Edward) to populate a world with characters who were more than merely available victims for Richard's evil. Two modern-dress productions marked an even sharper break with the Olivier tradition: Barry Kyle's *Richard III* at The Other Place in Stratford-upon-Avon in 1975, suggesting to critic Eric Shorter a "medieval nightmare in some royal asylum," and Michael Bogdanov's production at London's Young Vic Theatre in 1978 in which Richard was a thug, differing from the corrupt world around him only in his daring. Robin Phillips directed a stylized, Senecan version of the play at Stratford, Ontario, in 1977, featuring Brian Bedford's desperate and histrionic Richard together with Maggie Smith's fierce Elizabeth. In 1979 Al Pacino played a clowning, contemptuous Richard in a much derided production directed by David Wheeler at New York's Cort Theater. More successfully, Jane Howell, using a nearly full text, directed Kevin Kline in a production for the New York Shakespeare Festival in 1983. Kline's Richard was comically inventive, juggling a crucifix and a prayer book, for example, as he made what *The New York Times* called "farcical art out of outrageous wickedness." Certainly the most remarkable of the recent productions was Bill Alexander's *Richard III* at Stratford-upon-Avon in 1984. Antony Sher starred as a charismatic, energetic Richard trapped in a crippled body. Propped by metal crutches that served to emphasize his spidery quality as he pulled himself furiously across stage with his legs dangling beneath him, Sher's Richard could both repel and draw laughs, as with his deadpan response to Elizabeth's charge of murdering his family: "men shall deal unadvisedly sometimes."

Still, it is Olivier's Richard that remains in the modern imagination, partly because it has been seen by so many people in its film version (1955). Olivier's film uses an adapted text, beginning with the coronation of Edward IV in *3 Henry VI*, cutting the role of Margaret, and rearranging scenes with vigor; the wooing of the Lady Anne is divided in two, with intervening material, as though to allow Anne time to think over what Richard is proposing. For all its cavalier treatment of the text, Olivier's film captures the extraordinary sense of theatrical dominance that has generated such success in performance ever since the play first appeared. Olivier uses camera closeups to show us the evil glint in Richard's eye. Visual juxtapositions, well attuned to the requirements of Shakespeare's text, accentuate the contrasts among Richard's various roles. Olivier focuses his camera on key objects like the throne and the crown in order to exploit their visual symbolism. When Richard, informed of Richmond's return to England to claim the kingdom, exclaims, "Is the chair empty? Is the sword unswayed?" (4.4.469), the camera lingers on the chair of state, showing it left empty when Richard departs for battle. In the film's last minutes, the crown, formerly on Richard's head, tumbles around the battlefield and ends up in a bush until picked up by Lord Stanley and placed on the victor's brow. The language of theatrical gesture, violently usurped by the superb but unnerving histrionic ability of the protagonist, is at last reclaimed in a true ceremony of coronation.

The Playhouse

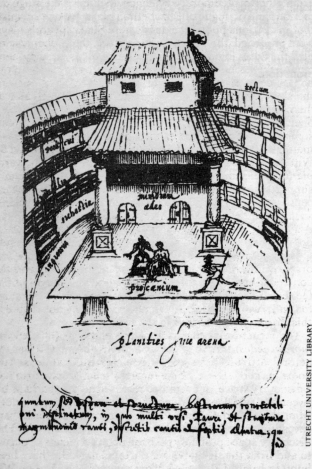

This early copy of a drawing by Johannes de Witt of the Swan Theatre in London (c. 1596), made by his friend Arend van Buchell, is the only surviving contemporary sketch of the interior of a public theater in the 1590s.

From other contemporary evidence, including the stage directions and dialogue of Elizabethan plays, we can surmise that the various public theaters where Shakespeare's plays were produced (the Theatre, the Curtain, the Globe) resembled the Swan in many important particulars, though there must have been some variations as well. The public playhouses were essentially round, or polygonal, and open to the sky, forming an acting arena approximately 70 feet in diameter; they did not have a large curtain with which to open and close a scene, such as we see today in opera and some traditional theater. A platform measuring approximately 43 feet across and 27 feet deep, referred to in the de Witt drawing as the *proscaenium*, projected into the yard, *planities sive arena*. The roof, *tectum*, above the stage and supported by two pillars, could contain machinery for ascents and descents, as were required in several of Shakespeare's late plays. Above this roof was a hut, shown in the drawing with a flag flying atop it and a trumpeter at its door announcing the performance of a play. The underside of the stage roof, called the heavens, was usually richly decorated with symbolic figures of the sun, the moon, and the constellations. The platform stage stood at a height of 5½ feet or so above the yard, providing room under the stage for underworldly effects. A trapdoor, which is not visible in this drawing, gave access to the space below.

The structure at the back of the platform (labeled *mimorum aedes*), known as the tiring-house because it was the actors' attiring (dressing) space, featured at least two doors, as shown here. Some theaters seem to have also had a discovery space, or curtained recessed alcove, perhaps between the two doors—in which Falstaff could have hidden from the sheriff (*1 Henry IV*, 2.4) or Polonius could have eavesdropped on Hamlet and his mother (*Hamlet*, 3.4). This discovery space probably gave the actors a means of access to and from the tiring-house. Curtains may also have been hung in front of the stage doors on occasion. The de Witt drawing shows a gallery above the doors that extends across the back and evidently contains spectators. On occasions when action "above" demanded the use of this space, as when Juliet appears at her "window" (*Romeo and Juliet*, 2.2 and 3.5), the gallery seems to have been used by the actors, but large scenes there were impractical.

The three-tiered auditorium is perhaps best described by
Thomas Platter, a visitor to London in 1599 who saw on that
occasion Shakespeare's *Julius Caesar* performed at the
Globe:

> The playhouses are so constructed that they play on a
> raised platform, so that everyone has a good view. There
> are different galleries and places [*orchestra, sedilia, porti-
> cus*], however, where the seating is better and more com-
> fortable and therefore more expensive. For whoever cares
> to stand below only pays one English penny, but if he
> wishes to sit, he enters by another door [*ingressus*] and
> pays another penny, while if he desires to sit in the most
> comfortable seats, which are cushioned, where he not only
> sees everything well but can also be seen, then he pays yet
> another English penny at another door. And during the
> performance food and drink are carried round the audi-
> ence, so that for what one cares to pay one may also have
> refreshment.

Scenery was not used, though the theater building itself
was handsome enough to invoke a feeling of order and hier-
archy that lent itself to the splendor and pageantry onstage.
Portable properties, such as thrones, stools, tables, and
beds, could be carried or thrust on as needed. In the scene
pictured here by de Witt, a lady on a bench, attended perhaps by her waiting-gentlewoman, receives the address of a
male figure. If Shakespeare had written *Twelfth Night* by
1596 for performance at the Swan, we could imagine
Malvolio appearing like this as he bows before the Countess Olivia and her gentlewoman, Maria.

RICHARD III

GHOSTS of King Henry VI, Edward Prince of Wales, and others murdered by Richard (Clarence, Rivers, Grey, Vaughan, Hastings, the two young princes, Anne, and Buckingham)

SIR ROBERT BRACKENBURY, *Lieutenant of the Tower*

TRESSEL,
BERKELEY, *attending the*
HALBERDIER, *Lady Anne*
GENTLEMAN,

Two MURDERERS
KEEPER *in the Tower*
Three CITIZENS
MESSENGER *to Queen Elizabeth*
LORD MAYOR OF LONDON
MESSENGER *to Lord Hastings*
PURSUIVANT
PRIEST
SCRIVENER
Two BISHOPS
PAGE *to Richard III*
Four MESSENGERS *to Richard III*
SHERIFF OF WILTSHIRE

Lords, Attendants, Aldermen, Citizens, Councilors, Soldiers

SCENE: *England.*]

1.1   *Enter Richard, Duke of Gloucester, solus.*

RICHARD
Now is the winter of our discontent
Made glorious summer by this sun of York,   2
And all the clouds that loured upon our house   3
In the deep bosom of the ocean buried.
Now are our brows bound with victorious wreaths,   5
Our bruisèd arms hung up for monuments,   6
Our stern alarums changed to merry meetings,   7
Our dreadful marches to delightful measures.   8
Grim-visaged War hath smoothed his wrinkled front;   9
And now, instead of mounting barbèd steeds   10
To fright the souls of fearful adversaries,   11
He capers nimbly in a lady's chamber
To the lascivious pleasing of a lute.
But I, that am not shaped for sportive tricks,   14
Nor made to court an amorous looking glass;
I, that am rudely stamped, and want love's majesty   16
To strut before a wanton ambling nymph;   17
I, that am curtailed of this fair proportion,   18
Cheated of feature by dissembling Nature,   19
Deformed, unfinished, sent before my time
Into this breathing world scarce half made up,
And that so lamely and unfashionable   22
That dogs bark at me as I halt by them—   23
Why, I, in this weak piping time of peace,   24
Have no delight to pass away the time,
Unless to see my shadow in the sun
And descant on mine own deformity.   27
And therefore, since I cannot prove a lover

1.1. Location: London. Near the Tower.
s.d. solus alone   **2 sun** (Edward IV's badge displayed three suns; with a
pun on *son*.)   **3 loured** looked threateningly   **5 brows** foreheads
6 arms armor.   **monuments** trophies   **7 alarums** calls to arms
8 dreadful formidable, awe-inspiring.   **measures** stately dances
9 wrinkled front furrowed forehead   **10 barbèd** armored   **11 fearful**
frightened   **14 sportive** amorous   **16 rudely** roughly.   **want** lack
17 ambling walking affectedly, i.e., wantonly   **18 curtailed** cut short,
denied.   **proportion** shape   **19 feature** shapeliness of body
22 unfashionable badly fashioned   **23 halt** limp   **24 piping time** i.e., a
time when the music heard is that of pipes and not fifes and drums
27 descant compose variations, warble, comment on

To entertain these fair well-spoken days,   29
I am determinèd to próve a villain
And hate the idle pleasures of these days.
Plots have I laid, inductions dangerous,   32
By drunken prophecies, libels, and dreams,
To set my brother Clarence and the King
In deadly hate the one against the other;
And if King Edward be as true and just
As I am subtle, false, and treacherous,
This day should Clarence closely be mewed up   38
About a prophecy, which says that G   39
Of Edward's heirs the murderer shall be.
Dive, thoughts, down to my soul; here Clarence comes.

    Enter Clarence, guarded, and Brackenbury,
    [*Lieutenant of the Tower*].

Brother, good day. What means this armèd guard
That waits upon Your Grace?
CLARENCE   His Majesty,
Tend'ring my person's safety, hath appointed   44
This conduct to convey me to the Tower.   45
RICHARD
Upon what cause?
CLARENCE   Because my name is George.
RICHARD
Alack, my lord, that fault is none of yours.
He should, for that, commit your godfathers.
O, belike His Majesty hath some intent   49
That you should be new christened in the Tower.   50
But what's the matter, Clarence, may I know?   51
CLARENCE
Yea, Richard, when I know; for I protest
As yet I do not. But, as I can learn,
He hearkens after prophecies and dreams,

---

29 entertain pass away pleasurably.   **well-spoken** refined, elegant
32 inductions preparations   **38 mewed up** confined (like a hawk)
39 prophecy . . . G (The prophecy is mentioned in the chronicles; the
quibble is that *G* stands for *Gloucester* and not for *George*, the given name
of the Duke of Clarence.)   **44 Tend'ring** having care for   **45 conduct**
escort   **49 belike** probably   **50 new christened** (Anticipates, ironically,
Clarence's death by drowning in 1.4.)   **51 matter** reason, cause

And from the crossrow plucks the letter G,   55
And says a wizard told him that by G
His issue disinherited should be;   57
And, for my name of George begins with G,   58
It follows in his thought that I am he.
These, as I learn, and suchlike toys as these   60
Hath moved His Highness to commit me now.   61

RICHARD
Why, this it is when men are ruled by women.
'Tis not the King that sends you to the Tower;
My Lady Grey his wife, Clarence, 'tis she   64
That tempers him to this extremity.   65
Was it not she, and that good man of worship,
Anthony Woodville, her brother there,   67
That made him send Lord Hastings to the Tower,
From whence this present day he is delivered?
We are not safe, Clarence, we are not safe.

CLARENCE
By heaven, I think there is no man secure
But the Queen's kindred and night-walking heralds   72
That trudge betwixt the King and Mistress Shore.   73
Heard you not what an humble suppliant
Lord Hastings was to her for his delivery?   75

RICHARD
Humbly complaining to Her Deity   76
Got my Lord Chamberlain his liberty.   77
I'll tell you what: I think it is our way,   78
If we will keep in favor with the King,

---

55 crossrow Christ-crossrow, or alphabet (so called from the cross printed before the alphabet in the hornbook)   **57 issue** offspring
58 for because   **60 toys** trifles   **61 commit** arrest   **64 My Lady Grey** (A disrespectful reference to the Queen, whose maiden name was Elizabeth Woodville and who, when the King married her, was the widow of Sir John Grey.)   **65 tempers** governs, directs   **67 Woodville** i.e., Earl Rivers (whom Richard also disrespectfully refers to by his family name rather than by his recently acquired title)   **72 night-walking heralds** i.e., secret messengers for an assignation   **73 Mistress Shore** Jane Shore, the King's mistress, and wife of a goldsmith in Lombard Street. (The title *Mistress* is a respectful form of address for any woman, married or unmarried.)   **75 her** i.e., Jane Shore   **76 Her Deity** (A mock title for Jane Shore, suggesting she is even more elevated than "Her Grace" or "Her Majesty.")   **77 Lord Chamberlain** i.e., Lord Hastings   **78 our way** i.e., our only way (to succeed)

To be her men and wear her livery.   80
The jealous o'erworn widow and herself,   81
Since that our brother dubbed them gentlewomen,   82
Are mighty gossips in our monarchy.   83

BRACKENBURY
I beseech Your Graces both to pardon me:
His Majesty hath straitly given in charge   85
That no man shall have private conference,
Of what degree soever, with your brother.   87

RICHARD
Even so? An 't please your worship, Brackenbury,   88
You may partake of anything we say.
We speak no treason, man. We say the King
Is wise and virtuous, and his noble queen
Well struck in years, fair, and not jealous.   92
We say that Shore's wife hath a pretty foot,
A cherry lip, a bonny eye, a passing pleasing tongue;   94
And that the Queen's kindred are made gentlefolks.
How say you, sir? Can you deny all this?

BRACKENBURY
With this, my lord, myself have naught to do.

RICHARD
Naught to do with Mistress Shore? I tell thee, fellow,   98
He that doth naught with her, excepting one,
Were best to do it secretly, alone.

BRACKENBURY   What one, my lord?

RICHARD
Her husband, knave. Wouldst thou betray me?   102

BRACKENBURY
I beseech Your Grace to pardon me, and withal   103
Forbear your conference with the noble Duke.

CLARENCE
We know thy charge, Brackenbury, and will obey.

---

80 men servants   **81 widow** i.e., Queen Elizabeth. (See l. 64, note.)   **herself**
i.e., Jane Shore   **82 gentlewomen** (A sneer at the Queen's family, which
was gentle but not noble until after her marriage with the King; Jane
Shore was, of course, neither gentle nor noble.)   **83 mighty gossips** i.e.,
influential busybodies   **85 straitly . . . charge** strictly ordered   **87 degree**
rank   **88 An 't** if it   **92 Well struck** i.e., well along.   **not jealous** (Implies
there are things she might be jealous about.)   **94 passing** surpassingly
98 Naught (Richard quibbles on the meanings "nothing" and "the sexual
act.")   **102 betray me** i.e., into naming the King as a person who does
"naught" with Mistress Shore   **103 withal** at the same time

RICHARD
We are the Queen's abjects, and must obey.   106
Brother, farewell. I will unto the King;
And whatsoe'er you will employ me in,
Were it to call King Edward's widow sister,   109
I will perform it to enfranchise you.   110
Meantime, this deep disgrace in brotherhood
Touches me deeper than you can imagine.   112

CLARENCE
I know it pleaseth neither of us well.

RICHARD
Well, your imprisonment shall not be long;
I will deliver you, or else lie for you.   115
Meantime, have patience.

CLARENCE   I must perforce. Farewell.   116
Exit Clarence [with Brackenbury and guard].

RICHARD
Go tread the path that thou shalt ne'er return.
Simple, plain Clarence, I do love thee so
That I will shortly send thy soul to heaven,
If heaven will take the present at our hands.
But who comes here? The new-delivered Hastings?   121

Enter Lord Hastings.

HASTINGS
Good time of day unto my gracious lord.

RICHARD
As much unto my good Lord Chamberlain.
Well are you welcome to the open air.
How hath your lordship brooked imprisonment?   125

HASTINGS
With patience, noble lord, as prisoners must.
But I shall live, my lord, to give them thanks   127
That were the cause of my imprisonment.

---

106 abjects abjectly servile subjects   **109 King Edward's widow** i.e., the widow whom Edward has made queen   **110 enfranchise** release from imprisonment   **112 Touches . . . imagine** (1) distresses me more than can be imagined (2) concerns me (in my personal ambition) more than you could possibly guess   **115 lie for you** (1) take your place in prison (2) tell lies about you   **116 perforce** necessarily   **121 new-delivered** recently released   **125 brooked** endured   **127 give them thanks** i.e., pay them back. (Said ironically.)

RICHARD
　No doubt, no doubt; and so shall Clarence too,
　For they that were your enemies are his,
　And have prevailed as much on him as you.

HASTINGS
　More pity that the eagles should be mewed,
　Whiles kites and buzzards prey at liberty.　　　　133

RICHARD　What news abroad?　　　　134

HASTINGS
　No news so bad abroad as this at home:
　The King is sickly, weak, and melancholy,
　And his physicians fear him mightily.　　　　137

RICHARD
　Now, by Saint John, that news is bad indeed!
　O, he hath kept an evil diet long　　　　139
　And overmuch consumed his royal person.
　'Tis very grievous to be thought upon.
　Where is he, in his bed?

HASTINGS　He is.

RICHARD
　Go you before, and I will follow you.　　　*Exit Hastings.*
　He cannot live, I hope, and must not die
　Till George be packed with post-horse up to heaven.　　146
　I'll in, to urge his hatred more to Clarence
　With lies well steeled with weighty arguments;　　148
　And, if I fail not in my deep intent,
　Clarence hath not another day to live.
　Which done, God take King Edward to his mercy,
　And leave the world for me to bustle in!
　For then I'll marry Warwick's youngest daughter.　　153
　What though I killed her husband and her father?　　154
　The readiest way to make the wench amends
　Is to become her husband and her father,
　The which will I; not all so much for love

---

133 kites scavengers of the hawk family　**134 abroad** at large, circulating　**137 fear** fear for　**139 diet** course of life, regimen　**146 with post-horse** by post-horses, i.e., by swiftest possible means　**148 steeled** reinforced　**153 Warwick's youngest daughter** the Lady Anne Neville (regarded by Shakespeare, following the chronicles, as widow of Edward, Prince of Wales, son of King Henry VI, though in fact they were only betrothed)　**154 father** i.e., father-in-law (Henry VI)

As for another secret close intent   158
By marrying her which I must reach unto.
But yet I run before my horse to market.
Clarence still breathes, Edward still lives and reigns;
When they are gone, then must I count my gains.

                              Exit.

❖

1.2   *Enter the corpse of [King] Henry the Sixth,*
        with Halberds to guard it; Lady Anne being the
        mourner [attended by Tressel and Berkeley].

ANNE
   Set down, set down your honorable load—
   If honor may be shrouded in a hearse—   2
   Whilst I awhile obsequiously lament   3
   Th' untimely fall of virtuous Lancaster.
                [The bearers set down the coffin.]
   Poor key-cold figure of a holy king,   5
   Pale ashes of the house of Lancaster,
   Thou bloodless remnant of that royal blood,
   Be it lawful that I invocate thy ghost   8
   To hear the lamentations of poor Anne,
   Wife to thy Edward, to thy slaughtered son,
   Stabbed by the selfsame hand that made these wounds!
   Lo, in these windows that let forth thy life   12
   I pour the helpless balm of my poor eyes.   13
   O, cursèd be the hand that made these holes!
   Cursèd the heart that had the heart to do it!
   Cursèd the blood that let this blood from hence!
   More direful hap betide that hated wretch   17
   That makes us wretched by the death of thee

---

158 intent design (i.e., Richard hopes to ally himself with the house of Lancaster to bolster his claim to the throne)

1.2. Location: London. A street.
s.d. Halberds halberdiers, guards with halberds, or long poleaxes
2 hearse (probably here an open coffin on a bier)   **3 obsequiously** as befits a funeral, mournfully   **5 key-cold** extremely cold, cold as a metal key. (Proverbial.)   **8 invocate** invoke   **12 windows** i.e., wounds
13 helpless useless, unavailing   **17 hap betide** fortune befall

Than I can wish to wolves, to spiders, toads,
Or any creeping venomed thing that lives!
If ever he have child, abortive be it,   21
Prodigious, and untimely brought to light,   22
Whose ugly and unnatural aspect   23
May fright the hopeful mother at the view,
And that be heir to his unhappiness!   25
If ever he have wife, let her be made
More miserable by the life of him
Than I am made by my young lord and thee!   28
Come, now towards Chertsey with your holy load,   29
Taken from Paul's to be interrèd there.   30
        [*The bearers take up the hearse.*]
And still as you are weary of this weight,   31
Rest you, whiles I lament King Henry's corpse.

Enter Richard, Duke of Gloucester.

RICHARD
Stay, you that bear the corpse, and set it down.
ANNE
What black magician conjures up this fiend
To stop devoted charitable deeds?   35
RICHARD
Villains, set down the corpse, or, by Saint Paul,
I'll make a corpse of him that disobeys.
HALBERDIER [*Advancing with his halberd lowered*]
My lord, stand back and let the coffin pass.
RICHARD
Unmannered dog, stand thou when I command!   39
Advance thy halberd higher than my breast,   40
Or, by Saint Paul, I'll strike thee to my foot
And spurn upon thee, beggar, for thy boldness.   42
        [*The bearers set down the hearse.*]
ANNE
What do you tremble? Are you all afraid?   43

21 abortive misshapen, monstrous   **22 Prodigious** monstrous, unnatural   **23 aspect** appearance   **25 unhappiness** evil nature   **28 by . . . thee** i.e., by the deaths of Prince Edward and King Henry VI   **29 Chertsey** monastery in Surrey, near London, where King Henry's body is to be buried   **30 Paul's** Saint Paul's Cathedral in London   **31 still as** as often as   **35 devoted** holy   **39 stand** halt   **40 Advance . . . breast** raise your halberd upright   **42 spurn** trample   **43 What** why

Alas, I blame you not, for you are mortal,
And mortal eyes cannot endure the devil.
Avaunt, thou dreadful minister of hell!   46
Thou hadst but power over his mortal body;
His soul thou canst not have. Therefore, begone.

RICHARD

Sweet saint, for charity, be not so curst.   49

ANNE

Foul devil, for God's sake hence and trouble us not,   50
For thou hast made the happy earth thy hell,
Filled it with cursing cries and deep exclaims.   52
If thou delight to view thy heinous deeds,
Behold this pattern of thy butcheries.   54

              [*She uncovers the corpse.*]
O, gentlemen, see, see dead Henry's wounds
Open their congealed mouths and bleed afresh!   56
Blush, blush, thou lump of foul deformity;
For 'tis thy presence that exhales this blood   58
From cold and empty veins where no blood dwells.
Thy deeds inhuman and unnatural
Provokes this deluge most unnatural.
O God, which this blood mad'st, revenge his death!
O earth, which this blood drink'st, revenge his death!
Either heaven with lightning strike the murderer dead,
Or earth gape open wide and eat him quick,   65
As thou dost swallow up this good king's blood,
Which his hell-governed arm hath butcherèd!

RICHARD

Lady, you know no rules of charity,
Which renders good for bad, blessings for curses.

ANNE

Villain, thou know'st nor law of God nor man.   70
No beast so fierce but knows some touch of pity.   71

RICHARD

But I know none, and therefore am no beast.

ANNE

O, wonderful, when devils tell the truth!

---

46 Avaunt begone   **49 curst** spiteful, shrewish   **50 hence** go hence,
depart   **52 exclaims** exclamations   **54 pattern** example   **56 bleed afresh**
(A phenomenon popularly supposed to occur in the presence of the
murderer.)   **58 exhales** draws out   **65 quick** alive   **70 nor . . . nor** neither . . . nor   **71 so fierce but knows** is so savage that it has not

RICHARD
    More wonderful, when angels are so angry.
    Vouchsafe, divine perfection of a woman,   75
    Of these supposèd crimes to give me leave
    By circumstance but to acquit myself.   77
ANNE
    Vouchsafe, defused infection of a man,   78
    Of these known evils but to give me leave
    By circumstance t' accuse thy cursèd self.
RICHARD
    Fairer than tongue can name thee, let me have
    Some patient leisure to excuse myself.
ANNE
    Fouler than heart can think thee, thou canst make
    No excuse current but to hang thyself.   84
RICHARD
    By such despair I should accuse myself.
ANNE
    And by despairing shalt thou stand excused
    For doing worthy vengeance on thyself
    That didst unworthy slaughter upon others.
RICHARD   Say that I slew them not?
ANNE   Then say they were not slain.
    But dead they are, and, devilish slave, by thee.
RICHARD   I did not kill your husband.
ANNE   Why, then he is alive.
RICHARD
    Nay, he is dead, and slain by Edward's hand.
ANNE
    In thy foul throat thou liest! Queen Margaret saw
    Thy murderous falchion smoking in his blood,   96
    The which thou once didst bend against her breast,   97
    But that thy brothers beat aside the point.
RICHARD
    I was provokèd by her slanderous tongue,
    That laid their guilt upon my guiltless shoulders.

---

75 Vouchsafe deign, consent **77 circumstance** detailed argument
78 defused diffused, disordered, shapeless; *defused infection* means
"spreading plague" **84 current** genuine, acceptable (as in coinage)
96 falchion curved sword **97 bend** direct, aim

ANNE
  Thou wast provokèd by thy bloody mind,
  That never dream'st on aught but butcheries.   102
  Didst thou not kill this king?
RICHARD   I grant ye.
ANNE
  Dost grant me, hedgehog? Then God grant me too   104
  Thou mayst be damnèd for that wicked deed!
  O, he was gentle, mild, and virtuous!
RICHARD
  The better for the King of Heaven that hath him.
ANNE
  He is in heaven, where thou shalt never come.
RICHARD
  Let him thank me that holp to send him thither;   109
  For he was fitter for that place than earth.
ANNE
  And thou unfit for any place but hell.
RICHARD
  Yes, one place else, if you will hear me name it.
ANNE   Some dungeon.
RICHARD   Your bedchamber.
ANNE
  Ill rest betide the chamber where thou liest!   115
RICHARD
  So will it, madam, till I lie with you.
ANNE
  I hope so.
RICHARD   I know so. But, gentle Lady Anne,
  To leave this keen encounter of our wits
  And fall something into a slower method,
  Is not the causer of the timeless deaths   120
  Of these Plantagenets, Henry and Edward,
  As blameful as the executioner?
ANNE
  Thou wast the cause and most accurst effect.   123
RICHARD
  Your beauty was the cause of that effect—   124

102 aught anything   **104 hedgehog** (Richard's heraldic emblem featured
a boar or wild hog.)   **109 holp** helped   **115 betide** befall   **120 timeless**
untimely   **123 effect** agent   **124 effect** result

Your beauty, that did haunt me in my sleep
To undertake the death of all the world,
So I might live one hour in your sweet bosom.

ANNE
If I thought that, I tell thee, homicide,   128
These nails should rend that beauty from my cheeks.   129

RICHARD
These eyes could not endure that beauty's wrack;   130
You should not blemish it, if I stood by.
As all the world is cheerèd by the sun,
So I by that. It is my day, my life.

ANNE
Black night o'ershade thy day, and death thy life!

RICHARD
Curse not thyself, fair creature—thou art both.

ANNE
I would I were, to be revenged on thee.

RICHARD
It is a quarrel most unnatural
To be revenged on him that loveth thee.

ANNE
It is a quarrel just and reasonable
To be revenged on him that killed my husband.

RICHARD
He that bereft thee, lady, of thy husband
Did it to help thee to a better husband.

ANNE
His better doth not breathe upon the earth.

RICHARD
He lives that loves thee better than he could.   144

ANNE
Name him.

RICHARD   Plantagenet.

ANNE   Why, that was he.

RICHARD
The selfsame name, but one of better nature.

ANNE
Where is he?

---

128 homicide murderer   **129 rend** tear   **130 wrack** destruction
144 He lives i.e., there is a man.   **he** i.e., Prince Edward

RICHARD   Here.   [*She*] *spits at him.*
                Why dost thou spit at me?

ANNE
  Would it were mortal poison for thy sake!

RICHARD
  Never came poison from so sweet a place.

ANNE
  Never hung poison on a fouler toad.   150
  Out of my sight! Thou dost infect mine eyes.

RICHARD
  Thine eyes, sweet lady, have infected mine.   152

ANNE
  Would they were basilisks, to strike thee dead!   153

RICHARD
  I would they were, that I might die at once;
  For now they kill me with a living death.
  Those eyes of thine from mine have drawn salt tears,
  Shamed their aspects with store of childish drops;   157
  These eyes, which never shed remorseful tear—
  No, when my father York and Edward wept
  To hear the piteous moan that Rutland made   160
  When black-faced Clifford shook his sword at him;   161
  Nor when thy warlike father, like a child,   162
  Told the sad story of my father's death
  And twenty times made pause to sob and weep,
  That all the standers-by had wet their cheeks   165
  Like trees bedashed with rain—in that sad time
  My manly eyes did scorn an humble tear;
  And what these sorrows could not thence exhale,   168
  Thy beauty hath, and made them blind with weeping.
  I never sued to friend nor enemy;   170
  My tongue could never learn sweet smoothing words;   171
  But, now thy beauty is proposed my fee,   172

---

150 poison . . . toad (Toads were popularly regarded as poisonous.)
152 infected i.e., with love (since love was thought to enter through the
eyes)   **153 basilisks** mythical reptiles reputed to kill by their looks
157 aspects appearance   **160 Rutland** second son of Richard, Duke of
York. (See *3 Henry VI*, 1.3, for his death scene.)   **161 black-faced** i.e.,
foreboding in appearance   **162 thy warlike father** i.e., the Earl of
Warwick   **165 That** so that   **168 exhale** draw out   **170 sued** suppli-
cated, appealed   **171 smoothing** flattering   **172 proposed my fee** offered as my reward

My proud heart sues and prompts my tongue to speak.
                    She looks scornfully at him.
Teach not thy lip such scorn, for it was made
For kissing, lady, not for such contempt.
If thy revengeful heart cannot forgive,
Lo, here I lend thee this sharp-pointed sword,
Which if thou please to hide in this true breast
And let the soul forth that adoreth thee,
I lay it naked to the deadly stroke
And humbly beg the death upon my knee.   181
                    He [kneels and] lays his breast open;
                    she offers at [it] with his sword.
Nay, do not pause; for I did kill King Henry—
But 'twas thy beauty that provokèd me.
Nay, now dispatch; 'twas I that stabbed young Edward—
But 'twas thy heavenly face that set me on.   185
                    She falls the sword.
Take up the sword again, or take up me.

ANNE
  Arise, dissembler. Though I wish thy death,
  I will not be thy executioner.

RICHARD [*rising*]
  Then bid me kill myself, and I will do it.

ANNE
  I have already.

RICHARD   That was in thy rage.
  Speak it again, and even with the word
  This hand, which for thy love did kill thy love,
  Shall for thy love kill a far truer love.
  To both their deaths shalt thou be accessory.

ANNE   I would I knew thy heart.   195

RICHARD   'Tis figured in my tongue.   196

ANNE   I fear me both are false.

RICHARD   Then never was man true.

ANNE   Well, well, put up your sword.

RICHARD   Say, then, my peace is made.

ANNE   That shalt thou know hereafter.

RICHARD   But shall I live in hope?

ANNE   All men, I hope, live so.

---

181 s.d. offers aims   **185 s.d. falls** lets fall   **195 would** wish
196 figured portrayed

RICHARD   Vouchsafe to wear this ring.   204
ANNE   To take is not to give.
                         [*He slips the ring on her finger.*]
RICHARD
  Look how my ring encompasseth thy finger,
  Even so thy breast encloseth my poor heart;
  Wear both of them, for both of them are thine.
  And if thy poor devoted servant may   209
  But beg one favor at thy gracious hand,
  Thou dost confirm his happiness forever.
ANNE   What is it?
RICHARD
  That it may please you leave these sad designs
  To him that hath most cause to be a mourner,
  And presently repair to Crosby House,   215
  Where, after I have solemnly interred
  At Chertsey monast'ry this noble king
  And wet his grave with my repentant tears,
  I will with all expedient duty see you.   219
  For divers unknown reasons, I beseech you,   220
  Grant me this boon.
ANNE
  With all my heart, and much it joys me too
  To see you are become so penitent.
  Tressel and Berkeley, go along with me.
RICHARD
  Bid me farewell.
ANNE   'Tis more than you deserve;
  But since you teach me how to flatter you,
  Imagine I have said farewell already.
                Exeunt two [*Tressel and Berkeley*] *with Anne.*
RICHARD
  Sirs, take up the corpse.
GENTLEMAN   Towards Chertsey, noble lord?
RICHARD
  No, to Whitefriars. There attend my coming.   229
                         Exeunt [*bearers with*] *corpse.*

204 Vouchsafe consent **209 servant** i.e., lover, one whom she may
command **215 presently** at once. **Crosby House** (One of Richard's
London dwellings; built originally by Sir John Crosby.) **219 expedient**
expeditious **220 unknown** secret **229 Whitefriars** the Carmelite
priory in London. **attend** await

Was ever woman in this humor wooed?
Was ever woman in this humor won?
I'll have her, but I will not keep her long.
What? I, that killed her husband and his father,
To take her in her heart's extremest hate,
With curses in her mouth, tears in her eyes,
The bleeding witness of my hatred by,
Having God, her conscience, and these bars against me, 237
And I no friends to back my suit at all
But the plain devil and dissembling looks?
And yet to win her! All the world to nothing!   240
Ha!
Hath she forgot already that brave prince,
Edward, her lord, whom I, some three months since,
Stabbed in my angry mood at Tewkesbury?
A sweeter and a lovelier gentleman,
Framed in the prodigality of nature,   246
Young, valiant, wise, and, no doubt, right royal,
The spacious world cannot again afford.
And will she yet abase her eyes on me,   249
That cropped the golden prime of this sweet prince   250
And made her widow to a woeful bed?
On me, whose all not equals Edward's moiety?   252
On me, that halts and am misshapen thus?   253
My dukedom to a beggarly denier,   254
I do mistake my person all this while.
Upon my life, she finds, although I cannot,
Myself to be a marvelous proper man.   257
I'll be at charges for a looking glass   258
And entertain a score or two of tailors   259
To study fashions to adorn my body.
Since I am crept in favor with myself,
I will maintain it with some little cost.
But first I'll turn yon fellow in his grave,   263
And then return lamenting to my love.

237 **bars** obstacles   240 **All . . . nothing** i.e., against infinite odds
246 **Framed . . . nature** i.e., formed in nature's most lavish mood
249 **abase** lower, devalue   250 **cropped** cut short   252 **moiety** half of
(Edward's virtues)   253 **halts** limps   254 **denier** small copper coin, the
twelfth part of a sou   257 **proper** handsome   258 **be . . . for** undertake
the expense of   259 **entertain** retain, employ   263 **in** into

Shine out, fair sun, till I have bought a glass,   265
That I may see my shadow as I pass.   *Exit.*

❖

1.3   *Enter the Queen Mother [Elizabeth], Lord*
        Rivers, [Marquess of Dorset,] and Lord Grey.

RIVERS
  Have patience, madam. There's no doubt His Majesty
  Will soon recover his accustomed health.
GREY
  In that you brook it ill, it makes him worse.   3
  Therefore, for God's sake, entertain good comfort   4
  And cheer His Grace with quick and merry eyes.
QUEEN ELIZABETH
  If he were dead, what would betide on me?   6
GREY
  No other harm but loss of such a lord.
QUEEN ELIZABETH
  The loss of such a lord includes all harms.
GREY
  The heavens have blessed you with a goodly son
  To be your comforter when he is gone.
QUEEN ELIZABETH
  Ah, he is young, and his minority
  Is put unto the trust of Richard Gloucester,
  A man that loves not me, nor none of you.
RIVERS
  Is it concluded he shall be Protector?
QUEEN ELIZABETH
  It is determined, not concluded yet;   15
  But so it must be, if the King miscarry.   16

    Enter Buckingham and [Lord Stanley, Earl of]
    Derby.

265 glass mirror

1.3. Location: London. The royal court.
3 brook endure   **4 comfort** cheer   **6 betide on** become of
15 determined, not concluded i.e., decided though not officially
announced   **16 miscarry** perish

GREY
  Here come the lords of Buckingham and Derby.

BUCKINGHAM
  Good time of day unto Your Royal Grace!

STANLEY
  God make Your Majesty joyful, as you have been!

QUEEN ELIZABETH
  The Countess Richmond, good my lord of Derby,   20
  To your good prayer will scarcely say amen.
  Yet, Derby, notwithstanding she's your wife
  And loves not me, be you, good lord, assured
  I hate not you for her proud arrogance.   24

STANLEY
  I do beseech you, either not believe
  The envious slanders of her false accusers,   26
  Or, if she be accused on true report,
  Bear with her weakness, which I think proceeds
  From wayward sickness and no grounded malice.   29

QUEEN ELIZABETH
  Saw you the King today, my lord of Derby?

STANLEY
  But now the Duke of Buckingham and I   31
  Are come from visiting His Majesty.

QUEEN ELIZABETH
  What likelihood of his amendment, lords?   33

BUCKINGHAM
  Madam, good hope; His Grace speaks cheerfully.

QUEEN ELIZABETH
  God grant him health! Did you confer with him?

BUCKINGHAM
  Ay, madam. He desires to make atonement   36
  Between the Duke of Gloucester and your brothers,   37
  And between them and my Lord Chamberlain,

20 Countess Richmond i.e., Margaret Beaufort (1443–1509), who married successively Edmund Tudor (Earl of Richmond), Lord Henry Stafford, and Thomas Lord Stanley (here called the Earl of Derby), to whom she is currently married. By the Earl of Richmond she was mother of the future Henry VII. **24 arrogance** i.e., ambition for her son **26 envious** malicious **29 wayward** erratic. **grounded** firmly fixed **31 But now** just now **33 amendment** recovery **36 atonement** reconciliation **37 brothers** (Only one brother, Earl Rivers, is mentioned in the play, though historically Elizabeth had others; Shakespeare may be thinking of other kinsmen, including her sons, whom she helped to advance.)

And sent to warn them to his royal presence.   39

QUEEN ELIZABETH
Would all were well! But that will never be.
I fear our happiness is at the height.

    *Enter Richard, [Duke of Gloucester, and Lord
    Hastings].*

RICHARD
They do me wrong, and I will not endure it!   ⚊
Who is it that complains unto the King
That I, forsooth, am stern and love them not?
By holy Paul, they love His Grace but lightly
That fill his ears with such dissentious rumors.   46
Because I cannot flatter and look fair,   47
Smile in men's faces, smooth, deceive, and cog,   48
Duck with French nods and apish courtesy,   49
I must be held a rancorous enemy.
Cannot a plain man live and think no harm,
But thus his simple truth must be abused
With silken, sly, insinuating Jacks?   53

GREY
To whom in all this presence speaks Your Grace?   54

RICHARD
To thee, that hast nor honesty nor grace.   55
When have I injured thee? When done thee wrong?
Or thee? Or thee? Or any of your faction?
A plague upon you all! His Royal Grace—
Whom God preserve better than you would wish!—
Cannot be quiet scarce a breathing while   60
But you must trouble him with lewd complaints.   61

QUEEN ELIZABETH
Brother of Gloucester, you mistake the matter.
The King, of his own royal disposition,   63
And not provoked by any suitor else,
Aiming, belike, at your interior hatred,   65

39 warn summon   **46 dissentious** quarrelsome, discordant   **47 fair** courteously   **48 smooth** flatter. **cog** employ deceit   **49 Duck . . . nods** i.e., bow affectedly   **53 With** by. **Jacks** lowbred persons   **54 presence** company   **55 grace** sense of duty or propriety (playing upon *Your Grace* in the preceding line)   **60 breathing while** i.e., brief time   **61 lewd** vile, base   **63 disposition** inclination   **65 Aiming** guessing. **belike** probably

That in your outward action shows itself
Against my children, brothers, and myself,
Makes him to send, that he may learn the ground   68
Of your ill will, and thereby to remove it.

RICHARD
I cannot tell. The world is grown so bad
That wrens make prey where eagles dare not perch.
Since every Jack became a gentleman,
There's many a gentle person made a Jack.

QUEEN ELIZABETH
Come, come, we know your meaning, brother
    Gloucester;
You envy my advancement and my friends'.   75
God grant we never may have need of you!

RICHARD
Meantime, God grants that I have need of you.
Our brother is imprisoned by your means,   78
Myself disgraced, and the nobility
Held in contempt, while great promotions
Are daily given to ennoble those
That scarce some two days since were worth a noble.   82

QUEEN ELIZABETH
By Him that raised me to this careful height   83
From that contented hap which I enjoyed,   84
I never did incense His Majesty
Against the Duke of Clarence, but have been
An earnest advocate to plead for him.
My lord, you do me shameful injury
Falsely to draw me in these vile suspects.   89

RICHARD
You may deny that you were not the means
Of my Lord Hastings' late imprisonment.

RIVERS   She may, my lord, for—

RICHARD
She may, Lord Rivers! Why, who knows not so?
She may do more, sir, than denying that:

---

68 Makes him causes him. (The implied subject is "The king's own disposition.")   **ground** cause (of your ill will)   **75 friends'** i.e., kinsmen's   **78 Our brother** i.e., Clarence.   **means** efforts   **82 noble** (1) gold coin worth 6 shillings 8 pence (2) nobleman   **83 careful** full of cares   **84 hap** fortune   **89 in** into.   **suspects** suspicions

She may help you to many fair preferments,   95
And then deny her aiding hand therein,
And lay those honors on your high desert.   97
What may she not? She may, ay, marry, may she—   98

RIVERS   What, marry, may she?

RICHARD
What, marry, may she? Marry with a king,
A bachelor, and a handsome stripling too!   101
Iwis your grandam had a worser match.   102

QUEEN ELIZABETH
My lord of Gloucester, I have too long borne
Your blunt upbraidings and your bitter scoffs.
By heaven, I will acquaint His Majesty
Of those gross taunts that oft I have endured.
I had rather be a country servant maid
Than a great queen with this condition,
To be so baited, scorned, and stormèd at.   109

     Enter old Queen Margaret [behind].

Small joy have I in being England's queen.

QUEEN MARGARET [*Aside*]
And lessened be that small, God I beseech him!
Thy honor, state, and seat is due to me.   112

RICHARD
What? Threat you me with telling of the King?   113
Tell him, and spare not. Look what I have said   114
I will avouch 't in presence of the King.
I dare adventure to be sent to the Tower.   116
'Tis time to speak; my pains are quite forgot.   117

QUEEN MARGARET [*Aside*]
Out, devil! I do remember them too well: 118
Thou killedst my husband Henry in the Tower,
And Edward, my poor son, at Tewkesbury.

---

95 preferments advantages, promotions   **97 lay . . . on** attribute these
high honors to   **98 marry** i.e., indeed (followed by a pun on "wed")
101 stripling young man   **102 Iwis** certainly   **109 baited** harassed
s.d. Queen Margaret (Historically, Queen Margaret was held prisoner in England for five years following Tewkesbury and then was sent
to France; see note to l. 167 below.)   **112 state** degree, high rank.   **seat**
throne   **113 Threat** threaten   **114 Look what** whatever   **116 adventure
to be** risk being   **117 pains** efforts (in King Edward's behalf)   **118 Out**
(An exclamation of anger.)

RICHARD
  Ere you were queen, ay, or your husband king,
  I was a packhorse in his great affairs,   122
  A weeder-out of his proud adversaries,
  A liberal rewarder of his friends.
  To royalize his blood I spent mine own.

QUEEN MARGARET [*Aside*]
  Ay, and much better blood than his or thine.

RICHARD
  In all which time you and your husband Grey
  Were factious for the house of Lancaster;   128
  And, Rivers, so were you. Was not your husband   129
  In Margaret's battle at Saint Albans slain?
  Let me put in your minds, if you forget,
  What you have been ere this, and what you are;
  Withal, what I have been, and what I am.   133

QUEEN MARGARET [*Aside*]
  A murderous villain, and so still thou art.

RICHARD
  Poor Clarence did forsake his father, Warwick,   135
  Ay, and forswore himself—which Jesu pardon!—

QUEEN MARGARET [*Aside*]   Which God revenge!

RICHARD
  To fight on Edward's party for the crown;
  And for his meed, poor lord, he is mewed up.   139
  I would to God my heart were flint, like Edward's,
  Or Edward's soft and pitiful, like mine.
  I am too childish-foolish for this world.

QUEEN MARGARET [*Aside*]
  Hie thee to hell for shame, and leave this world,   143
  Thou cacodemon! There thy kingdom is.   144

RIVERS
  My lord of Gloucester, in those busy days
  Which here you urge to prove us enemies,   146

---

122 packhorse workhorse, beast of burden   **128 factious** promoting
dissension.   **for** on the side of   **129 husband** (Queen Elizabeth's first
husband, Sir John Grey, fell fighting on the Lancastrian side at Saint
Albans.)   **133 Withal** in addition   **135 father** i.e., father-in-law. (See *3
Henry VI*, 4.1, when Clarence deserted his brothers to marry Warwick's
daughter Isabella and supported the Lancastrian cause for a time;
thereafter he forswore his oath to Warwick by returning to fight on
Edward's *party* [l. 138] or side.)   **139 meed** reward.   **mewed** caged (like a
hawk)   **143 Hie** hasten   **144 cacodemon** evil spirit   **146 urge** cite

We followed then our lord, our sovereign king.
So should we you, if you should be our king.

RICHARD

If I should be? I had rather be a peddler.
Far be it from my heart, the thought thereof!

QUEEN ELIZABETH

As little joy, my lord, as you suppose
You should enjoy were you this country's king,
As little joy you may suppose in me
That I enjoy, being the queen thereof.

QUEEN MARGARET [*Aside*]

Ah, little joy enjoys the queen thereof,
For I am she, and altogether joyless.
I can no longer hold me patient.   [*Advancing.*]
Hear me, you wrangling pirates, that fall out
In sharing that which you have pilled from me!   159
Which of you trembles not that looks on me?
If not, that I am queen, you bow like subjects,   161
Yet that, by you deposed, you quake like rebels?   162
[*To Richard.*] Ah, gentle villain, do not turn away!   163

RICHARD

Foul wrinkled witch, what mak'st thou in my sight?   164

QUEEN MARGARET

But repetition of what thou hast marred;   165
That will I make before I let thee go.

RICHARD

Wert thou not banishèd on pain of death?   167

QUEEN MARGARET

I was; but I do find more pain in banishment
Than death can yield me here by my abode.
A husband and a son thou ow'st to me,   170
And thou a kingdom; all of you allegiance.   171
This sorrow that I have by right is yours,
And all the pleasures you usurp are mine.

---

159 pilled pillaged, robbed   **161–162 If . . . rebels** i.e., even if you do not
bow low to me as your queen, you quake as rebels who have deposed
me   **163 gentle** nobly born   **164 mak'st thou** are you doing   **165 But
. . . marred** only reciting your crimes   **167 banishèd** (Margaret was
banished in 1464, returned to England in 1471, and after the Battle of
Tewkesbury was confined in the Tower until 1476 when she returned to
France, dying there in 1482, one year before the historical time of this
scene.)   **170 thou** i.e., Richard   **171 thou** i.e., Elizabeth

RICHARD

  The curse my noble father laid on thee   174
  When thou didst crown his warlike brows with paper
  And with thy scorns drew'st rivers from his eyes,
  And then, to dry them, gav'st the Duke a clout   177
  Steeped in the faultless blood of pretty Rutland—
  His curses then, from bitterness of soul
  Denounced against thee, are all fall'n upon thee;
  And God, not we, hath plagued thy bloody deed.

QUEEN ELIZABETH

  So just is God, to right the innocent.

HASTINGS

  O, 'twas the foulest deed to slay that babe,   183
  And the most merciless, that e'er was heard of!

RIVERS

  Tyrants themselves wept when it was reported.

DORSET

  No man but prophesied revenge for it.   186

BUCKINGHAM

  Northumberland, then present, wept to see it.

QUEEN MARGARET

  What? Were you snarling all before I came,
  Ready to catch each other by the throat,
  And turn you all your hatred now on me?
  Did York's dread curse prevail so much with heaven
  That Henry's death, my lovely Edward's death,
  Their kingdom's loss, my woeful banishment,
  Should all but answer for that peevish brat?   194
  Can curses pierce the clouds and enter heaven?
  Why then give way, dull clouds, to my quick curses!   196
  Though not by war, by surfeit die your king,   197
  As ours by murder, to make him a king!
  Edward thy son, that now is Prince of Wales,
  For Edward our son, that was Prince of Wales,
  Die in his youth by like untimely violence!
  Thyself a queen, for me that was a queen,
  Outlive thy glory, like my wretched self!

---

174 The curse (See *3 Henry VI*, 1.4.164–166.)   **177 clout** cloth, handkerchief   **183 that babe** i.e., Rutland   **186 No . . . prophesied** there was no one who did not prophesy   **194 but answer for** merely atone for, equal.   **peevish** silly, senseless   **196 quick** lively, piercing   **197 surfeit** dissipated living

Long mayst thou live to wail thy children's death
And see another, as I see thee now,
Decked in thy rights, as thou art stalled in mine!   206
Long die thy happy days before thy death,
And, after many lengthened hours of grief,
Die neither mother, wife, nor England's queen!
Rivers and Dorset, you were standers-by,   210
And so wast thou, Lord Hastings, when my son   211
Was stabbed with bloody daggers: God, I pray him,
That none of you may live his natural age,   213
But by some unlooked accident cut off!   214

RICHARD
Have done thy charm, thou hateful withered hag!   215

QUEEN MARGARET
And leave out thee? Stay, dog, for thou shalt hear me.
If heaven have any grievous plague in store
Exceeding those that I can wish upon thee,
O, let them keep it till thy sins be ripe,   219
And then hurl down their indignation
On thee, the troubler of the poor world's peace!
The worm of conscience still begnaw thy soul!   222
Thy friends suspect for traitors while thou liv'st,
And take deep traitors for thy dearest friends!
No sleep close up that deadly eye of thine,
Unless it be while some tormenting dream
Affrights thee with a hell of ugly devils!
Thou elvish-marked, abortive, rooting hog,   228
Thou that wast sealed in thy nativity   229
The slave of nature and the son of hell!   230
Thou slander of thy heavy mother's womb,   231
Thou loathèd issue of thy father's loins,
Thou rag of honor, thou detested—

RICHARD
Margaret.

---

206 Decked dressed.   **stalled** installed   **210–211 Rivers, Dorset, Hastings** (Not present in Shakespeare's dramatization of the event in *3 Henry VI*, 5.5, but named in the chronicles as having been present.)
213 natural age full course of life   **214 unlooked** unanticipated
215 charm magic curse, pronounced by a witch   **219 them** i.e., the heavens, heaven   **222 still begnaw** continually gnaw   **228 elvish-marked** marked by elves at birth.   **hog** (Alludes to Richard's badge, the wild boar.)   **229 sealed** stamped   **230 slave of nature** i.e., by the malignancy of nature (as seen in his deformity)   **231 heavy** sorrowful

QUEEN MARGARET Richard!

RICHARD   Ha?

QUEEN MARGARET   I call thee not.

RICHARD
I cry thee mercy then, for I did think   235
That thou hadst called me all these bitter names.

QUEEN MARGARET
Why, so I did, but looked for no reply.
O, let me make the period to my curse!   238

RICHARD
'Tis done by me, and ends in "Margaret."

QUEEN ELIZABETH
Thus have you breathed your curse against yourself.

QUEEN MARGARET
Poor painted queen, vain flourish of my fortune!   241
Why strew'st thou sugar on that bottled spider,   242
Whose deadly web ensnareth thee about?
Fool, fool, thou whet'st a knife to kill thyself.
The day will come that thou shalt wish for me
To help thee curse this poisonous bunch-backed toad.   246

HASTINGS
False-boding woman, end thy frantic curse,   247
Lest to thy harm thou move our patience.

QUEEN MARGARET
Foul shame upon you! You have all moved mine.

RIVERS
Were you well served, you would be taught your duty.   250

QUEEN MARGARET
To serve me well, you all should do me duty,   251
Teach me to be your queen, and you my subjects.
O, serve me well, and teach yourselves that duty!

DORSET
Dispute not with her; she is lunatic.

---

235 **cry thee mercy** beg your pardon. (Said sarcastically.)   238 **period**
conclusion   241 **painted** counterfeit.   **vain . . . fortune** i.e., mere
ornament of a position that is mine by right   242 **bottled** bottle-shaped,
swollen   246 **bunch-backed** hunchbacked   247 **False-boding** falsely
prophesying   250 **well served** treated as you deserve. (But Margaret
turns the phrase around to mean "served as befitting one of royal
rank.")   **your duty** your place (i.e., to be obedient)   251 **duty**
reverence

QUEEN MARGARET
　Peace, Master Marquess, you are malapert.   255
　Your fire-new stamp of honor is scarce current.   256
　O, that your young nobility could judge
　What 'twere to lose it and be miserable!
　They that stand high have many blasts to shake them,
　And if they fall, they dash themselves to pieces.

RICHARD
　Good counsel, marry! Learn it, learn it, Marquess.

DORSET
　It touches you, my lord, as much as me.

RICHARD
　Ay, and much more; but I was born so high.
　Our aerie buildeth in the cedar's top,   264
　And dallies with the wind and scorns the sun.

QUEEN MARGARET
　And turns the sun to shade; alas, alas!   266
　Witness my son, now in the shade of death,
　Whose bright outshining beams thy cloudy wrath
　Hath in eternal darkness folded up.
　Your aerie buildeth in our aerie's nest.
　O God, that seest it, do not suffer it!
　As it is won with blood, lost be it so!

BUCKINGHAM
　Peace, peace, for shame, if not for charity!

QUEEN MARGARET
　Urge neither charity nor shame to me.
　　　　　　　　　　　[*Turning to the others.*]
　Uncharitably with me have you dealt,
　And shamefully my hopes by you are butchered.
　My charity is outrage, life my shame,   277
　And in that shame still live my sorrow's rage!

BUCKINGHAM　Have done, have done.

QUEEN MARGARET
　O princely Buckingham, I'll kiss thy hand
　In sign of league and amity with thee.
　Now fair befall thee and thy noble house!   282

---

255 malapert impudent　**256 fire-new** newly coined.　**current** genuine
as legal tender　**264 aerie** eagle's brood　**266 sun** (with a play on *son* in
the next line)　**277 My . . . outrage** i.e., instead of charity I receive
outrage　**282 fair befall** good luck to

Thy garments are not spotted with our blood,
Nor thou within the compass of my curse.   284

BUCKINGHAM
Nor no one here; for curses never pass   285
The lips of those that breathe them in the air.   286

QUEEN MARGARET
I will not think but they ascend the sky   287
And there awake God's gentle-sleeping peace.
O Buckingham, take heed of yonder dog!
Look when he fawns, he bites; and when he bites,   290
His venom tooth will rankle to the death.   291
Have not to do with him, beware of him;
Sin, death, and hell have set their marks on him,
And all their ministers attend on him.

RICHARD
What doth she say, my lord of Buckingham?

BUCKINGHAM
Nothing that I respect, my gracious lord.   296

QUEEN MARGARET
What, dost thou scorn me for my gentle counsel?
And soothe the devil that I warn thee from?   298
O, but remember this another day,
When he shall split thy very heart with sorrow,
And say poor Margaret was a prophetess!
Live each of you the subjects to his hate,
And he to yours, and all of you to God's!   *Exit.*

BUCKINGHAM
My hair doth stand on end to hear her curses.

RIVERS
And so doth mine. I muse why she's at liberty.   305

RICHARD
I cannot blame her. By God's holy mother,
She hath had too much wrong, and I repent
My part thereof that I have done to her.

QUEEN ELIZABETH
I never did her any, to my knowledge.

---

284 compass scope, boundary **285–286 curses . . . air** i.e., curses have
no effect, are mere speech **287 I . . . but** I must believe that **290 Look
when** whenever **291 venom** envenomed. **rankle** cause a festering
wound **296 respect** heed **298 soothe** flatter **305 muse** wonder

RICHARD

Yet you have all the vantage of her wrong.   310
I was too hot to do somebody good   311
That is too cold in thinking of it now.   312
Marry, as for Clarence, he is well repaid;
He is franked up to fatting for his pains—   314
God pardon them that are the cause thereof!

RIVERS

A virtuous and a Christian-like conclusion,
To pray for them that have done scathe to us.   317

RICHARD

So do I ever—(*Speaks to himself*) being well advised.
For had I cursed now, I had cursed myself.

    Enter Catesby.

CATESBY

Madam, His Majesty doth call for you,
And for Your Grace, and yours, my gracious lord.

QUEEN ELIZABETH

Catesby, I come. Lords, will you go with me?

RIVERS   We wait upon Your Grace.   323

    Exeunt all but [Richard, Duke of] Gloucester.

RICHARD

I do the wrong, and first begin to brawl.
The secret mischiefs that I set abroach   325
I lay unto the grievous charge of others.   326
Clarence, who I indeed have cast in darkness,
I do beweep to many simple gulls—   328
Namely, to Derby, Hastings, Buckingham—
And tell them 'tis the Queen and her allies
That stir the King against the Duke my brother.
Now they believe it, and withal whet me   332
To be revenged on Rivers, Dorset, Grey.
But then I sigh and, with a piece of Scripture,
Tell them that God bids us do good for evil.   335

---

310 vantage of advantage derived from   **311 hot** eager (in helping
Edward to the throne)   **312 That . . . cold** who is too ungrateful
314 franked up shut up in a frank or sty.   **to fatting** to be fattened (for
slaughter)   **317 scathe** harm   **323 wait upon** attend   **325 set abroach**
set flowing, begin   **326 lay . . . of** impute as a serious accusation
against   **328 gulls** credulous persons   **332 whet** urge, incite   **335 for** in
return for

And thus I clothe my naked villainy
With odd old ends stol'n forth of Holy Writ,   337
And seem a saint when most I play the devil.

    Enter two Murderers.

But, soft! Here come my executioners.
How now, my hardy, stout, resolvèd mates,   340
Are you now going to dispatch this thing?
FIRST MURDERER
We are, my lord, and come to have the warrant
That we may be admitted where he is.
RICHARD
Well thought upon. I have it here about me.
                     [He gives the warrant.]
When you have done, repair to Crosby Place.   345
But, sirs, be sudden in the execution,
Withal obdurate; do not hear him plead;   347
For Clarence is well-spoken, and perhaps
May move your hearts to pity if you mark him.   349
FIRST MURDERER
Tut, tut, my lord, we will not stand to prate;
Talkers are no good doers. Be assured
We go to use our hands and not our tongues.
RICHARD
Your eyes drop millstones when fools' eyes fall tears.   353
I like you, lads; about your business straight.
Go, go, dispatch.
FIRST MURDERER   We will, my noble lord.   *[Exeunt.]*

                      ✶

1.4   *Enter Clarence and Keeper.*

KEEPER
Why looks Your Grace so heavily today?   1

---

337 ends fragments, tags **340 resolvèd** resolute **345 repair** betake
yourselves. **347 Withal** at the same time **349 mark** pay attention to
353 millstones heavy stone disks used for grinding. (To *drop millstones*
was proverbially to show signs of hardheartedness.) **353 fall** let fall

1.4. Location: London. The Tower.
1 heavily sad

CLARENCE

  O, I have passed a miserable night,
  So full of fearful dreams, of ugly sights,
  That, as I am a Christian faithful man,
  I would not spend another such a night
  Though 'twere to buy a world of happy days,
  So full of dismal terror was the time!

KEEPER

  What was your dream, my lord? I pray you, tell me.

CLARENCE

  Methought that I had broken from the Tower   9
  And was embarked to cross to Burgundy,   10
  And in my company my brother Gloucester,
  Who from my cabin tempted me to walk
  Upon the hatches. Thence we looked toward England   13
  And cited up a thousand heavy times,   14
  During the wars of York and Lancaster,
  That had befall'n us. As we paced along
  Upon the giddy footing of the hatches,   17
  Methought that Gloucester stumbled, and in falling
  Struck me, that thought to stay him, overboard   19
  Into the tumbling billows of the main.   20
  O Lord, methought what pain it was to drown!
  What dreadful noise of waters in my ears!
  What sights of ugly death within my eyes!
  Methought I saw a thousand fearful wracks;   24
  Ten thousand men that fishes gnawed upon;
  Wedges of gold, great anchors, heaps of pearl,
  Inestimable stones, unvalued jewels,   27
  All scattered in the bottom of the sea.
  Some lay in dead men's skulls, and in the holes
  Where eyes did once inhabit there were crept,
  As 'twere in scorn of eyes, reflecting gems,
  That wooed the slimy bottom of the deep
  And mocked the dead bones that lay scattered by.

---

9 Methought it seemed to me   **10 Burgundy** (Clarence and Richard, according to the chronicles, had been sent to Burgundy for protection following their father's death.)   **13 hatches** movable planks forming a deck   **14 cited up** recalled   **17 giddy** dizzying   **19 stay** hold, steady   **20 main** ocean   **24 wracks** shipwrecked vessels   **27 Inestimable** precious and innumerable.   **unvalued** priceless

KEEPER
  Had you such leisure in the time of death
  To gaze upon these secrets of the deep?

CLARENCE
  Methought I had, and often did I strive
  To yield the ghost; but still the envious flood   37
  Stopped in my soul, and would not let it forth   38
  To seek the empty, vast, and wandering air,
  But smothered it within my panting bulk,   40
  Which almost burst to belch it in the sea.

KEEPER
  Awaked you not in this sore agony?

CLARENCE
  No, no, my dream was lengthened after life.
  O, then began the tempest to my soul!
  I passed, methought, the melancholy flood,   45
  With that sour ferryman which poets write of,   46
  Unto the kingdom of perpetual night.
  The first that there did greet my stranger soul   48
  Was my great father-in-law, renownèd Warwick,
  Who spake aloud, "What scourge for perjury
  Can this dark monarchy afford false Clarence?"
  And so he vanished. Then came wandering by
  A shadow like an angel, with bright hair   53
  Dabbled in blood, and he shrieked out aloud,
  "Clarence is come—false, fleeting, perjured Clarence,   55
  That stabbed me in the field by Tewkesbury.
  Seize on him, Furies, take him unto torment!"
  With that, methought, a legion of foul fiends
  Environed me, and howlèd in mine ears
  Such hideous cries that with the very noise
  I trembling waked, and for a season after   61
  Could not believe but that I was in hell,
  Such terrible impression made my dream.

KEEPER
  No marvel, my lord, though it affrighted you.
  I am afraid, methinks, to hear you tell it.

---

37 envious malicious   **38 Stopped** held   **40 bulk** body   **45 melancholy flood** i.e., River Styx   **46 ferryman** i.e., Charon, who ferried souls to Hades, *the kingdom of perpetual night* (l. 47)   **48 stranger** i.e., newly arrived   **53 shadow** i.e., ghost of Edward, Prince of Wales, son of Henry VI   **55 fleeting** fickle, deceitful   **61 season** time

CLARENCE
Ah, keeper, keeper, I have done these things,
That now give evidence against my soul,
For Edward's sake, and see how he requites me!   68
O God! If my deep prayers cannot appease thee,
But thou wilt be avenged on my misdeeds,
Yet execute thy wrath in me alone!
O, spare my guiltless wife and my poor children!
Keeper, I prithee, sit by me awhile.
My soul is heavy, and I fain would sleep.   74

KEEPER
I will, my lord. God give Your Grace good rest!
                 [Clarence sleeps.]

    Enter Brackenbury, the Lieutenant.

BRACKENBURY
Sorrow breaks seasons and reposing hours,   76
Makes the night morning and the noontide night.
Princes have but their titles for their glories,
An outward honor for an inward toil,
And, for unfelt imaginations,   80
They often feel a world of restless cares;
So that between their titles and low name   82
There's nothing differs but the outward fame.   83

    Enter two Murderers.

FIRST MURDERER   Ho! Who's here?
BRACKENBURY
What would'st thou, fellow, and how cam'st thou
hither?
FIRST MURDERER   I would speak with Clarence, and I
came hither on my legs.
BRACKENBURY   What, so brief?
SECOND MURDERER   'Tis better, sir, than to be tedious.
Let him see our commission, and talk no more.
                 [Brackenbury] reads [it].

---

68 requites repays   **74 fain** willingly   **76 breaks seasons** i.e., disrupts
the normal rhythms of life.   **reposing hours** i.e., hours properly devoted
to sleep   **80 for unfelt imaginations** in return for glories that are only
imagined   **82 low name** i.e., the lowly position of ordinary men
83 fame reputation

BRACKENBURY
I am in this commanded to deliver
The noble Duke of Clarence to your hands.
I will not reason what is meant hereby,
Because I will be guiltless from the meaning.   94
There lies the Duke asleep, and there the keys.

[*He gives keys.*]

I'll to the King and signify to him
That thus I have resigned to you my charge.

FIRST MURDERER   You may, sir; 'tis a point of wisdom.
Fare you well.   *Exit [Brackenbury with Keeper].*

SECOND MURDERER   What, shall I stab him as he
sleeps?

FIRST MURDERER   No. He'll say 'twas done cowardly,
when he wakes.

SECOND MURDERER   Why, he shall never wake until the
great Judgment Day.

FIRST MURDERER   Why, then he'll say we stabbed him
sleeping.

SECOND MURDERER   The urging of that word "judgment" hath bred a kind of remorse in me.

FIRST MURDERER   What, art thou afraid?

SECOND MURDERER   Not to kill him, having a warrant,
but to be damned for killing him, from the which no
warrant can defend me.

FIRST MURDERER   I thought thou hadst been resolute.

SECOND MURDERER   So I am—to let him live.

FIRST MURDERER   I'll back to the Duke of Gloucester and
tell him so.

SECOND MURDERER   Nay, I prithee, stay a little. I hope
this passionate humor of mine will change. It was   119
wont to hold me but while one tells twenty.   120

FIRST MURDERER   How dost thou feel thyself now?

SECOND MURDERER   Faith, some certain dregs of conscience are yet within me.

FIRST MURDERER   Remember our reward when the deed's
done.

SECOND MURDERER   Zounds, he dies! I had forgot the   126
reward.

---

94 will be wish to be   **119 passionate humor** compassionate mood
120 tells counts   **126 Zounds** i.e., by God's (Christ's) wounds

FIRST MURDERER   Where's thy conscience now?

SECOND MURDERER   O, in the Duke of Gloucester's purse.

FIRST MURDERER   When he opens his purse to give us our reward, thy conscience flies out.

SECOND MURDERER   'Tis no matter; let it go. There's few or none will entertain it.   134

FIRST MURDERER   What if it come to thee again?

SECOND MURDERER   I'll not meddle with it; it makes a man a coward. A man cannot steal but it accuseth him; a man cannot swear but it checks him; a man 138 cannot lie with his neighbor's wife but it detects him. 'Tis a blushing shamefaced spirit that mutinies in a man's bosom. It fills a man full of obstacles. It made me once restore a purse of gold that by chance I found. It beggars any man that keeps it. It is turned out of towns and cities for a dangerous thing, and every man that means to live well endeavors to trust to himself and live without it.

FIRST MURDERER   Zounds, 'tis even now at my elbow, persuading me not to kill the Duke.

SECOND MURDERER   Take the devil in thy mind, and be- 149 lieve him not. He would insinuate with thee but to 150 make thee sigh.

FIRST MURDERER   Tut, I am strong-framed; he cannot prevail with me.

SECOND MURDERER   Spoke like a tall man that respects 154 thy reputation. Come, shall we fall to work?

FIRST MURDERER   Take him on the costard with the hilts 156 of thy sword, and then throw him into the malmsey 157 butt in the next room. 158

SECOND MURDERER   O, excellent device! And make a sop 159 of him.

FIRST MURDERER   Soft, he wakes.

SECOND MURDERER   Strike!

---

134 entertain it receive it, give it welcome   **138 checks** reproves
149–150 Take . . . not i.e., listen to the devil and don't heed the devil conscience   **150 insinuate** ingratiate himself   **154 tall** brave   **156 Take** strike.   **costard** head. (Literally, a kind of apple.)   **157–158 malmsey butt** wine barrel. (Malmsey is a sweet wine.)   **159 sop** bread or cake soaked in wine

FIRST MURDERER   No, we'll reason with him.   163

[*Clarence wakes.*]

CLARENCE
Where art thou, keeper? Give me a cup of wine.

SECOND MURDERER
You shall have wine enough, my lord, anon.

CLARENCE   In God's name, what art thou?

FIRST MURDERER   A man, as you are.

CLARENCE   But not, as I am, royal.

FIRST MURDERER   Nor you, as we are, loyal.

CLARENCE
Thy voice is thunder, but thy looks are humble.

FIRST MURDERER
My voice is now the King's, my looks mine own.

CLARENCE
How darkly and how deadly dost thou speak!
Your eyes do menace me. Why look you pale?
Who sent you hither? Wherefore do you come?

SECOND MURDERER   To, to, to—

CLARENCE   To murder me?

BOTH   Ay, ay.

CLARENCE
You scarcely have the hearts to tell me so,
And therefore cannot have the hearts to do it.
Wherein, my friends, have I offended you?

FIRST MURDERER
Offended us you have not, but the King.

CLARENCE
I shall be reconciled to him again.

SECOND MURDERER
Never, my lord; therefore prepare to die.

CLARENCE
Are you drawn forth among a world of men   184
To slay the innocent? What is my offense?
Where is the evidence that doth accuse me?
What lawful quest have given their verdict up   187
Unto the frowning judge? Or who pronounced
The bitter sentence of poor Clarence' death
Before I be convict by course of law?   190

---

163 reason talk   **184 drawn . . . men** especially selected from the whole
human race   **187 quest** inquest, i.e., jury   **190 convict** convicted

To threaten me with death is most unlawful.
I charge you, as you hope to have redemption
By Christ's dear blood shed for our grievous sins,
That you depart and lay no hands on me.
The deed you undertake is damnable.

FIRST MURDERER
What we will do, we do upon command.

SECOND MURDERER
And he that hath commanded is our king.

CLARENCE
Erroneous vassals! The great King of kings   198
Hath in the table of his law commanded   199
That thou shalt do no murder. Will you then
Spurn at his edict, and fulfill a man's?
Take heed; for he holds vengeance in his hand
To hurl upon their heads that break his law.

SECOND MURDERER
And that same vengeance doth he hurl on thee
For false forswearing and for murder too.
Thou didst receive the Sacrament to fight   206
In quarrel of the house of Lancaster.

FIRST MURDERER
And, like a traitor to the name of God,
Didst break that vow, and with thy treacherous blade
Unrippedst the bowels of thy sovereign's son.   210

SECOND MURDERER
Whom thou wast sworn to cherish and defend.

FIRST MURDERER
How canst thou urge God's dreadful law to us
When thou hast broke it in such dear degree?   213

CLARENCE
Alas! For whose sake did I that ill deed?
For Edward, for my brother, for his sake.
He sends you not to murder me for this,
For in that sin he is as deep as I.
If God will be avengèd for the deed,
O, know you yet he doth it publicly!
Take not the quarrel from his powerful arm.

198 Erroneous vassals sinful and mistaken wretches   **199 table** tablet
206 receive the Sacrament i.e., swear upon the Sacrament   **210 sovereign's son** i.e., Prince Edward, son of Henry VI   **213 dear** grievous

He needs no indirect or lawless course
To cut off those that have offended him.

FIRST MURDERER
Who made thee, then, a bloody minister   223
When gallant-springing brave Plantagenet,   224
That princely novice, was struck dead by thee? 225

CLARENCE
My brother's love, the devil, and my rage.   226

FIRST MURDERER
Thy brother's love, our duty, and thy faults
Provoke us hither now to slaughter thee.

CLARENCE
If you do love my brother, hate not me!
I am his brother, and I love him well.
If you are hired for meed, go back again,   231
And I will send you to my brother Gloucester,
Who shall reward you better for my life
Than Edward will for tidings of my death.   234

SECOND MURDERER
You are deceived. Your brother Gloucester hates you.

CLARENCE
O, no, he loves me, and he holds me dear.
Go you to him from me.

FIRST MURDERER   Ay, so we will.

CLARENCE
Tell him, when that our princely father York
Blessed his three sons with his victorious arm
And charged us from his soul to love each other,
He little thought of this divided friendship.
Bid Gloucester think of this, and he will weep.

FIRST MURDERER
Ay, millstones, as he lessoned us to weep.   243

CLARENCE
O, do not slander him, for he is kind.

---

223 **minister** agent of God   224 **gallant-springing** i.e., gallant and
sprightly, aspiring.   **Plantagenet** (Originally, a nickname for Geoffrey of
Anjou, father of Henry II and founder of the dynasty that ruled England until 1485; the name is thus appropriate to the Lancastrian Prince
Edward, though the Yorkist Richard Plantagenet had attempted to take
the name for his own.)   225 **novice** youth   226 **My brother's love** i.e.,
my love for my brother   231 **meed** financial reward   234 **tidings**
news   243 **lessoned** taught

FIRST MURDERER
  Right, as snow in harvest. Come, you deceive yourself. 245
  'Tis he that sends us to destroy you here.
CLARENCE
  It cannot be, for he bewept my fortune,
  And hugged me in his arms, and swore with sobs
  That he would labor my delivery.   249
FIRST MURDERER
  Why, so he doth, when he delivers you
  From this earth's thralldom to the joys of heaven.   251
SECOND MURDERER
  Make peace with God, for you must die, my lord.
CLARENCE
  Have you that holy feeling in your souls
  To counsel me to make my peace with God,
  And are you yet to your own souls so blind
  That you will war with God by murdering me?
  O, sirs, consider, they that set you on
  To do this deed will hate you for the deed.
SECOND MURDERER [*To First Murderer*]
  What shall we do?
CLARENCE   Relent, and save your souls.
  Which of you, if you were a prince's son,
  Being pent from liberty, as I am now,   261
  If two such murderers as yourselves came to you,
  Would not entreat for life?   263
FIRST MURDERER
  Relent? No. 'Tis cowardly and womanish.
CLARENCE
  Not to relent is beastly, savage, devilish.
  My friend [*To Second Murderer*], I spy some pity in
    thy looks.
  O, if thine eye be not a flatterer,
  Come thou on my side, and entreat for me,
  As you would beg, were you in my distress.
  A begging prince what beggar pities not?
SECOND MURDERER   Look behind you, my lord.

245 Right . . . harvest i.e., he's just as kind and natural—that is, both
affectionate and with the natural feelings of a brother—as is snow at
harvest time   **249 labor my delivery** work for my release   **251 thralldom**
bondage, captivity   **261 pent** shut up   **263 entreat** beseech, beg

FIRST MURDERER
  Take that, and that! (*Stabs him.*) If all this will not do,
  I'll drown you in the malmsey butt within.
                              Exit [with the body].
SECOND MURDERER
  A bloody deed, and desperately dispatched!
  How fain, like Pilate, would I wash my hands   275
  Of this most grievous murder!

    Enter First Murderer.

FIRST MURDERER
  How now? What mean'st thou that thou help'st me not?
  By heaven, the Duke shall know how slack you have
    been.
SECOND MURDERER
  I would he knew that I had saved his brother!
  Take thou the fee, and tell him what I say,
  For I repent me that the Duke is slain.   *Exit.*
FIRST MURDERER
  So do not I. Go, coward as thou art.
  Well, I'll go hide his body in some hole
  Till that the Duke give order for his burial;
  And when I have my meed, I will away,
  For this will out, and then I must not stay.   *Exit.* 286

❖

275 **fain** gladly   286 **this** i.e., this murder

2.1　　*Flourish. Enter the King [Edward], sick, the Queen [Elizabeth], Lord Marquess Dorset, [Grey,] Rivers, Hastings, Catesby, Buckingham, [and others].*

KING EDWARD

Why, so. Now have I done a good day's work.
You peers, continue this united league.
I every day expect an embassage
From my Redeemer to redeem me hence;
And more in peace my soul shall part to heaven,
Since I have made my friends at peace on earth.
Rivers and Hastings, take each other's hand;
Dissemble not your hatred, swear your love.　　　　　8

RIVERS [*Taking Hastings' hand*]

By heaven, my soul is purged from grudging hate,
And with my hand I seal my true heart's love.

HASTINGS

So thrive I, as I truly swear the like!

KING EDWARD

Take heed you dally not before your king,　　　　　12
Lest he that is the supreme King of kings
Confound your hidden falsehood, and award　　　　　14
Either of you to be the other's end.　　　　　15

HASTINGS

So prosper I, as I swear perfect love!

RIVERS

And I, as I love Hastings with my heart!

KING EDWARD

Madam, yourself is not exempt from this,
Nor you, son Dorset, Buckingham, nor you;　　　　　19
You have been factious one against the other.　　　　　20
Wife, love Lord Hastings; let him kiss your hand;
And what you do, do it unfeignedly.

QUEEN ELIZABETH

There, Hastings, I will nevermore remember

2.1. Location: London. The royal court.
s.d. Flourish trumpet call to announce the arrival of a distinguished person　**8 Dissemble** conceal, disguise (under a false appearance of love)　**12 dally** trifle　**14 Confound** defeat　**15 Either . . . end** i.e., each of you to be the agent of death of the other　**19 son** i.e., stepson
20 factious quarrelsome

Our former hatred, so thrive I and mine!
                    [*Hastings kisses her hand.*]

KING EDWARD
  Dorset, embrace him. Hastings, love Lord Marquess.
DORSET
  This interchange of love, I here protest,
  Upon my part shall be inviolable.
HASTINGS   And so swear I.   [*They embrace.*]
KING EDWARD
  Now, princely Buckingham, seal thou this league
  With thy embracements to my wife's allies,
  And make me happy in your unity.
BUCKINGHAM [*To the Queen*]
  Whenever Buckingham doth turn his hate
  Upon Your Grace, but with all duteous love   33
  Doth cherish you and yours, God punish me
  With hate in those where I expect most love!
  When I have most need to employ a friend,
  And most assurèd that he is a friend,
  Deep, hollow, treacherous, and full of guile   38
  Be he unto me! This do I beg of God,
  When I am cold in love to you or yours.
                              [*They*] *embrace.*

KING EDWARD
  A pleasing cordial, princely Buckingham,   41
  Is this thy vow unto my sickly heart.
  There wanteth now our brother Gloucester here   43
  To make the blessèd period of this peace.   44
BUCKINGHAM   And, in good time,
  Here comes Sir Richard Ratcliffe and the Duke.

    Enter Ratcliffe and [*Richard, Duke of*]
    Gloucester.

RICHARD
  Good morrow to my sovereign king and queen;
  And, princely peers, a happy time of day!
KING EDWARD
  Happy, indeed, as we have spent the day.
  Gloucester, we have done deeds of charity,

33 **but** i.e., nor   **38 Deep** subtle, crafty   **41 cordial** restorative
43 wanteth is lacking   **44 period** conclusion

Made peace of enmity, fair love of hate,
Between these swelling wrong-incensèd peers.   52

RICHARD
A blessèd labor, my most sovereign lord.
Among this princely heap, if any here,   54
By false intelligence, or wrong surmise,   55
Hold me a foe;
If I unwittingly, or in my rage,
Have aught committed that is hardly borne   58
By any in this presence, I desire
To reconcile me to his friendly peace.
'Tis death to me to be at enmity;
I hate it, and desire all good men's love.
First, madam, I entreat true peace of you,
Which I will purchase with my duteous service;
Of you, my noble cousin Buckingham,
If ever any grudge were lodged between us;
Of you and you, Lord Rivers, and of Dorset,
That all without desert have frowned on me;   68
Dukes, earls, lords, gentlemen—indeed, of all.
I do not know that Englishman alive
With whom my soul is any jot at odds
More than the infant that is born tonight.   72
I thank my God for my humility.

QUEEN ELIZABETH
A holy day shall this be kept hereafter.
I would to God all strifes were well compounded.   75
My sovereign lord, I do beseech Your Highness
To take our brother Clarence to your grace.

RICHARD
Why, madam, have I offered love for this,
To be so flouted in this royal presence?   79
Who knows not that the gentle Duke is dead?
                           They all start.
You do him injury to scorn his corpse.

KING EDWARD
Who knows not he is dead? Who knows he is?

---

52 swelling i.e., with anger or rivalry   **54 heap** assembly   **55 false
intelligence** being misinformed   **58 hardly borne** taken amiss, deeply
resented   **68 all without desert** wholly without my having deserved it
72 More than the infant i.e., more than is that infant's soul
75 compounded settled   **79 flouted** mocked

QUEEN ELIZABETH
  All-seeing heaven, what a world is this!
BUCKINGHAM
  Look I so pale, Lord Dorset, as the rest?
DORSET
  Ay, my good lord, and no man in the presence   85
  But his red color hath forsook his cheeks.
KING EDWARD
  Is Clarence dead? The order was reversed.
RICHARD
  But he, poor man, by your first order died,
  And that a wingèd Mercury did bear;
  Some tardy cripple bare the countermand,   90
  That came too lag to see him buried.   91
  God grant that some, less noble and less loyal,   92
  Nearer in bloody thoughts but not in blood,   93
  Deserve not worse than wretched Clarence did,   94
  And yet go current from suspicion!   95

  Enter [Lord Stanley,] Earl of Derby.

STANLEY [*Kneeling*]
  A boon, my sovereign, for my service done!   96
KING EDWARD
  I prithee, peace. My soul is full of sorrow.
STANLEY
  I will not rise unless Your Highness hear me.
KING EDWARD
  Then say at once what is it thou requests.
STANLEY
  The forfeit, sovereign, of my servant's life,   100
  Who slew today a riotous gentleman   101
  Lately attendant on the Duke of Norfolk.
KING EDWARD
  Have I a tongue to doom my brother's death,   103

---

85 presence i.e., royal presence **90 bare** bore **91 lag** late **92–95 God . . .
suspicion** i.e., (ironically) pray God there be not persons who deserve
worse than Clarence got, persons less noble or related by blood to the
King than he although closely involved in bloody plots, who yet go unde-
tected. (Richard means the Queen and her kindred.) **go current** are
accepted at face value (like legal currency). **from** free from **96 A boon** (I
crave) a favor **100 the forfeit** i.e., the remission of the forfeit
101 riotous disorderly, wild **103 doom** decree

And shall that tongue give pardon to a slave?   104
My brother killed no man; his fault was thought,
And yet his punishment was bitter death.
Who sued to me for him? Who, in my wrath,
Kneeled at my feet and bid me be advised?   108
Who spoke of brotherhood? Who spoke of love?
Who told me how the poor soul did forsake
The mighty Warwick and did fight for me?
Who told me, in the field at Tewkesbury,
When Oxford had me down, he rescued me   113
And said, "Dear brother, live, and be a king"?
Who told me, when we both lay in the field
Frozen almost to death, how he did lap me   116
Even in his garments, and did give himself,
All thin and naked, to the numb-cold night?
All this from my remembrance brutish wrath
Sinfully plucked, and not a man of you
Had so much grace to put it in my mind.
But when your carters or your waiting vassals   122
Have done a drunken slaughter and defaced
The precious image of our dear Redeemer,
You straight are on your knees for pardon, pardon;
And I, unjustly too, must grant it you.
                                        [*Stanley rises.*]
But for my brother not a man would speak,
Nor I, ungracious, speak unto myself
For him, poor soul. The proudest of you all
Have been beholding to him in his life;   130
Yet none of you would once beg for his life.
O God, I fear thy justice will take hold
On me and you, and mine and yours, for this!
Come, Hastings, help me to my closet. Ah, poor
    Clarence!   *Exeunt some with King and Queen.* 134
RICHARD
    This is the fruits of rashness! Marked you not
    How that the guilty kindred of the Queen
    Looked pale when they did hear of Clarence' death?
    O, they did urge it still unto the King!

104 **slave** wretch   108 **advised** cautious   113 **Oxford** (See *3 Henry VI*,
5.5.2; this episode has no historical basis.)   116 **lap** wrap   122 **carters**
cart drivers   130 **beholding** beholden   134 **closet** private chambers

God will revenge it. Come, lords, will you go
To comfort Edward with our company?
BUCKINGHAM   We wait upon Your Grace.   *Exeunt.*

＊

2.2   *Enter the old Duchess of York, with the two
children of Clarence, [Edward and Margaret
Plantagenet].*

BOY
Good grandam, tell us, is our father dead?
DUCHESS   No, boy.
GIRL
Why do you weep so oft, and beat your breast,
And cry, "O Clarence, my unhappy son"?
BOY
Why do you look on us, and shake your head,
And call us orphans, wretches, castaways,
If that our noble father were alive?
DUCHESS
My pretty cousins, you mistake me both.   8
I do lament the sickness of the King,
As loath to lose him, not your father's death;
It were lost sorrow to wail one that's lost.
BOY
Then, you conclude, my grandam, he is dead.
The King mine uncle is to blame for it.
God will revenge it, whom I will importune   14
With earnest prayers all to that effect.
GIRL   And so will I.
DUCHESS
Peace, children, peace! The King doth love you well.
Incapable and shallow innocents,   18
You cannot guess who caused your father's death.
BOY
Grandam, we can; for my good uncle Gloucester
Told me the King, provoked to it by the Queen,
Devised impeachments to imprison him;   22

2.2. Location: London. The royal court.
8 cousins kinsmen   **14 importune** solicit, beg   **18 Incapable** unable to
understand   **22 impeachments** accusations

And when my uncle told me so, he wept,
And pitied me, and kindly kissed my cheek;
Bade me rely on him as on my father,
And he would love me dearly as a child.

DUCHESS
Ah, that deceit should steal such gentle shape,
And with a virtuous visor hide deep vice!   28
He is my son—ay, and therein my shame;
Yet from my dugs he drew not this deceit.   30

BOY
Think you my uncle did dissemble, grandam?

DUCHESS   Ay, boy.

BOY
I cannot think it. Hark, what noise is this?

*Enter the Queen [Elizabeth], with her hair about
her ears; Rivers and Dorset after her.*

QUEEN ELIZABETH
Ah, who shall hinder me to wail and weep,
To chide my fortune and torment myself?
I'll join with black despair against my soul,
And to myself become an enemy.

DUCHESS
What means this scene of rude impatience?   38

QUEEN ELIZABETH
To make an act of tragic violence.   39
Edward, my lord, thy son, our king, is dead!   40
Why grow the branches when the root is gone?
Why wither not the leaves that want their sap?
If you will live, lament; if die, be brief,   43
That our swift-wingèd souls may catch the King's
Or, like obedient subjects, follow him
To his new kingdom of ne'er-changing night.

DUCHESS
Ah, so much interest have I in thy sorrow
As I had title in thy noble husband!   48
I have bewept a worthy husband's death

---

28 visor mask   **30 dugs** breasts   **38 rude** violent   **39 make** perform.
(Continues the theatrical metaphor in the previous line.)   **40 Edward
... dead** (Clarence's death, February 1478, and Edward IV's death, April
1483, are treated as if they had occurred near together.)   **43 brief**
quick   **48 title** i.e., as mother of the King

And lived with looking on his images;   50
But now two mirrors of his princely semblance   51
Are cracked in pieces by malignant death,
And I for comfort have but one false glass,   53
That grieves me when I see my shame in him.
Thou art a widow; yet thou art a mother,
And hast the comfort of thy children left;
But death hath snatched my husband from mine arms
And plucked two crutches from my feeble hands,
Clarence and Edward. O, what cause have I,   59
Thine being but a moiety of my moan,   60
To overgo thy woes and drown thy cries!   61

BOY
Ah, aunt! You wept not for our father's death.
How can we aid you with our kindred tears?   63

GIRL
Our fatherless distress was left unmoaned;
Your widow-dolor likewise be unwept!   65

QUEEN ELIZABETH
Give me no help in lamentation;
I am not barren to bring forth complaints.   67
All springs reduce their currents to mine eyes,   68
That I, being governed by the watery moon,
May send forth plenteous tears to drown the world!
Ah for my husband, for my dear lord Edward!

CHILDREN
Ah for our father, for our dear lord Clarence!

DUCHESS
Alas for both, both mine, Edward and Clarence!

QUEEN ELIZABETH
What stay had I but Edward? And he's gone.   74

CHILDREN
What stay had we but Clarence? And he's gone.

DUCHESS
What stays had I but they? And they are gone.

---

50 images likenesses; here, children   **51 two mirrors** i.e., Edward and
Clarence. (She does not count Rutland.)   **53 false glass** i.e., Richard
59 what . . . I what a cause have I   **60 moiety of my moan** half (the
cause) of my grief   **61 overgo** exceed   **63 kindred tears** i.e., tears of
kinsmen   **65 widow-dolor** widow's grief   **67 barren to** unable to
68 All springs reduce let all springs bring   **74 stay** support

QUEEN ELIZABETH
  Was never widow had so dear a loss!   77
CHILDREN
  Were never orphans had so dear a loss!
DUCHESS
  Was never mother had so dear a loss!
  Alas, I am the mother of these griefs;
  Their woes are parceled, mine is general.   81
  She for an Edward weeps, and so do I;
  I for a Clarence weep, so doth not she.
  These babes for Clarence weep, and so do I;
  I for an Edward weep, so do not they.
  Alas, you three, on me, threefold distressed,
  Pour all your tears! I am your sorrow's nurse,
  And I will pamper it with lamentation.   88
DORSET [*To Queen Elizabeth*]
  Comfort, dear Mother. God is much displeased
  That you take with unthankfulness his doing.
  In common worldly things 'tis called ungrateful
  With dull unwillingness to repay a debt
  Which with a bounteous hand was kindly lent;
  Much more to be thus opposite with heaven   94
  For it requires the royal debt it lent you.   95
RIVERS
  Madam, bethink you like a careful mother
  Of the young Prince your son. Send straight for him;
  Let him be crowned. In him your comfort lives.
  Drown desperate sorrow in dead Edward's grave
  And plant your joys in living Edward's throne.

        Enter Richard, [Duke of Gloucester,] Buckingham,
        [Lord Stanley, Earl of] Derby, Hastings, and
        Ratcliffe.

RICHARD
  Sister, have comfort. All of us have cause
  To wail the dimming of our shining star,
  But none can help our harms by wailing them.—

77 **dear** grievous   81 **Their . . . parceled** i.e., the woes of Queen Elizabeth and these children are single   88 **pamper** i.e., sustain   94 **opposite
with** hostile toward   95 **For it requires** because it calls back

Madam, my mother, I do cry you mercy;   104
I did not see Your Grace. Humbly on my knee
I crave your blessing.   [*He kneels.*]

DUCHESS
God bless thee, and put meekness in thy breast,
Love, charity, obedience, and true duty!

RICHARD
Amen! [*Aside.*] And make me die a good old man!
That is the butt end of a mother's blessing;
I marvel that Her Grace did leave it out.

BUCKINGHAM
You cloudy princes and heart-sorrowing peers,   112
That bear this heavy mutual load of moan,   113
Now cheer each other in each other's love.
Though we have spent our harvest of this king,
We are to reap the harvest of his son.
The broken rancor of your high-swoll'n hates,
But lately splintered, knit, and joined together,   118
Must gently be preserved, cherished, and kept.   119
Meseemeth good that with some little train   120
Forthwith from Ludlow the young Prince be fet   121
Hither to London, to be crowned our king.

RIVERS
Why with some little train, my lord of Buckingham?

BUCKINGHAM
Marry, my lord, lest by a multitude   124
The new-healed wound of malice should break out,
Which would be so much the more dangerous
By how much the estate is green and yet ungoverned.   127
Where every horse bears his commanding rein   128
And may direct his course as please himself,   129
As well the fear of harm, as harm apparent,   130
In my opinion, ought to be prevented.

---

104 cry you mercy beg your pardon   **112 cloudy** clouded with grief
113 moan lamentation   **118 But lately splintered** only recently bound
together (as with a splint)   **119 Must . . . preserved** i.e., the recent mend-
ing of differences must be preserved   **120 Meseemeth** it seems to me.
train entourage   **121 Ludlow** royal castle in Shropshire, near the Welsh
border.   **fet** fetched   **124 multitude** i.e., large train or entourage
127 estate state, government.   **green** i.e., newly established   **128 bears**
. . . rein controls the reins that ought to control him   **129 as please** as it
pleases   **130 As well . . . as** both . . . and.   **apparent** evident, real

RICHARD
  I hope the King made peace with all of us;
  And the compact is firm and true in me.

RIVERS
  And so in me, and so, I think, in all.
  Yet since it is but green, it should be put
  To no apparent likelihood of breach,
  Which haply by much company might be urged.   137
  Therefore I say with noble Buckingham
  That it is meet so few should fetch the Prince.   139

HASTINGS   And so say I.

RICHARD
  Then be it so; and go we to determine
  Who they shall be that straight shall post to Ludlow. 142
  Madam, and you, my sister, will you go
  To give your censures in this business?   144

QUEEN ELIZABETH, DUCHESS   With all our hearts.   145

            Exeunt. Manent Buckingham and Richard.

BUCKINGHAM
  My lord, whoever journeys to the Prince,
  For God's sake let not us two stay at home;
  For by the way I'll sort occasion,   148
  As index to the story we late talked of,   149
  To part the Queen's proud kindred from the Prince.

RICHARD
  My other self, my counsel's consistory,   151
  My oracle, my prophet! My dear cousin,
  I, as a child, will go by thy direction.
  Toward Ludlow then, for we'll not stay behind.

                                          Exeunt.

                       ✣

2.3   *Enter one Citizen at one door, and another at
          the other.*

FIRST CITIZEN
  Good morrow, neighbor. Whither away so fast?

---

137 haply perhaps.   **urged** encouraged, provoked   **139 meet** fitting
142 post hasten   **144 censures** judgments   **145 s.d. Manent** they remain
onstage   **148 by** on.   **sort** find, contrive   **149 index** prologue.   **late**
lately   **151 consistory** council chamber

2.3. Location: London. A street.

SECOND CITIZEN
I promise you, I scarcely know myself. 2
Hear you the news abroad?
FIRST CITIZEN   Yes, that the King is dead.
SECOND CITIZEN
Ill news, by 'r Lady; seldom comes the better. 5
I fear, I fear 'twill prove a giddy world. 6

Enter another Citizen.

THIRD CITIZEN
Neighbors, God speed!
FIRST CITIZEN   Give you good morrow, sir.
THIRD CITIZEN
Doth the news hold of good King Edward's death? 8
SECOND CITIZEN
Ay, sir, it is too true, God help the while!
THIRD CITIZEN
Then, masters, look to see a troublous world. 10
FIRST CITIZEN
No, no; by God's good grace his son shall reign.
THIRD CITIZEN
Woe to that land that's governed by a child! 12
SECOND CITIZEN
In him there is a hope of government,
Which in his nonage, council under him, 14
And in his full and ripened years, himself,
No doubt shall then, and till then, govern well.
FIRST CITIZEN
So stood the state when Henry the Sixth
Was crowned in Paris but at nine months old.
THIRD CITIZEN
Stood the state so? No, no, good friends, God wot, 19
For then this land was famously enriched
With politic grave counsel; then the King 21
Had virtuous uncles to protect His Grace.

---

2 promise assure   **5 by 'r Lady** by Our Lady.   **seldom comes the better**
i.e., rarely is the news good   **6 giddy** mad   **8 Doth the news hold** is the
news true   **10 troublous** troubled, disorderly   **12 Woe . . . child** (Compare Ecclesiastes 10:16: "Woe to thee, O land, when thy king is a
child.")   **14 nonage** minority.   **council under him** i.e., aided by wise
counsel   **19 wot** knows   **21 politic** sagacious

FIRST CITIZEN
Why, so hath this, both by his father and mother.
THIRD CITIZEN
Better it were they all came by his father,
Or by his father there were none at all;
For emulation who shall now be nearest   26
Will touch us all too near, if God prevent not.
O, full of danger is the Duke of Gloucester,
And the Queen's sons and brothers haught and proud!   29
And were they to be ruled, and not to rule,
This sickly land might solace as before.   31
FIRST CITIZEN
Come, come, we fear the worst. All will be well.
THIRD CITIZEN
When clouds are seen, wise men put on their cloaks;
When great leaves fall, then winter is at hand;
When the sun sets, who doth not look for night?
Untimely storms make men expect a dearth.
All may be well; but if God sort it so,   37
'Tis more than we deserve or I expect.
SECOND CITIZEN
Truly, the hearts of men are full of fear.
You cannot reason almost with a man   40
That looks not heavily and full of dread.   41
THIRD CITIZEN
Before the days of change, still is it so.   42
By a divine instinct men's minds mistrust   43
Ensuing danger; as, by proof, we see   44
The water swell before a boisterous storm.
But leave it all to God. Whither away?
SECOND CITIZEN
Marry, we were sent for to the justices.
THIRD CITIZEN
And so was I. I'll bear you company.   *Exeunt.*

❦

26 emulation ambitious rivalry   **29 haught** haughty   **31 solace** be
happy, have comfort   **37 sort** dispose   **40 You . . . man** there is scarcely
anyone with whom you can talk   **41 heavily** sad   **42 still** ever
43 mistrust suspect, fear   **44 proof** experience

2.4   *Enter [the] Archbishop [of York], [the] young*
         [Duke of] York, the Queen [Elizabeth], and the
         Duchess [of York].

ARCHBISHOP
  Last night, I hear, they lay at Stony Stratford,   1
  And at Northampton they do rest tonight.   2
  Tomorrow, or next day, they will be here.

DUCHESS
  I long with all my heart to see the Prince.
  I hope he is much grown since last I saw him.

QUEEN ELIZABETH
  But I hear, no; they say my son of York
  Has almost overta'en him in his growth.

YORK
  Ay, Mother, but I would not have it so.

DUCHESS
  Why, my young cousin? It is good to grow.

YORK
  Grandam, one night as we did sit at supper,
  My uncle Rivers talked how I did grow
  More than my brother. "Ay," quoth my uncle
      Gloucester,
  "Small herbs have grace; great weeds do grow apace."   13
  And since, methinks, I would not grow so fast,   14
  Because sweet flowers are slow and weeds make haste.

DUCHESS
  Good faith, good faith, the saying did not hold   16
  In him that did object the same to thee.   17
  He was the wretched'st thing when he was young,
  So long a-growing and so leisurely,
  That, if his rule were true, he should be gracious.

ARCHBISHOP
  And so no doubt he is, my gracious madam.

2.4. Location: London. The royal court.
1 Stony Stratford town in Buckinghamshire   **2 Northampton** town in
Northamptonshire, and hence farther from London than Stony Stratford. The Prince was taken back to Northampton after the arrest of
Rivers, Grey, and Vaughan; but since the Archbishop does not yet know
of that arrest, his speech doesn't make sense dramatically. The quartos
reverse the order in which the two towns are named.   **13 grace** virtuous
qualities. **apace** rapidly   **14 since** ever since   **16 hold** pertain   **17 In
him** i.e., in Richard.   **object . . . to** i.e., apply this saying to

DUCHESS
  I hope he is, but yet let mothers doubt.
YORK
  Now, by my troth, if I had been remembered,   23
  I could have given my uncle's Grace a flout   24
  To touch his growth nearer than he touched mine.   25
DUCHESS
  How, my young York? I prithee, let me hear it.
YORK
  Marry, they say my uncle grew so fast
  That he could gnaw a crust at two hours old;
  'Twas full two years ere I could get a tooth.
  Grandam, this would have been a biting jest.   30
DUCHESS
  I prithee, pretty York, who told thee this?
YORK   Grandam, his nurse.
DUCHESS
  His nurse? Why, she was dead ere thou wast born.
YORK
  If 'twere not she, I cannot tell who told me.
QUEEN ELIZABETH
  A parlous boy! Go to, you are too shrewd.   35
DUCHESS
  Good madam, be not angry with the child.
QUEEN ELIZABETH   Pitchers have ears.   37

          Enter a Messenger.

ARCHBISHOP
  Here comes a messenger. What news?
MESSENGER
  Such news, my lord, as grieves me to report.
QUEEN ELIZABETH
  How doth the Prince?
MESSENGER   Well, madam, and in health.
DUCHESS   What is thy news?

23 troth truth, faith.   **been remembered** considered, recollected   **24 my
. . . flout** His Grace, my uncle, a mocking gibe   **25 touch . . . nearer** i.e.,
taunt him about his growth more tellingly   **30 biting** (with a play on the
idea of teething)   **35 parlous** cunning, precocious.   **Go to** (An expression of remonstrance.)   **shrewd** sharp-tongued   **37 Pitchers have ears**
i.e., little pitchers have large ears. (Proverbial.)

MESSENGER
  Lord Rivers and Lord Grey are sent to Pomfret,   42
  And with them Sir Thomas Vaughan, prisoners.

DUCHESS
  Who hath committed them?   The mighty dukes

MESSENGER
  Gloucester and Buckingham.

ARCHBISHOP   For what offense?

MESSENGER
  The sum of all I can, I have disclosed.   46
  Why or for what the nobles were committed
  Is all unknown to me, my gracious lord.

QUEEN ELIZABETH
  Ay me, I see the ruin of my house!
  The tiger now hath seized the gentle hind;   50
  Insulting tyranny begins to jut   51
  Upon the innocent and aweless throne.   52
  Welcome, destruction, blood, and massacre!
  I see, as in a map, the end of all.   54

DUCHESS
  Accursèd and unquiet wrangling days,
  How many of you have mine eyes beheld!
  My husband lost his life to get the crown,
  And often up and down my sons were tossed
  For me to joy and weep their gain and loss;
  And being seated, and domestic broils   60
  Clean overblown, themselves the conquerors
  Make war upon themselves, brother to brother,
  Blood to blood, self against self. O, preposterous   63
  And frantic outrage, end thy damnèd spleen,   64
  Or let me die, to look on death no more!

QUEEN ELIZABETH
  Come, come, my boy, we will to sanctuary.   66
  Madam, farewell.

DUCHESS   Stay, I will go with you.

---

42 Pomfret the castle at Pontefract in Yorkshire   **46 can** know   **50 hind** doe   **51 jut** encroach   **52 aweless** inspiring no awe (because of the youth of the King)   **54 map** i.e., of future events   **60 seated** i.e., on the throne   **63 preposterous** monstrous, perverse   **64 spleen** i.e., malice, hatred   **66 sanctuary** (Queen Elizabeth, with her son, daughters, and kinsmen, lodged in the precincts of Westminster Abbey, which served as a legal refuge for criminals and persons in danger of their lives.)

QUEEN ELIZABETH
You have no cause.

ARCHBISHOP [*To the Queen*]   My gracious lady, go,
And thither bear your treasure and your goods.
For my part, I'll resign unto Your Grace
The seal I keep; and so betide to me   71
As well I tender you and all of yours!   72
Go, I'll conduct you to the sanctuary.   *Exeunt.*

✤

3.1 *The trumpets sound. Enter [the] young Prince
[Edward], the Dukes of Gloucester and
Buckingham, [Lord] Cardinal [Bourchier,
Catesby], etc.*

BUCKINGHAM
  Welcome, sweet Prince, to London, to your chamber.

RICHARD
  Welcome, dear cousin, my thoughts' sovereign!
  The weary way hath made you melancholy.

PRINCE EDWARD
  No, uncle, but our crosses on the way
  Have made it tedious, wearisome, and heavy.
  I want more uncles here to welcome me.

RICHARD
  Sweet Prince, the untainted virtue of your years
  Hath not yet dived into the world's deceit.
  Nor more can you distinguish of a man
  Than of his outward show—which, God he knows,
  Seldom or never jumpeth with the heart.
  Those uncles which you want were dangerous.
  Your Grace attended to their sugared words
  But looked not on the poison of their hearts.
  God keep you from them, and from such false friends!

PRINCE EDWARD
  God keep me from false friends! But they were none.

RICHARD
  My lord, the Mayor of London comes to greet you.

    Enter [the] Lord Mayor [and his train].

MAYOR
  God bless Your Grace with health and happy days!

PRINCE EDWARD
  I thank you, good my lord, and thank you all.
            [*The Mayor and his train stand aside.*]
  I thought my mother and my brother York
  Would long ere this have met us on the way.
  Fie, what a slug is Hastings, that he comes not

3.1. Location: London. A street.
1 chamber (London was called the *camera regis*, or King's chamber.)
4 crosses vexations (i.e., the arrests of the Queen's kindred)   **6 want**
(1) lack (2) wish   **11 jumpeth** agrees   **22 slug** sluggard

To tell us whether they will come or no!

Enter Lord Hastings.

BUCKINGHAM
And, in good time, here comes the sweating lord.

PRINCE EDWARD
Welcome, my lord. What, will our mother come?

HASTINGS
On what occasion God he knows, not I,   26
The Queen your mother and your brother York
Have taken sanctuary. The tender Prince
Would fain have come with me to meet Your Grace
But by his mother was perforce withheld.   30

BUCKINGHAM
Fie, what an indirect and peevish course   31
Is this of hers! Lord Cardinal, will Your Grace
Persuade the Queen to send the Duke of York
Unto his princely brother presently?   34
If she deny, Lord Hastings, go with him,
And from her jealous arms pluck him perforce.   36

CARDINAL
My lord of Buckingham, if my weak oratory
Can from his mother win the Duke of York,
Anon expect him here; but if she be obdurate   39
To mild entreaties, God in heaven forbid
We should infringe the holy privilege
Of blessèd sanctuary! Not for all this land
Would I be guilty of so deep a sin.

BUCKINGHAM
You are too senseless-obstinate, my lord,
Too ceremonious and traditional.   45
Weigh it but with the grossness of this age,   46
You break not sanctuary in seizing him.
The benefit thereof is always granted
To those whose dealings have deserved the place
And those who have the wit to claim the place.
This Prince hath neither claimed it nor deserved it,
And therefore, in mine opinion, cannot have it.

26 **On what occasion** for what reason   **30 perforce** by force   **31 peevish** perverse   **34 presently** at once   **36 jealous** suspicious   **39 Anon** shortly   **45 ceremonious** bound by formalities   **46 grossness** lack of moral refinement

Then, taking him from thence that is not there,
You break no privilege nor charter there.
Oft have I heard of sanctuary men,
But sanctuary children never till now.

CARDINAL
My lord, you shall o'errule my mind for once.
Come on, Lord Hastings, will you go with me?

HASTINGS   I go, my lord.

PRINCE EDWARD
Good lords, make all the speedy haste you may.
                    [*Exeunt Cardinal and Hastings.*]
Say, uncle Gloucester, if our brother come,
Where shall we sojourn till our coronation?   62

RICHARD
Where it seems best unto your royal self.
If I may counsel you, some day or two
Your Highness shall repose you at the Tower;   65
Then where you please and shall be thought most fit
For your best health and recreation.

PRINCE EDWARD
I do not like the Tower of any place.   68
Did Julius Caesar build that place, my lord?

BUCKINGHAM
He did, my gracious lord, begin that place,
Which, since, succeeding ages have re-edified.   71

PRINCE EDWARD
Is it upon record, or else reported   72
Successively from age to age, he built it?

BUCKINGHAM   Upon record, my gracious lord.

PRINCE EDWARD
But say, my lord, it were not registered,   75
Methinks the truth should live from age to age,
As 'twere retailed to all posterity,   77
Even to the general all-ending day.   78

---

62 sojourn reside   **65 Tower** (Although in the fifteenth century, the
historical time this play represents, the Tower of London was a royal
palace, by Shakespeare's day it had acquired a sinister reputation.)
68 of any place of all places   **71 re-edified** rebuilt   **72 upon record)** in
the written record.   **reported** i.e., by oral tradition   **75 say** suppose.
registered written down   **77 retailed** handed down from one to another   **78 general . . . day** Day of Judgment

RICHARD [*Aside*]
  So wise so young, they say, do never live long.
PRINCE EDWARD   What say you, uncle?
RICHARD
  I say, without characters fame lives long.   81
  [*Aside*.] Thus, like the formal Vice, Iniquity,   82
  I moralize two meanings in one word.   83
PRINCE EDWARD
  That Julius Caesar was a famous man;
  With what his valor did enrich his wit,   85
  His wit set down to make his valor live.   86
  Death makes no conquest of this conqueror,
  For now he lives in fame, though not in life.
  I'll tell you what, my cousin Buckingham—
BUCKINGHAM   What, my gracious lord?
PRINCE EDWARD
  An if I live until I be a man,   91
  I'll win our ancient right in France again
  Or die a soldier, as I lived a king.
RICHARD [*Aside*]
  Short summers lightly have a forward spring.   94

       Enter young York, Hastings, [and the] Cardinal.

BUCKINGHAM
  Now, in good time, here comes the Duke of York.
PRINCE EDWARD
  Richard of York, how fares our loving brother?   96
YORK
  Well, my dread lord—so must I call you now.   97

81 without characters (1) even lacking written records (2) even in the
absence of moral character   **82 formal Vice** i.e., the conventional Vice
figure of the morality play, a comic tempter to evil who would habitu-
ally *moralize two meanings in one word*, that is, play on double meanings in a single phrase as Richard does in the phrase *live long*
83 moralize interpret, discover   **85–86 With . . . live** i.e., taking his
military achievements, whereby his bravery as a soldier added stature
to his understanding, he used his understanding to set down in writing
an account (the *Gallic Wars*) that would make his valor immortal.
With what with that with which   **91 An if** if   **94 lightly** commonly,
often   **forward** early. (Alludes to Edward's precociousness.)   **96 our** i.e.,
my. (The royal "we.")   **97 dread** inspiring reverential fear (as King)

PRINCE EDWARD
Ay, brother, to our grief, as it is yours.
Too late he died that might have kept that title,   99
Which by his death hath lost much majesty.

RICHARD
How fares our cousin, noble lord of York?

YORK
I thank you, gentle uncle. O my lord,
You said that idle weeds are fast in growth;   103
The Prince my brother hath outgrown me far.

RICHARD
He hath, my lord.

YORK   And therefore is he idle?

RICHARD
O my fair cousin, I must not say so.

YORK
Then he is more beholding to you than I.   107

RICHARD
He may command me as my sovereign,
But you have power in me as in a kinsman.

YORK
I pray you, uncle, give me this dagger.

RICHARD
My dagger, little cousin? With all my heart.

PRINCE EDWARD   A beggar, brother?

YORK
Of my kind uncle, that I know will give;   112
And being but a toy, which is no grief to give.   113

RICHARD
A greater gift than that I'll give my cousin.

YORK
A greater gift? O, that's the sword to it.

RICHARD
Ay, gentle cousin, were it light enough.

YORK
O, then I see you will part but with light gifts;   118
In weightier things you'll say a beggar nay.

RICHARD
It is too heavy for Your Grace to wear.

---

99 late lately   **103 idle** useless   **107 beholding** beholden   **112 that**
who   **113 toy** trifle   **118 light** trivial

YORK
I weigh it lightly, were it heavier.   121

RICHARD
What, would you have my weapon, little lord?

YORK
I would, that I might thank you as you call me.

RICHARD How?

YORK Little.

PRINCE EDWARD
My lord of York will still be cross in talk.   126
Uncle, Your Grace knows how to bear with him.

YORK
You mean, to bear me, not to bear with me.
Uncle, my brother mocks both you and me:
Because that I am little, like an ape,
He thinks that you should bear me on your shoulders.   131

BUCKINGHAM [*Aside to Hastings*]
With what a sharp-provided wit he reasons!   132
To mitigate the scorn he gives his uncle,
He prettily and aptly taunts himself.
So cunning and so young is wonderful.

RICHARD
My lord, will 't please you pass along?
Myself and my good cousin Buckingham
Will to your mother, to entreat of her
To meet you at the Tower and welcome you.

YORK
What, will you go unto the Tower, my lord?

PRINCE EDWARD
My Lord Protector needs will have it so.

YORK
I shall not sleep in quiet at the Tower.

RICHARD Why, what should you fear?

YORK
Marry, my uncle Clarence' angry ghost.
My grandam told me he was murdered there.

---

121 weigh it lightly consider it a trifle (playing on the literal meanings of "light" and "heavy")   **126 still** always.   **cross in talk** perverse in twisting words   **131 bear me . . . shoulders** (At fairs, the bear commonly carried an ape on his back. The speech is doubtless an allusion to Richard's hump, and puns triply on *bear with*, put up with, *bear*, carry, and *bear*, an animal.)   **132 sharp-provided** keenly thought out

PRINCE EDWARD   I fear no uncles dead.

RICHARD   Nor none that live, I hope.

PRINCE EDWARD

An if they live, I hope I need not fear.   148
But come, my lord; with a heavy heart,
Thinking on them, go I unto the Tower.   150
[*A sennet.*] *Exeunt Prince, York, Hastings,*
[Cardinal, and others]. Manent Richard,
Buckingham, [and Catesby].

BUCKINGHAM

Think you, my lord, this little prating York   151
Was not incensèd by his subtle mother   152
To taunt and scorn you thus opprobriously?

RICHARD

No doubt, no doubt. O, 'tis a parlous boy,   154
Bold, quick, ingenious, forward, capable.
He is all the mother's, from the top to toe.

BUCKINGHAM

Well, let them rest. Come hither, Catesby.   157
Thou art sworn as deeply to effect what we intend
As closely to conceal what we impart.
Thou know'st our reasons urged upon the way.   160
What think'st thou? Is it not an easy matter
To make William, Lord Hastings, of our mind
For the installment of this noble duke   163
In the seat royal of this famous isle?

CATESBY

He for his father's sake so loves the Prince   165
That he will not be won to aught against him.

BUCKINGHAM

What think'st thou, then, of Stanley? Will not he?

CATESBY

He will do all in all as Hastings doth.

BUCKINGHAM

Well, then, no more but this: go, gentle Catesby,

148 An if if. **they** i.e., Rivers and Grey. (Grey was in fact Edward's step-brother, not his uncle.) **150 s.d. sennet** trumpet call to announce the approach or departure of processions. **Manent** they remain onstage **151 prating** babbling **152 incensèd** incited **154 parlous** clever, but also dangerous **157 let them rest** leave them for the moment **160 the way** i.e., the journey to London from Ludlow **163 installment** installation **165 He . . . sake** i.e., Hastings for King Edward IV's sake

nd hopes to find you forward   46
for the gain thereof;   47
n he sends you this good news,
ne very day your enemies,
d of the Queen, must die at Pomfret.

am no mourner for that news,
they have been still my adversaries.   52
at I'll give my voice on Richard's side
r my master's heirs in true descent,
knows I will not do it, to the death.   55

SBY
d keep your lordship in that gracious mind!

STINGS
But I shall laugh at this a twelvemonth hence,
That they which brought me in my master's hate,   58
I live to look upon their tragedy.   59
Well, Catesby, ere a fortnight make me older,
I'll send some packing that yet think not on 't.

CATESBY
'Tis a vile thing to die, my gracious lord,
When men are unprepared and look not for it.

HASTINGS
O, monstrous, monstrous! And so falls it out
With Rivers, Vaughan, Grey; and so 'twill do
With some men else, that think themselves as safe
As thou and I—who, as thou know'st, are dear
To princely Richard and to Buckingham.

CATESBY
The princes both make high account of you—   69
[*Aside*.] For they account his head upon the Bridge.   70

HASTINGS
I know they do, and I have well deserved it.

Enter Lord Stanley, [Earl of Derby].

46 **forward** inclined   47 **Upon his party** on his side   52 **still** always
55 **to the death** i.e., though I lose my life   58 **they which** i.e., regarding those who   59 **I live** i.e., I shall live   69 **high account** great
estimation. (The quibble on *high* appears in the next line.)   70 **account**
expect, reckon (punning on *account* in the previous line).   **the Bridge**
London Bridge, on a tower of which the heads of traitors were
exposed

And, as it were far off, sound thou Lord Hastings   170
How he doth stand affected to our purpose,   171
And summon him tomorrow to the Tower
To sit about the coronation.   173
If thou dost find him tractable to us,
Encourage him, and tell him all our reasons.
If he be leaden, icy, cold, unwilling,
Be thou so too; and so break off the talk,
And give us notice of his inclination.
For we tomorrow hold divided councils,   179
Wherein thyself shalt highly be employed.
RICHARD
Commend me to Lord William. Tell him, Catesby,   181
His ancient knot of dangerous adversaries   182
Tomorrow are let blood at Pomfret Castle;   183
And bid my lord, for joy of this good news,
Give Mistress Shore one gentle kiss the more.   185
BUCKINGHAM
Good Catesby, go, effect this business soundly.   186
CATESBY
My good lords both, with all the heed I can.   187
RICHARD
Shall we hear from you, Catesby, ere we sleep?
CATESBY   You shall, my lord.
RICHARD
At Crosby House, there shall you find us both.
                                        Exit Catesby.
BUCKINGHAM
Now, my lord, what shall we do if we perceive
Lord Hastings will not yield to our complots?   192
RICHARD
Chop off his head. Something we will determine.
And look when I am king, claim thou of me   194

170 **sound** sound out   171 **doth stand affected** is disposed   173 **sit** sit
in council   179 **divided councils** (While the regular Council meets
about the coronation, Richard plans also to have his own private consul-
tation at Crosby House.)   181 **Lord William** i.e., Hastings   182 **knot**
group, company   183 **are let blood** i.e., will be executed   185 **Mistress
Shore** (According to Thomas More, Jane Shore had become the mistress
of Hastings after the death of Edward IV.)   186 **soundly** thoroughly
187 **heed** attention, care   192 **complots** conspiracies   194 **look when** as
soon as

The earldom of Hereford, and all the movables   195
Whereof the King my brother was possessed.

BUCKINGHAM
I'll claim that promise at Your Grace's hand.

RICHARD
And look to have it yielded with all kindness.
Come, let us sup betimes, that afterwards   199
We may digest our complots in some form.   *Exeunt.*   200

✤

3.2   *Enter a Messenger to the door of Hastings.*

MESSENGER   My lord! My lord!
HASTINGS [*Within*]   Who knocks?
MESSENGER   One from the Lord Stanley.
HASTINGS [*Within*]   What is 't o'clock?   4
MESSENGER   Upon the stroke of four.

Enter Lord Hastings.

HASTINGS
Cannot my Lord Stanley sleep these tedious nights?

MESSENGER
So it appears by that I have to say.
First, he commends him to your noble self.

HASTINGS   What then?

MESSENGER
Then certifies your lordship that this night   10
He dreamt the boar had razèd off his helm.   11
Besides, he says there are two councils kept,
And that may be determined at the one
Which may make you and him to rue at th' other.   14
Therefore he sends to know your lordship's pleasure,
If you will presently take horse with him   16

And with all speed post
To shun the danger tha

HASTINGS
Go, fellow, go, retu
Bid him not fear
His honor and mys
And at the other is my
Where nothing can proce
Whereof I shall not have inte
Tell him his fears are shallow, w
And for his dreams, I wonder he's
To trust the mockery of unquiet slum
To fly the boar before the boar pursues
Were to incense the boar to follow us,
And make pursuit where he did mean no chase.
Go, bid thy master rise and come to me,
And we will both together to the Tower,
Where he shall see the boar will use us kindly.

MESSENGER
I'll go, my lord, and tell him what you say.   *Exit.*

Enter Catesby.

CATESBY
Many good morrows to my noble lord!

HASTINGS
Good morrow, Catesby. You are early stirring.
What news, what news, in this our tottering state?

CATESBY
It is a reeling world, indeed, my lord,
And I believe will never stand upright
Till Richard wear the garland of the realm.

HASTINGS
How? Wear the garland? Dost thou mean the crown?

CATESBY   Ay, my good lord.

HASTINGS
I'll have this crown of mine cut from my shoulders   43
Before I'll see the crown so foul misplaced.
But canst thou guess that he doth aim at it?

---

195 **movables** personal property, other than real estate   199 **betimes** soon   200 **digest** arrange, perfect.   **form** good order

3.2. Location: Before Lord Hastings's house.
4 **What is 't o'clock** what time is it   10 **certifies** informs   11 **boar** i.e., Richard.   **razèd** torn, slashed   14 **at th' other** i.e., the regular Council meeting in the Tower, in which Hastings and Stanley will participate   16 **presently** immediately

24 **intelligence** information   25 **without instance** lacking evidence
27 **To** as to   28 **fly** flee   43 **crown** i.e., head. (Recalls Stanley's dream in l. 11 and anticipates Hastings's execution by beheading.)

Come on, come on, where is your boar spear, man?
Fear you the boar, and go so unprovided?

STANLEY
My lord, good morrow. Good morrow, Catesby.
You may jest on, but, by the Holy Rood,   75
I do not like these several councils, I.   76

HASTINGS   My lord,
I hold my life as dear as you do yours,
And never in my days, I do protest,
Was it so precious to me as 'tis now.
Think you, but that I know our state secure,
I would be so triumphant as I am?

STANLEY
The lords at Pomfret, when they rode from London,   83
Were jocund and supposed their states were sure,   84
And they indeed had no cause to mistrust;
But yet you see how soon the day o'ercast.   86
This sudden stab of rancor I misdoubt.   87
Pray God, I say, I prove a needless coward!
What, shall we toward the Tower? The day is spent.   89

HASTINGS
Come, come, have with you. Wot you what, my lord?   90
Today the lords you talk of are beheaded.

STANLEY
They, for their truth, might better wear their heads   92
Than some that have accused them wear their hats.   93
But come, my lord, let's away.   94

Enter a Pursuivant.

HASTINGS
Go on before. I'll talk with this good fellow.
     Exit Lord Stanley, [Earl of Derby,] and Catesby.
How now, sirrah? How goes the world with thee?   96

PURSUIVANT
The better that your lordship please to ask.

75 the Holy Rood i.e., the cross of Christ   **76 several** separate
83 London (An error for "Ludlow"?)   **84 jocund** merry   **86 o'ercast**
became overcast   **87 misdoubt** fear (i.e., I fear more such sudden
attacks)   **89 spent** i.e., well advanced (although the scene began at 4:00
A.M.)   **90 have with you** I'll go with you.   **Wot** know   **92 for their truth**
as far as their honesty is concerned   **93 wear their hats** i.e., hold their
offices   **94 s.d. Pursuivant** attendant on a herald with authority to serve
warrants   **96 sirrah** (Form of address to inferiors.)

HASTINGS
  I tell thee, man, 'tis better with me now
  Than when thou mett'st me last where now we meet.
  Then was I going prisoner to the Tower,
  By the suggestion of the Queen's allies;   101
  But now, I tell thee—keep it to thyself—
  This day those enemies are put to death,
  And I in better state than e'er I was.

PURSUIVANT
  God hold it, to your honor's good content!   105

HASTINGS
  Gramercy, fellow. There, drink that for me.   106
                     Throws him his purse.

PURSUIVANT I thank your honor.   *Exit Pursuivant.*

    Enter a Priest.

PRIEST
  Well met, my lord. I am glad to see your honor.

HASTINGS
  I thank thee, good Sir John, with all my heart.   109
  I am in your debt for your last exercise;   110
  Come the next Sabbath, and I will content you.   111
                 [He whispers in his ear.]

PRIEST I'll wait upon your lordship.

    Enter Buckingham.

BUCKINGHAM
  What, talking with a priest, Lord Chamberlain?
  Your friends at Pomfret, they do need the priest;
  Your honor hath no shriving work in hand.   115

HASTINGS
  Good faith, and when I met this holy man,
  The men you talk of came into my mind.
  What, go you toward the Tower?

BUCKINGHAM
  I do, my lord, but long I cannot stay there.
  I shall return before your lordship thence.

---

101 suggestion instigation   **105 hold it** continue it (i.e., the better
state)   **106 Gramercy** much thanks   **109 Sir** (Common title for address-
ing any priest.)   **110 exercise** sermon or religious service   **111 content**
compensate   **115 shriving work** confession and absolution

HASTINGS
  Nay, like enough, for I stay dinner there.   121

BUCKINGHAM [*Aside*]
  And supper too, although thou know'st it not.—
  Come, will you go?

HASTINGS   I'll wait upon your lordship.

                        Exeunt.

♣

3.3   *Enter Sir Richard Ratcliffe, with Halberds,*
       carrying the nobles [Rivers, Grey, and Vaughan]
       to death at Pomfret.

RATCLIFFE Come, bring forth the prisoners.

RIVERS
  Sir Richard Ratcliffe, let me tell thee this:
  Today shalt thou behold a subject die
  For truth, for duty, and for loyalty.

GREY
  God bless the Prince from all the pack of you!   5
  A knot you are of damnèd bloodsuckers.   6

VAUGHAN
  You live that shall cry woe for this hereafter.

RATCLIFFE
  Dispatch. The limit of your lives is out.   8

RIVERS
  O Pomfret, Pomfret! O thou bloody prison,
  Fatal and ominous to noble peers!
  Within the guilty closure of thy walls   11
  Richard the Second here was hacked to death;
  And, for more slander to thy dismal seat,   13
  We give to thee our guiltless blood to drink.

GREY
  Now Margaret's curse is fall'n upon our heads,
  When she exclaimed on Hastings, you, and I,
  For standing by when Richard stabbed her son.

---

121 stay stay for

3.3. Location: Pomfret (Pontefract) Castle.
5 pack gang **6 knot** group **8 Dispatch** hurry. **is out** has been
reached **11 closure** enclosure **13 for . . . seat** i.e., to add further to the
evil reputation of this place

RIVERS
  Then cursed she Richard, then cursed she Buckingham,
  Then cursed she Hastings. O, remember, God,
  To hear her prayer for them, as now for us!
  And for my sister and her princely sons,
  Be satisfied, dear God, with our true blood,
  Which, as thou know'st, unjustly must be spilt.

RATCLIFFE
  Make haste. The hour of death is expiate.   24

RIVERS
  Come, Grey, come, Vaughan, let us here embrace.
                              [*They embrace.*]
  Farewell, until we meet again in heaven.   *Exeunt.*

❖

3.4   *Enter Buckingham, [Lord Stanley, Earl of]*
        Derby, Hastings, Bishop of Ely, Norfolk,
        Ratcliffe, Lovell, with others, at a table.

HASTINGS
  Now, noble peers, the cause why we are met
  Is to determine of the coronation.   2
  In God's name, speak. When is the royal day?

BUCKINGHAM
  Is all things ready for the royal time?

STANLEY
  It is, and wants but nomination.   5

ELY
  Tomorrow, then, I judge a happy day.   6

BUCKINGHAM
  Who knows the Lord Protector's mind herein?
  Who is most inward with the noble Duke?   8

ELY
  Your Grace, we think, should soonest know his mind.

BUCKINGHAM
  We know each other's faces; for our hearts,   10

---

24 expiate fully come
3.4. Location: London. The Tower.
2 determine of decide upon   **5 nomination** naming of a date   **6 happy**
favorable   **8 inward** intimate   **10 for** as for

He knows no more of mine than I of yours,
Or I of his, my lord, than you of mine.
Lord Hastings, you and he are near in love.

HASTINGS
I thank His Grace, I know he loves me well;
But, for his purpose in the coronation,
I have not sounded him, nor he delivered
His gracious pleasure any way therein.
But you, my honorable lords, may name the time,
And in the Duke's behalf I'll give my voice,   19
Which I presume he'll take in gentle part.

    Enter [Richard, Duke of] Gloucester.

ELY
In happy time, here comes the Duke himself.

RICHARD
My noble lords and cousins all, good morrow.
I have been long a sleeper; but I trust
My absence doth neglect no great design   24
Which by my presence might have been concluded.

BUCKINGHAM
Had you not come upon your cue, my lord,
William, Lord Hastings, had pronounced your part,
I mean your voice for crowning of the King.

RICHARD
Than my Lord Hastings no man might be bolder.
His lordship knows me well, and loves me well.—
My lord of Ely, when I was last in Holborn,
I saw good strawberries in your garden there.
I do beseech you send for some of them.

ELY
Marry, and will, my lord, with all my heart.
                        Exit Bishop.

RICHARD
Cousin of Buckingham, a word with you.
                [Drawing him aside.]
Catesby hath sounded Hastings in our business,
And finds the testy gentleman so hot
That he will lose his head ere give consent

---

19 voice vote   **24 neglect** cause the neglect of

His master's child, as worshipfully he terms it,   39
Shall lose the royalty of England's throne.

BUCKINGHAM
Withdraw yourself awhile. I'll go with you.
          Exeunt [Richard and Buckingham].

STANLEY
We have not yet set down this day of triumph.
Tomorrow, in my judgment, is too sudden,
For I myself am not so well provided   44
As else I would be, were the day prolonged.   45

     Enter the Bishop of Ely.

ELY
Where is my lord the Duke of Gloucester?
I have sent for these strawberries.

HASTINGS
His Grace looks cheerfully and smooth this morning;   48
There's some conceit or other likes him well   49
When that he bids good morrow with such spirit.
I think there's never a man in Christendom
Can lesser hide his love or hate than he,
For by his face straight shall you know his heart.

STANLEY
What of his heart perceive you in his face
By any livelihood he showed today?   55

HASTINGS
Marry, that with no man here he is offended;
For, were he, he had shown it in his looks.

STANLEY   I pray God he be not, I say.

     Enter Richard and Buckingham.

RICHARD
I pray you all, tell me what they deserve
That do conspire my death with devilish plots
Of damnèd witchcraft, and that have prevailed
Upon my body with their hellish charms?

HASTINGS
The tender love I bear Your Grace, my lord,   63

---

39 worshipfully reverently. (Said contemptuously.)   **44 provided**
equipped   **45 prolonged** postponed   **48 smooth** pleasant   **49 conceit**
fancy, idea. **likes** pleases   **55 livelihood** liveliness   **63 tender** dear

Makes me most forward in this princely presence   64
To doom th' offenders, whosoe'er they be:
I say, my lord, they have deservèd death.

RICHARD
Then be your eyes the witness of their evil.
                              [*He bares his arm.*]
Look how I am bewitched! Behold, mine arm
Is like a blasted sapling withered up.   69
And this is Edward's wife, that monstrous witch,
Consorted with that harlot strumpet Shore,   71
That by their witchcraft thus have markèd me.

HASTINGS
If they have done this deed, my noble lord—

RICHARD
If? Thou protector of this damnèd strumpet,
Talk'st thou to me of "ifs"? Thou art a traitor.
Off with his head! Now, by Saint Paul I swear,
I will not dine until I see the same.
Lovell and Ratcliffe, look that it be done.   78
The rest that love me, rise and follow me.   79
                    Exeunt. Manent Lovell and Ratcliffe,
                              with the Lord Hastings.

HASTINGS
Woe, woe for England! Not a whit for me,
For I, too fond, might have prevented this.   81
Stanley did dream the boar did raze our helms,
And I did scorn it and disdain to fly.
Three times today my footcloth horse did stumble,   84
And started, when he looked upon the Tower,
As loath to bear me to the slaughterhouse.
O, now I need the priest that spake to me!
I now repent I told the pursuivant,
As too triumphing, how mine enemies
Today at Pomfret bloodily were butchered,
And I myself secure in grace and favor.
O Margaret, Margaret, now thy heavy curse
Is lighted on poor Hastings' wretched head!

---

64 forward eager **69 blasted** shriveled **71 Consorted** associated **78 look**
see to it **79 s.d. Manent** they remain onstage **81 fond** foolish **84 footcloth** large, richly ornamented cloth laid over the back of a horse and
hanging to the ground on each side. **stumble** (An omen of misfortune.)

RATCLIFFE

Come, come, dispatch. The Duke would be at dinner.
Make a short shrift. He longs to see your head.   95

HASTINGS

O momentary grace of mortal men,   96
Which we more hunt for than the grace of God!
Who builds his hope in air of your good looks   98
Lives like a drunken sailor on a mast,
Ready with every nod to tumble down
Into the fatal bowels of the deep.

LOVELL

Come, come, dispatch. 'Tis bootless to exclaim.   102

HASTINGS

O bloody Richard! Miserable England!
I prophesy the fearfull'st time to thee
That ever wretched age hath looked upon.
Come, lead me to the block; bear him my head.
They smile at me who shortly shall be dead.

                               Exeunt.

                  ❧

3.5   *Enter Richard [Duke of Gloucester] and*
         Buckingham in rotten armor, marvelous
         ill-favored.

RICHARD

Come, cousin, canst thou quake and change thy color,
Murder thy breath in middle of a word,   2
And then again begin, and stop again,
As if thou wert distraught and mad with terror?

BUCKINGHAM

Tut, I can counterfeit the deep tragedian,
Speak and look back, and pry on every side,   6
Tremble and start at wagging of a straw;
Intending deep suspicion, ghastly looks   8

---

95 shrift confession   **96 grace** favor, fortune   **98 Who** he who.   **in . . . looks** on the insubstantial foundation of your favor   **102 bootless** unavailing

3.5. Location: London. The Tower.
s.d. rotten rusty.   **marvelous ill-favored** remarkably unattractive
2 Murder i.e., stop, catch   **6 pry** peer   **8 Intending** pretending

Are at my service, like enforcèd smiles;
And both are ready in their offices,   10
At any time, to grace my stratagems.
But what, is Catesby gone?

RICHARD
He is; and, see, he brings the Mayor along.

Enter the Mayor and Catesby.

BUCKINGHAM   Lord Mayor—
RICHARD   Look to the drawbridge there!
BUCKINGHAM   Hark, a drum!
RICHARD   Catesby, o'erlook the walls.   [*Exit Catesby.*] 17
BUCKINGHAM
Lord Mayor, the reason we have sent—
RICHARD
Look back, defend thee, here are enemies!
BUCKINGHAM
God and our innocence defend and guard us!

Enter Lovell and Ratcliffe, with Hastings' head.

RICHARD
Be patient. They are friends, Ratcliffe and Lovell.
LOVELL
Here is the head of that ignoble traitor,
The dangerous and unsuspected Hastings.
RICHARD
So dear I loved the man that I must weep.
I took him for the plainest harmless creature
That breathed upon the earth a Christian;
Made him my book wherein my soul recorded   27
The history of all her secret thoughts.
So smooth he daubed his vice with show of virtue
That, his apparent open guilt omitted—   30
I mean, his conversation with Shore's wife—   31
He lived from all attainder of suspects.   32
BUCKINGHAM
Well, well, he was the covert'st sheltered traitor   33

---

10 offices uses, functions   **17 o'erlook** inspect   **27 book** i.e., table book
or diary   **30 his . . . omitted** apart from his manifest open guilt   **31 conversation** sexual intimacy   **32 from** free from.   **attainder of suspects**
stain of suspicion   **33 covert'st** most secret.   **sheltered** most hidden

That ever lived. Look ye, my Lord Mayor,
Would you imagine, or almost believe,   35
Were 't not that, by great preservation   36
We live to tell it, that the subtle traitor
This day had plotted, in the Council House,
To murder me and my good lord of Gloucester?

MAYOR   Had he done so?   39

RICHARD
What, think you we are Turks or infidels?
Or that we would, against the form of law,
Proceed thus rashly in the villain's death,
But that the extreme peril of the case,
The peace of England, and our persons' safety,
Enforced us to this execution?

MAYOR
Now fair befall you! He deserved his death,   47
And your good graces both have well proceeded   48
To warn false traitors from the like attempts.

BUCKINGHAM
I never looked for better at his hands
After he once fell in with Mistress Shore.
Yet had we not determined he should die
Until your lordship came to see his end,
Which now the loving haste of these our friends,
Something against our meaning, have prevented;   55
Because, my lord, we would have had you heard   56
The traitor speak and timorously confess
The manner and the purpose of his treasons,
That you might well have signified the same
Unto the citizens, who haply may   60
Misconster us in him and wail his death.   61

MAYOR
But, my good lord, Your Grace's words shall serve
As well as I had seen and heard him speak.   63
And do not doubt, right noble princes both,

---

35 almost even **36 great preservation** i.e., fortunate escape through
forestalling evil **39 Had he** would he have **47 fair** good fortune
48 proceeded done **55 Something . . . meaning** somewhat contrary to our
intent. **have prevented** has anticipated **56 we . . . heard** we would have
wished you to have heard **60 haply** perhaps **61 Misconster . . . him** i.e.,
misconstrue our intentions regarding him **63 as** as if

But I'll acquaint our duteous citizens   65
With all your just proceedings in this cause.

RICHARD
And to that end we wished your lordship here,
T' avoid the censures of the carping world.

BUCKINGHAM
Which since you come too late of our intent,   69
Yet witness what you hear we did intend.   70
And so, my good Lord Mayor, we bid farewell.

Exit Mayor.

RICHARD
Go, after, after, cousin Buckingham.
The Mayor towards Guildhall hies him in all post.   73
There, at your meet'st advantage of the time,   74
Infer the bastardy of Edward's children.   75
Tell them how Edward put to death a citizen
Only for saying he would make his son
Heir to the Crown—meaning indeed his house,   78
Which, by the sign thereof, was termèd so.
Moreover, urge his hateful luxury   80
And bestial appetite in change of lust,   81
Which stretched unto their servants, daughters, wives,
Even where his raging eye or savage heart,
Without control, lusted to make a prey.
Nay, for a need, thus far come near my person: 85
Tell them, when that my mother went with child   86
Of that insatiate Edward, noble York   87
My princely father then had wars in France,
And by true computation of the time
Found that the issue was not his begot—
Which well appearèd in his lineaments,   91

---

65 duteous obedient   **69 of** regarding   **70 witness** bear witness to
73 Guildhall central hall for municipal affairs.   **hies** hastens.   **post**
haste   **74 meet'st advantage** most suitable opportunity   **75 Infer** allege,
adduce   **78 the Crown** i.e., a tavern in Cheapside identified by the sign
of the Crown. (King Edward is portrayed as having been so sensitive to
possible rivals that he put to death a man merely for naming his son
heir to "the Crown," even though the poor fellow innocently meant
nothing more than his own tavern. The story is from Sir Thomas More's
History of King Richard III.)   **80 luxury** lechery   **81 in . . . lust** i.e.,
constantly desiring new mistresses   **85 for a need** if necessary
86–87 went . . . Of was pregnant with   **91 lineaments** features

Being nothing like the noble Duke my father.
Yet touch this sparingly, as 'twere far off,
Because, my lord, you know my mother lives.

BUCKINGHAM
Doubt not, my lord, I'll play the orator   95
As if the golden fee for which I plead   96
Were for myself. And so, my lord, adieu.

RICHARD
If you thrive well, bring them to Baynard's Castle,   98
Where you shall find me well accompanied
With reverend fathers and well-learnèd bishops.

BUCKINGHAM
I go; and towards three or four o'clock
Look for the news that the Guildhall affords.
                                    Exit Buckingham.

RICHARD
Go, Lovell, with all speed to Doctor Shaw.   103
[*To Ratcliffe.*] Go thou to Friar Penker. Bid them both 104
Meet me within this hour at Baynard's Castle.
                                Exeunt [all but Richard].
Now will I go to take some privy order   106
To draw the brats of Clarence out of sight,
And to give order that no manner person   108
Have any time recourse unto the princes.   *Exit.* 109

✤

3.6   *Enter a Scrivener [with a paper in his hand].*

SCRIVENER
Here is the indictment of the good Lord Hastings,
Which in a set hand fairly is engrossed   2
That it may be today read o'er in Paul's.   3

95 Doubt fear   **96 golden fee** i.e., the crown   **98 Baynard's Castle**
residence on the north bank of the Thames. It was founded by Baynard,
a nobleman in the time of the Conquest, and belonged to Richard's
father.   **103, 104 Doctor Shaw, Friar Penker** (Well-known divines who
delivered sermons in Richard's favor.)   **106 take . . . order** make some
secret disposition   **108 no manner person** no one at all   **109 any time**
at any time.   **recourse** access, admittance

3.6. Location: London. A street.
2 in . . . engrossed is written out in a style of script used for legal
documents   **3 Paul's** i.e., Saint Paul's Cathedral

And mark how well the sequel hangs together: 4
Eleven hours I have spent to write it over,
For yesternight by Catesby was it sent me;
The precedent was full as long a-doing.   7
And yet within these five hours Hastings lived,
Untainted, unexamined, free, at liberty.   9
Here's a good world the while! Who is so gross   10
That cannot see this palpable device?
Yet who's so bold but says he sees it not?
Bad is the world, and all will come to naught
When such ill dealing must be seen in thought.   14

Exit.

✱

3.7   *Enter Richard [Duke of Gloucester] and*
         Buckingham, at several doors.

RICHARD
How now, how now, what say the citizens?
BUCKINGHAM
Now, by the holy mother of our Lord,
The citizens are mum, say not a word.
RICHARD
Touched you the bastardy of Edward's children?   4
BUCKINGHAM
I did; with his contract with Lady Lucy   5
And his contract by deputy in France;   6
Th' unsatiate greediness of his desire   7
And his enforcement of the city wives;   8
His tyranny for trifles; his own bastardy,   9

---

4 the sequel what follows   **7 precedent** prepared indictment serving as
a first draft   **9 Untainted** unaccused   **10 the while** meanwhile.   **gross**
dull, stupid   **14 seen in thought** i.e., perceived in silence

3.7. Location: The courtyard of Baynard's Castle.
s.d. several separate   **4 Touched you** did you deal with, touch upon,
discuss   **5 contract** betrothal.   **Lady Lucy** Elizabeth Lucy (by whom
Edward had a child, though there was no formal contract of betrothal)   **6 deputy** (See *3 Henry VI*, 3.3.49 ff., where Warwick, as deputy,
contracts with Louis XI of France for the marriage of King Edward to
Lady Bona, sister of the French queen.)   **7 unsatiate** insatiable
8 enforcement forcible seduction   **9 tyranny for trifles** harsh punishment of minor offenses

As being got, your father then in France,　　　　　　10
And his resemblance, being not like the Duke.
Withal I did infer your lineaments,　　　　　　　　　12
Being the right idea of your father　　　　　　　　　13
Both in your form and nobleness of mind;
Laid open all your victories in Scotland,　　　　　　15
Your discipline in war, wisdom in peace,　　　　　　16
Your bounty, virtue, fair humility;
Indeed, left nothing fitting for your purpose
Untouched or slightly handled in discourse.
And when mine oratory drew toward end,
I bid them that did love their country's good
Cry, "God save Richard, England's royal king!"

RICHARD　And did they so?

BUCKINGHAM
No, so God help me, they spake not a word,
But, like dumb statues or breathing stones,
Stared each on other and looked deadly pale.
Which when I saw, I reprehended them,
And asked the Mayor what meant this willful silence.
His answer was, the people were not used
To be spoke to but by the Recorder.　　　　　　　　30
Then he was urged to tell my tale again:
"Thus saith the Duke, thus hath the Duke inferred"—　32
But nothing spake in warrant from himself.　　　　　33
When he had done, some followers of mine own,
At lower end of the hall, hurled up their caps,
And some ten voices cried, "God save King Richard!"
And thus I took the vantage of those few:　　　　　37
"Thanks, gentle citizens and friends," quoth I,
"This general applause and cheerful shout
Argues your wisdoms and your love to Richard"—
And even here brake off and came away.　　　　　　41

RICHARD
What tongueless blocks were they! Would they not
　speak?

---

10 got begot　**12 Withal** in addition.　**infer** mention, relate.　**lineaments** features　**13 right idea** exact image　**15 victories in Scotland**
(Richard had commanded the English forces in the Scottish expedition
of 1482.)　**16 discipline** skill, training　**30 the Recorder** a city official
32 inferred alleged, asserted　**33 in . . . himself** on his own authority
37 vantage of opportunity from　**41 brake** broke

BUCKINGHAM No, by my troth, my lord.

RICHARD

Will not the Mayor then and his brethren come?

BUCKINGHAM

The Mayor is here at hand. Intend some fear; 45
Be not you spoke with but by mighty suit. 46
And look you get a prayer book in your hand,
And stand between two churchmen, good my lord,
For on that ground I'll make a holy descant; 49
And be not easily won to our requests.
Play the maid's part: still answer nay and take it.

RICHARD

I go; and if you plead as well for them
As I can say nay to thee for myself,
No doubt we'll bring it to a happy issue. 54

BUCKINGHAM

Go, go, up to the leads. The Lord Mayor knocks. 55

[Exit Richard.]

Enter the Mayor, [aldermen,] and citizens.

Welcome, my lord. I dance attendance here; 56
I think the Duke will not be spoke withal. 57

Enter Catesby.

Now, Catesby, what says your lord to my request?

CATESBY

He doth entreat Your Grace, my noble lord,
To visit him tomorrow or next day.
He is within, with two right reverend fathers,
Divinely bent to meditation,
And in no worldly suits would he be moved
To draw him from his holy exercise.

BUCKINGHAM

Return, good Catesby, to the gracious Duke.
Tell him myself, the Mayor and aldermen,
In deep designs, in matter of great moment,
No less importing than our general good, 68

---

45 Intend pretend **46 mighty suit** importunate entreaty **49 descant**
variation composed on a theme (called a *ground*) **54 issue** outcome
55 leads flat lead coverings for roof; hence, the roof itself **56 dance
attendance** i.e., am kept waiting **57 withal** with **68 No less importing**
concerned with nothing less

Are come to have some conference with His Grace.

CATESBY
I'll signify so much unto him straight.   *Exit.*

BUCKINGHAM
Aha, my lord, this prince is not an Edward!
He is not lolling on a lewd love bed
But on his knees at meditation;
Not dallying with a brace of courtesans
But meditating with two deep divines;   75
Not sleeping, to engross his idle body,   76
But praying, to enrich his watchful soul.
Happy were England, would this virtuous prince
Take on His Grace the sovereignty thereof;
But sure I fear we shall not win him to it.

MAYOR
Marry, God defend His Grace should say us nay!   81

BUCKINGHAM
I fear he will.—Here Catesby comes again.

        Enter Catesby.

Now, Catesby, what says His Grace?

CATESBY   My lord,
He wonders to what end you have assembled
Such troops of citizens to come to him,
His Grace not being warned thereof before.
He fears, my lord, you mean no good to him.

BUCKINGHAM
Sorry I am my noble cousin should
Suspect me that I mean no good to him.
By heaven, we come to him in perfect love,
And so once more return and tell His Grace.
                                    Exit [Catesby].

When holy and devout religious men
Are at their beads, 'tis much to draw them thence,   93
So sweet is zealous contemplation.   94

        Enter Richard aloft, between two bishops.
        [Catesby returns to the main stage.]

---

75 deep learned   **76 engross** fatten   **81 defend** forbid   **93 beads** i.e.,
prayers   **94 s.d. aloft** i.e., on the gallery above the stage, rear. (The
tiring-house facade in this scene is imagined to be the facade of Baynard's Castle.)

MAYOR

See where His Grace stands, 'tween two clergymen!

BUCKINGHAM

Two props of virtue for a Christian prince,
To stay him from the fall of vanity.   97
And, see, a book of prayer in his hand,
True ornaments to know a holy man.—   99
Famous Plantagenet, most gracious prince,
Lend favorable ear to our requests,
And pardon us the interruption
Of thy devotion and right Christian zeal.

RICHARD

My lord, there needs no such apology.
I do beseech Your Grace to pardon me,
Who, earnest in the service of my God,
Deferred the visitation of my friends.
But, leaving this, what is Your Grace's pleasure?

BUCKINGHAM

Even that, I hope, which pleaseth God above
And all good men of this ungoverned isle.

RICHARD

I do suspect I have done some offense
That seems disgracious in the city's eye,   112
And that you come to reprehend my ignorance.

BUCKINGHAM

You have, my lord. Would it might please Your Grace,
On our entreaties, to amend your fault!

RICHARD

Else wherefore breathe I in a Christian land?   116

BUCKINGHAM

Know then, it is your fault that you resign
The supreme seat, the throne majestical,
The sceptered office of your ancestors,   119
Your state of fortune and your due of birth,   120
The lineal glory of your royal house,
To the corruption of a blemished stock;
Whiles, in the mildness of your sleepy thoughts,   123
Which here we waken to our country's good,

97 stay prevent. **of** caused by   **99 ornaments** i.e., the bishops as well
as the prayer book   **112 disgracious** unbecoming, displeasing   **116 Else**
otherwise   **119 office** duty   **120 state of fortune** position to which
fortune entitles you   **123 sleepy** reposeful

The noble isle doth want her proper limbs;   125
Her face defaced with scars of infamy,   127
Her royal stock graft with ignoble plants,   128
And almost shouldered in the swallowing gulf
Of dark forgetfulness and deep oblivion.
Which to recure, we heartily solicit   130
Your gracious self to take on you the charge
And kingly government of this your land—
Not as protector, steward, substitute,
Or lowly factor for another's gain,   134
But as successively from blood to blood,   135
Your right of birth, your empery, your own.   136
For this, consorted with the citizens,   137
Your very worshipful and loving friends,
And by their vehement instigation,
In this just cause come I to move Your Grace.

RICHARD
I cannot tell if to depart in silence
Or bitterly to speak in your reproof
Best fitteth my degree or your condition.   143
If not to answer, you might haply think   144
Tongue-tied ambition, not replying, yielded   145
To bear the golden yoke of sovereignty,
Which fondly you would here impose on me.   147
If to reprove you for this suit of yours,
So seasoned with your faithful love to me,   149
Then on the other side I checked my friends.   150
Therefore, to speak, and to avoid the first,
And then, in speaking, not to incur the last,
Definitively thus I answer you.   153
Your love deserves my thanks, but my desert
Unmeritable shuns your high request.   155
First, if all obstacles were cut away,
And that my path were even to the crown   157

125 **want her proper** lack its own   127 **graft** engrafted   128 **shouldered
in** jostled into, or immersed up to the shoulders in   130 **recure** restore,
make whole   134 **factor** agent   135 **successively** in order of succes-
sion   136 **empery** realm of your sole rule   137 **consorted** associated,
leagued   143 **degree** rank.   **condition** social status   144 **haply** perhaps   145 **Tongue-tied** silent (i.e., silence gives consent.   **yielded** consented   147 **fondly** foolishly   149 **seasoned** i.e., made agreeable or
palatable   150 **checked** rebuked, i.e., would rebuke   153 **Definitively**
once and for all   155 **Unmeritable** undeserving   157 **even** smooth

As the ripe revenue and due of birth,   158
Yet so much is my poverty of spirit,
So mighty and so many my defects,
That I would rather hide me from my greatness—   161
Being a bark to brook no mighty sea—   162
Than in my greatness covet to be hid   163
And in the vapor of my glory smothered.
But, God be thanked, there is no need of me,
And much I need to help you, were there need.   166
The royal tree hath left us royal fruit,
Which, mellowed by the stealing hours of time,
Will well become the seat of majesty,
And make, no doubt, us happy by his reign.
On him I lay that you would lay on me,
The right and fortune of his happy stars,
Which God defend that I should wring from him!   173

BUCKINGHAM
My lord, this argues conscience in Your Grace;
But the respects thereof are nice and trivial,   175
All circumstances well considerèd.
You say that Edward is your brother's son.
So say we too, but not by Edward's wife;
For first was he contract to Lady Lucy—   179
Your mother lives a witness to his vow—   180
And afterward by substitute betrothed   181
To Bona, sister to the King of France.   182
These both put off, a poor petitioner,
A care-crazed mother to a many sons,
A beauty-waning and distressèd widow,
Even in the afternoon of her best days,
Made prize and purchase of his wanton eye,   187

---

158 ripe revenue possession ready to be inherited   **161 my greatness**
i.e., my claim to the throne   **162 bark** ship.   **brook** endure   **163 Than**
. . . **hid** than wish to be enveloped in and protected by my greatness, i.e.,
the throne   **166 I need** I lack the ability requisite   **173 defend** forbid
175 respects thereof considerations by which you support your argument.   **nice** overscrupulous   **179 contract** contracted   **180 Your . . .
vow** (According to the chronicles, Richard's mother, in opposing
Edward's intention of marrying Lady Grey because it was interfering
with the negotiations for his marriage to Lady Bona of Savoy, asserted
that Lady Elizabeth Lucy was already Edward's trothplight wife.
Cf. 3.5.75 and 3.7.6.)   **181 substitute** proxy   **182 sister** i.e., sister-in-law,
the Queen's sister   **187 purchase** booty

Seduced the pitch and height of his degree   188
To base declension and loathed bigamy.   189
By her, in his unlawful bed, he got
This Edward, whom our manners call the Prince.   191
More bitterly could I expostulate,   192
Save that, for reverence to some alive,   193
I give a sparing limit to my tongue.
Then, good my lord, take to your royal self   195
This proffered benefit of dignity;
If not to bless us and the land withal,
Yet to draw forth your noble ancestry   198
From the corruption of abusing times
Unto a lineal true-derivèd course.

MAYOR
Do, good my lord; your citizens entreat you.

BUCKINGHAM
Refuse not, mighty lord, this proffered love.

CATESBY
O, make them joyful, grant their lawful suit!

RICHARD
Alas, why would you heap this care on me?
I am unfit for state and majesty.
I do beseech you, take it not amiss;
I cannot nor I will not yield to you.

BUCKINGHAM
If you refuse it—as, in love and zeal,   208
Loath to depose the child, your brother's son;
As well we know your tenderness of heart   210
And gentle, kind, effeminate remorse,   211
Which we have noted in you to your kindred
And equally indeed to all estates—   213
Yet know, whe'er you accept our suit or no,   214

---

188 Seduced debased. **pitch** height, highest point (as in falconry).
degree rank **189 declension** falling away from a high standard.
bigamy (Edward was not only bound by previous contracts as indicated
in lines 178–182 above, but, by marrying a widow, entered into a union
that canon law regarded as bigamous.) **191 manners** sense of polite-
ness **192 expostulate** discuss, dilate **193 some alive** i.e., the Duchess
of York. (See 3.5.93–94.) **195 good my lord** my good lord **198 draw
forth** rescue **208 as** from being **210 As . . . know** since we know
well **211 kind, effeminate remorse** natural, tender pity **213 estates**
ranks (i.e., this virtue is found in Richard's treatment of everyone)
214 whe'er whether

Your brother's son shall never reign our king,
But we will plant some other in the throne
To the disgrace and downfall of your house.
And in this resolution here we leave you.—
Come, citizens. Zounds! I'll entreat no more.

RICHARD
O, do not swear, my lord of Buckingham.

Exeunt [Buckingham, Mayor, aldermen,
and the citizens].

CATESBY
Call him again, sweet prince. Accept their suit.
If you deny them, all the land will rue it.

RICHARD
Will you enforce me to a world of cares?
Call them again. I am not made of stones,
But penetrable to your kind entreaties,
Albeit against my conscience and my soul.

Enter Buckingham and the rest.

Cousin of Buckingham, and sage, grave men,
Since you will buckle fortune on my back,
To bear her burden, whe'er I will or no,
I must have patience to endure the load.
But if black scandal or foul-faced reproach
Attend the sequel of your imposition,   232
Your mere enforcement shall acquittance me   233
From all the impure blots and stains thereof;
For God doth know, and you may partly see,
How far I am from the desire of this.

MAYOR
God bless Your Grace! We see it and will say it.

RICHARD
In saying so, you shall but say the truth.

BUCKINGHAM
Then I salute you with this royal title:
Long live Richard, England's worthy king!

MAYOR AND CITIZENS   Amen.

BUCKINGHAM
Tomorrow may it please you to be crowned?

---

232 your imposition the duty that you lay upon me   **233 mere** absolute,
downright.   **acquittance** acquit

RICHARD
  Even when you please, for you will have it so.
BUCKINGHAM
  Tomorrow, then, we will attend Your Grace.
  And so most joyfully we take our leave.
RICHARD [*To the Bishops*]
  Come, let us to our holy work again.—
  Farewell, my cousin; farewell, gentle friends. *Exeunt.*

❧

4.1   *Enter [at one door] the Queen [Elizabeth,] the
Duchess of York, and Marquess [of] Dorset; [at
another door] Anne, Duchess of Gloucester,
[leading Lady Margaret Plantagenet, Clarence's
young daughter].*

DUCHESS
  Who meets us here? My niece Plantagenet   1
  Led in the hand of her kind aunt of Gloucester?
  Now, for my life, she's wandering to the Tower,   3
  On pure heart's love to greet the tender Prince.   4
  Daughter, well met.
ANNE   God give Your Graces both   5
  A happy and a joyful time of day!
QUEEN ELIZABETH
  As much to you, good sister. Whither away?   7
ANNE
  No farther than the Tower, and, as I guess,
  Upon the like devotion as yourselves,
  To gratulate the gentle princes there.   9
QUEEN ELIZABETH   10
  Kind sister, thanks. We'll enter all together.

    Enter [Brackenbury] the Lieutenant.

  And, in good time, here the Lieutenant comes.
  Master Lieutenant, pray you, by your leave,
  How doth the Prince and my young son of York?
BRACKENBURY
  Right well, dear madam. By your patience,
  I may not suffer you to visit them;   16
  The King hath strictly charged the contrary.
QUEEN ELIZABETH
  The King? Who's that?
BRACKENBURY   I mean the Lord Protector.
QUEEN ELIZABETH
  The Lord protect him from that kingly title!

4.1. Location: London. Before the Tower.
1 niece i.e., granddaughter   **3 for my life** i.e., I'd bet my life   **4 On** out
of.   **tender** young   **5 Daughter** i.e., daughter-in-law   **7 sister** i.e., sister-
in-law   **9 like devotion** same devout errand   **10 gratulate** greet, salute
16 suffer permit

Hath he set bounds between their love and me?   20
I am their mother; who shall bar me from them?

DUCHESS
I am their father's mother; I will see them.

ANNE
Their aunt I am in law, in love their mother;
Then bring me to their sights. I'll bear thy blame
And take thy office from thee, on my peril.   25

BRACKENBURY
No, madam, no; I may not leave it so.   26
I am bound by oath, and therefore pardon me.
                                        Exit Lieutenant.

        Enter [Lord] Stanley, [Earl of Derby].

STANLEY
Let me but meet you, ladies, one hour hence,
And I'll salute Your Grace of York as mother,   29
And reverend looker-on, of two fair queens.   30
[*To Anne.*] Come, madam, you must straight to
        Westminster,
There to be crownèd Richard's royal queen.

QUEEN ELIZABETH   Ah, cut my lace asunder,   33
That my pent heart may have some scope to beat,
Or else I swoon with this dead-killing news!

ANNE
Despiteful tidings! O unpleasing news!   36

DORSET
Be of good cheer. Mother, how fares Your Grace?

QUEEN ELIZABETH
O Dorset, speak not to me, get thee gone!
Death and destruction dogs thee at thy heels;
Thy mother's name is ominous to children.
If thou wilt outstrip death, go cross the seas
And live with Richmond, from the reach of hell.   42
Go, hie thee, hie thee from this slaughterhouse,   43

20 bounds barriers   **25 take … thee** i.e., relieve you of the responsibility   **26 leave it** i.e., fail to perform my office   **29 mother** i.e., mother-in-law (of Elizabeth as widow of Edward, and of Anne as wife of King Richard)   **30 looker-on** beholder.   **two fair queens** i.e., Elizabeth and Anne, since Anne's husband, Richard, is about to be crowned   **33 cut my lace** i.e., of my bodice   **36 Despiteful** cruel   **42 with Richmond** i.e., with Henry Tudor, Earl of Richmond, at this time in Brittany   **43 hie** hasten

Lest thou increase the number of the dead
And make me die the thrall of Margaret's curse,   45
Nor mother, wife, nor England's counted queen.   46

STANLEY
Full of wise care is this your counsel, madam.
[*To Dorset.*] Take all the swift advantage of the hours.
You shall have letters from me to my son   49
In your behalf, to meet you on the way.   50
Be not ta'en tardy by unwise delay.   51

DUCHESS
O ill-dispersing wind of misery!   52
O my accursèd womb, the bed of death!
A cockatrice hast thou hatched to the world,   54
Whose unavoided eye is murderous.

STANLEY
Come, madam, come. I in all haste was sent.

ANNE
And I with all unwillingness will go.
O, would to God that the inclusive verge   58
Of golden metal that must round my brow
Were red-hot steel, to sear me to the brains!
Anointed let me be with deadly venom   61
And die ere men can say, "God save the Queen!"

QUEEN ELIZABETH
Go, go, poor soul, I envy not thy glory,
To feed my humor wish thyself no harm.   64

ANNE
No? Why? When he that is my husband now
Came to me, as I followed Henry's corpse,
When scarce the blood was well washed from his hands
Which issued from my other angel husband
And that dear saint which then I weeping followed—
O, when, I say, I looked on Richard's face,
This was my wish: "Be thou," quoth I, "accurst

45 thrall subject, victim **46 Nor** neither. **counted** accepted, esteemed
49 You . . . from me i.e., I'll dispatch letters in your behalf. **son** i.e.,
stepson **50 meet . . . way** i.e., catch up with you **51 ta'en** taken, caught
52 ill-dispersing scattering ill fortune **54 cockatrice** basilisk. (See 1.2.153,
note.) **58 inclusive verge** enclosing circle, i.e., the crown, here likened to
an instrument of torture used to punish regicides or other criminals
61 Anointed (Anne desires to be anointed with poison rather than with
holy oil, as in the ceremony of coronation.) **64 To . . . harm** I do not wish
you harm just to satisfy my vengeful mood

For making me, so young, so old a widow!   72
And, when thou wedd'st, let sorrow haunt thy bed;
And be thy wife—if any be so mad—
More miserable by the life of thee
Than thou hast made me by my dear lord's death!"
Lo, ere I can repeat this curse again,
Within so small a time, my woman's heart
Grossly grew captive to his honey words   79
And proved the subject of mine own soul's curse,
Which hitherto hath held mine eyes from rest;
For never yet one hour in his bed
Did I enjoy the golden dew of sleep,
But with his timorous dreams was still awaked.   84
Besides, he hates me for my father Warwick,   85
And will, no doubt, shortly be rid of me.

QUEEN ELIZABETH
Poor heart, adieu! I pity thy complaining.

ANNE
No more than with my soul I mourn for yours.

DORSET
Farewell, thou woeful welcomer of glory!

ANNE
Adieu, poor soul, that tak'st thy leave of it!

DUCHESS [*To Dorset*]
Go thou to Richmond, and good fortune guide thee!
[*To Anne.*] Go thou to Richard, and good angels
    tend thee!
[*To Queen Elizabeth.*] Go thou to sanctuary, and
    good thoughts possess thee!
I to my grave, where peace and rest lie with me!
Eighty-odd years of sorrow have I seen,
And each hour's joy wracked with a week of teen.   96
                                    [*They start to go.*]

QUEEN ELIZABETH
Stay, yet look back with me unto the Tower.
Pity, you ancient stones, those tender babes
Whom envy hath immured within your walls—   99
Rough cradle for such little pretty ones!
Rude ragged nurse, old sullen playfellow   101

72 so old a widow i.e., destined to live so long as a widow   **79 Grossly**
stupidly   **84 timorous** full of fears.   **still** continually   **85 for** on account
of   **96 wracked** destroyed.   **teen** woe   **99 envy** malice   **101 Rude** rough

For tender princes, use my babies well!
So foolish sorrows bids your stones farewell. *Exeunt.*

❖

4.2   *Sound a sennet. Enter Richard, in pomp;*
Buckingham, Catesby, Ratcliffe, Lovell, [a Page,
and others].

KING RICHARD
  Stand all apart. Cousin of Buckingham!   1
            [The others stand aside, out of earshot.]

BUCKINGHAM   My gracious sovereign?

KING RICHARD
  Give me thy hand.
       Sound [trumpets. Here he ascends the throne.]
               Thus high, by thy advice
  And thy assistance, is King Richard seated.
  But shall we wear these glories for a day?
  Or shall they last, and we rejoice in them?

BUCKINGHAM
  Still live they, and forever let them last!

KING RICHARD
  Ah, Buckingham, now do I play the touch,   8
  To try if thou be current gold indeed: 9
  Young Edward lives. Think now what I would speak.

BUCKINGHAM   Say on, my loving lord.

KING RICHARD
  Why, Buckingham, I say I would be king.

BUCKINGHAM
  Why, so you are, my thrice-renownèd lord.

KING RICHARD
  Ha! Am I king? 'Tis so. But Edward lives.

BUCKINGHAM
  True, noble prince.

KING RICHARD   O bitter consequence,   15

4.2. Location: London. The royal court.
1 apart aside   **8 play the touch** play the part of a touchstone (to test the
quality of gold)   **9 current** sterling, genuine   **15 bitter consequence** i.e.,
intolerable answer to my words, and an intolerable fact

That Edward still should live "true, noble prince"!   16
Cousin, thou wast not wont to be so dull.   17
Shall I be plain? I wish the bastards dead,
And I would have it suddenly performed.   19
What sayst thou now? Speak suddenly; be brief.

BUCKINGHAM   Your Grace may do your pleasure.

KING RICHARD
Tut, tut, thou art all ice; thy kindness freezes.
Say, have I thy consent that they shall die?

BUCKINGHAM
Give me some little breath, some pause, dear lord,
Before I positively speak in this.
I will resolve you herein presently.   *Exit Buckingham.*   26

CATESBY [*To those standing aside*]
The King is angry. See, he gnaws his lip.

KING RICHARD
I will converse with iron-witted fools   28
And unrespective boys. None are for me   29
That look into me with considerate eyes.   30
High-reaching Buckingham grows circumspect.   31
Boy!

PAGE [*Approaching*]   My lord?

KING RICHARD
Know'st thou not any whom corrupting gold
Will tempt unto a close exploit of death?   35

PAGE
My lord, I know a discontented gentleman
Whose humble means match not his haughty spirit.
Gold were as good as twenty orators,
And will, no doubt, tempt him to anything.

KING RICHARD
What is his name?

PAGE   His name, my lord, is Tyrrel.

KING RICHARD
I partly know the man. Go call him hither, boy.
            Exit [Page].

16 **"true, noble prince"** (Richard mockingly repeats Buckingham's evasive
reply in l. 15 and applies it to the irritating fact that young Edward still lives
and is a noble prince.)   17 **wast not wont** used not   19 **suddenly** swiftly
26 **resolve** answer   28 **converse** associate.   **iron-witted** unfeeling, stupid
29 **unrespective** thoughtless   30 **considerate** deliberate, reflective
31 **High-reaching** ambitious.   **circumspect** cautious   35 **close** secret

The deep-revolving witty Buckingham   42
No more shall be the neighbor to my counsels.
Hath he so long held out with me untired,
And stops he now for breath? Well, be it so.

Enter [Lord] Stanley, [Earl of Derby].

How now, Lord Stanley? What's the news?
STANLEY   Know, my loving lord,
    The Marquess Dorset, as I hear, is fled
    To Richmond, in the parts where he abides.
                                        [He stands apart.]
KING RICHARD
    Come hither, Catesby. Rumor it abroad
    That Anne my wife is very grievous sick;
    I will take order for her keeping close.   52
    Inquire me out some mean poor gentleman,   53
    Whom I will marry straight to Clarence' daughter.
    The boy is foolish, and I fear not him.   55
    Look how thou dream'st! I say again, give out
    That Anne my queen is sick and like to die.   57
    About it, for it stands me much upon   58
    To stop all hopes whose growth may damage me.
                                        [Exit Catesby.]
    I must be married to my brother's daughter,   60
    Or else my kingdom stands on brittle glass.
    Murder her brothers, and then marry her—
    Uncertain way of gain! But I am in
    So far in blood that sin will pluck on sin.   64
    Tear-falling pity dwells not in this eye.

Enter [Page, with] Tyrrel.

Is thy name Tyrrel?
TYRREL
    James Tyrrel, and your most obedient subject.

42 deep-revolving deeply scheming. **witty** cunning **52 take** give.
close imprisoned, confined **53 mean poor** of low degree **55 boy** i.e.,
Clarence's eldest son, Edward Plantagenet, Earl of Warwick **57 like**
likely **58 stands . . . upon** is a matter of the utmost importance to
me **60 brother's daughter** i.e., Elizabeth of York, daughter to Edward
IV, who will in fact later become the queen of Henry VII; see 4.5.7–9 and
5.5.29–31 **64 pluck on** draw on

KING RICHARD
  Art thou, indeed?
TYRREL   Prove me, my gracious lord.   68
KING RICHARD
  Dar'st thou resolve to kill a friend of mine?
TYRREL   Please you;   70
  But I had rather kill two enemies.
KING RICHARD
  Why, there thou hast it: two deep enemies,
  Foes to my rest and my sweet sleep's disturbers
  Are they that I would have thee deal upon—   74
  Tyrrel, I mean those bastards in the Tower.
TYRREL
  Let me have open means to come to them,   76
  And soon I'll rid you from the fear of them.
KING RICHARD
  Thou sing'st sweet music. Hark, come hither, Tyrrel.
  Go, by this token. [*He gives him a token.*] Rise, and
      lend thine ear.   *Whispers.*
  There is no more but so. Say it is done,
  And I will love thee and prefer thee for it.   81
TYRREL   I will dispatch it straight.   *Exit.*

      Enter Buckingham.

BUCKINGHAM
  My lord, I have considered in my mind
  The late request that you did sound me in.   84
KING RICHARD
  Well, let that rest. Dorset is fled to Richmond.
BUCKINGHAM   I hear the news, my lord.
KING RICHARD
  Stanley, he is your wife's son. Well, look unto it.   87
BUCKINGHAM
  My lord, I claim the gift, my due by promise,
  For which your honor and your faith is pawned: 89
  Th' earldom of Hereford and the movables

---

68 Prove test   **70 Please** if it please   **74 deal upon** proceed against
76 open unhampered   **81 prefer** promote, advance   **84 late** recent.
sound me in ask me about   **87 he** i.e., Richmond   **89 pawned** pledged

Which you have promisèd I shall possess.

KING RICHARD
Stanley, look to your wife. If she convey
Letters to Richmond, you shall answer it.　　　93

BUCKINGHAM
What says Your Highness to my just request?

KING RICHARD
I do remember me, Henry the Sixth
Did prophesy that Richmond should be king,
When Richmond was a little peevish boy.
A king! Perhaps, perhaps—

BUCKINGHAM　My lord!

KING RICHARD
How chance the prophet could not at that time
Have told me, I being by, that I should kill him?　　　101

BUCKINGHAM
My lord, your promise for the earldom!

KING RICHARD
Richmond! When last I was at Exeter,
The Mayor in courtesy showed me the castle
And called it Rougemont, at which name I started,　　　105
Because a bard of Ireland told me once
I should not live long after I saw Richmond.

BUCKINGHAM　My lord!

KING RICHARD　Ay, what's o'clock?　　　109

BUCKINGHAM
I am thus bold to put Your Grace in mind
Of what you promised me.

KING RICHARD　Well, but what's o'clock?

BUCKINGHAM　Upon the stroke of ten.

KING RICHARD　Well, let it strike.

BUCKINGHAM　Why let it strike?

KING RICHARD
Because that, like a jack, thou keep'st the stroke　　　116

---

93 it i.e., for it　**101 by** nearby　**105 Rougemont** i.e., Red Hill (with a play on "Richmond")　**109 what's o'clock** what time is it　**116 jack** the figure of a man that strikes the bell on the outside of a clock (with a play on the meaning "lowbred fellow." Richard's complaint is that Buckingham, like the jack of a clock, being on the point of striking the hour—i.e., speaking his request—breaks the continuity of Richard's reflections.)

Betwixt thy begging and my meditation.
I am not in the giving vein today.   118

BUCKINGHAM
May it please you to resolve me in my suit.   119

KING RICHARD
Thou troublest me. I am not in the vein.
          Exit [with all but Buckingham].

BUCKINGHAM
And is it thus? Repays he my deep service
With such contempt? Made I him king for this?
O, let me think on Hastings, and be gone
To Brecknock, while my fearful head is on!   *Exit.* 124

❖

4.3   *Enter Tyrrel.*

TYRREL
The tyrannous and bloody act is done,
The most arch deed of piteous massacre   2
That ever yet this land was guilty of.
Dighton and Forrest, whom I did suborn   4
To do this piece of ruthless butchery,
Albeit they were fleshed villains, bloody dogs,   6
Melted with tenderness and mild compassion,
Wept like to children in their deaths' sad story.
"O, thus," quoth Dighton, "lay the gentle babes."
"Thus, thus," quoth Forrest, "girdling one another
Within their alabaster innocent arms.
Their lips were four red roses on a stalk,
Which in their summer beauty kissed each other.
A book of prayers on their pillow lay,
Which once," quoth Forrest, "almost changed my mind;
But O! the devil"—there the villain stopped;
When Dighton thus told on: "We smotherèd
The most replenishèd sweet work of Nature   18
That from the prime creation e'er she framed."   19

118 vein mood   **119 resolve me** give me a final answer   **124 Brecknock**
i.e., Brecon, Buckingham's family seat in Wales.   **fearful** full of fears

4.3. Location: London. The royal court.
2 arch deed i.e., chief or notorious act   **4 suborn** bribe   **6 fleshed** experienced in bloodshed   **18 replenishèd** complete, perfect   **19 prime** first

Hence both are gone; with conscience and remorse
They could not speak; and so I left them both,
To bear this tidings to the bloody king.

  Enter [King] Richard.

And here he comes.—All health, my sovereign lord!

KING RICHARD
Kind Tyrrel, am I happy in thy news?

TYRREL
If to have done the thing you gave in charge   25
Beget your happiness, be happy then,
For it is done.

KING RICHARD   But didst thou see them dead?

TYRREL
I did, my lord.

KING RICHARD   And buried, gentle Tyrrel?

TYRREL
The chaplain of the Tower hath buried them;
But where, to say the truth, I do not know.

KING RICHARD
Come to me, Tyrrel, soon at after-supper,   31
When thou shalt tell the process of their death.   32
Meantime, but think how I may do thee good,
And be inheritor of thy desire.
Farewell till then.

TYRREL   I humbly take my leave.   [*Exit.*]

KING RICHARD
The son of Clarence have I pent up close,   36
His daughter meanly have I matched in marriage,   37
The sons of Edward sleep in Abraham's bosom,   38
And Anne my wife hath bid this world good night.
Now, for I know the Breton Richmond aims   40
At young Elizabeth, my brother's daughter,   41
And by that knot looks proudly on the crown,   42
To her go I, a jolly thriving wooer.

25 gave in charge ordered, commanded **31 after-supper** dessert after
supper **32 process** story **36 pent up close** strictly confined **37 His . . .
marriage** (Margaret Plantagenet was about twelve years old when Richard
died. Shakespeare may have confused her with Lady Cicely, a daughter of
Edward IV, whom Richard, according to Holinshed, intended to marry to
"a man found in a cloud, and of an unknown lineage and family.")
38 Abraham's bosom (See Luke 16:22.) **40 for** because **41 my brother's**
Edward's **42 by that knot** by virtue of that alliance

Enter Ratcliffe.

RATCLIFFE My lord!

KING RICHARD

Good or bad news, that thou com'st in so bluntly?

RATCLIFFE

Bad news, my lord. Morton is fled to Richmond,   46
And Buckingham, backed with the hardy Welshmen,
Is in the field, and still his power increaseth.   48

KING RICHARD

Ely with Richmond troubles me more near   49
Than Buckingham and his rash-levied strength.   50
Come, I have learned that fearful commenting   51
Is leaden servitor to dull delay;   52
Delay leads impotent and snail-paced beggary.   53
Then fiery expedition be my wing,   54
Jove's Mercury, and herald for a king!   55
Go muster men. My counsel is my shield;   56
We must be brief when traitors brave the field.   57

                                              Exeunt.

❖

4.4   *Enter old Queen Margaret.*

QUEEN MARGARET

So now prosperity begins to mellow   1
And drop into the rotten mouth of death.
Here in these confines slyly have I lurked
To watch the waning of mine enemies.
A dire induction am I witness to,   5
And will to France, hoping the consequence   6
Will prove as bitter, black, and tragical.

46 **Morton** i.e., John Morton, Bishop of Ely, who had been kept prisoner
at Brecknock (or Brecon) Castle; he is the Ely of 3.4   48 **power** army
49 **near** deeply   50 **rash-levied** hastily recruited   51 **fearful commenting** timorous talk   52 **leaden servitor** sluggish attendant   53 **leads**
leads to.   **beggary** ruin   54 **expedition** speed   55 **Mercury** messenger
of the gods   56 **counsel** sagacity   57 **brave** challenge

4.4. Location: London. Near the royal court.
1 **mellow** mature   5 **induction** beginning (as of a play)   6 **will** will go.
consequence what follows, the sequel and conclusion (as in a play)

Withdraw thee, wretched Margaret. Who comes here?
       [*She steps aside.*]

 Enter Duchess [of York] and Queen [Elizabeth].

QUEEN ELIZABETH
 Ah, my poor princes! Ah, my tender babes!
 My unblown flowers, new-appearing sweets!   10
 If yet your gentle souls fly in the air
 And be not fixed in doom perpetual,   12
 Hover about me with your airy wings
 And hear your mother's lamentation!

QUEEN MARGARET [*Aside*]
 Hover about her; say that right for right   15
 Hath dimmed your infant morn to agèd night. 16

DUCHESS
 So many miseries have crazed my voice   17
 That my woe-wearied tongue is still and mute.
 Edward Plantagenet, why art thou dead?

QUEEN MARGARET [*Aside*]
 Plantagenet doth quit Plantagenet.   20
 Edward for Edward pays a dying debt.   21

QUEEN ELIZABETH
 Wilt thou, O God, fly from such gentle lambs 22
 And throw them in the entrails of the wolf?
 When didst thou sleep when such a deed was done? 24

QUEEN MARGARET [*Aside*]
 When holy Harry died, and my sweet son.   25

DUCHESS
 Dead life, blind sight, poor mortal-living ghost, 26
 Woe's scene, world's shame, grave's due by life usurped, 27
 Brief abstract and record of tedious days,   28

---

10 unblown unopened. **sweets** flowers   **12 doom perpetual** i.e., eternal
punishment or reward   **15 right for right** i.e., a just punishment for an
offense against justice   **16 dimmed . . . night** i.e., brought the youthful
promise of your children to ruin and death   **17 crazed** cracked   **20 quit**
requite   **21 Edward for Edward** i.e., Edward V, the Yorkist Prince, for
Edward, the son of Margaret and Henry VI. **dying debt** debt paid
through death   **22 fly from** abandon   **24 When** i.e., whenever till now
25 Harry i.e., Henry VI   **26 mortal-living ghost** i.e., a dead person still
among the living   **27 grave's . . . usurped** i.e., one who, by living too
long, deprives the grave of its due   **28 abstract** epitome

Rest thy unrest on England's lawful earth,
                           [*Sitting down*]
Unlawfully made drunk with innocent blood!

QUEEN ELIZABETH
Ah, that thou wouldst as soon afford a grave   31
As thou canst yield a melancholy seat!
Then would I hide my bones, not rest them here.
Ah, who hath any cause to mourn but we?
                    [*Sitting down by her.*]

QUEEN MARGARET [*Coming forward*]
If ancient sorrow be most reverend,   35
Give mine the benefit of seniory   36
And let my griefs frown on the upper hand.   37
If sorrow can admit society, [*Sitting down with them*]
Tell o'er your woes again by viewing mine:
I had an Edward, till a Richard killed him;   40
I had a Harry, till a Richard killed him: 41
Thou hadst an Edward, till a Richard killed him; 42
Thou hadst a Richard, till a Richard killed him. 43

DUCHESS
I had a Richard too, and thou didst kill him;   44
I had a Rutland too, thou holp'st to kill him.   45

QUEEN MARGARET
Thou hadst a Clarence too, and Richard killed him.
From forth the kennel of thy womb hath crept
A hellhound that doth hunt us all to death.
That dog, that had his teeth before his eyes   49
To worry lambs and lap their gentle blood,   50
That foul defacer of God's handiwork,
That excellent grand tyrant of the earth   52
That reigns in gallèd eyes of weeping souls,   53
Thy womb let loose, to chase us to our graves.
O upright, just, and true-disposing God,

---

31 that would that. **thou** i.e., the earth   **35 reverend** worthy of respect
36 seniory seniority of claim   **37 on . . . hand** i.e., from a place of prece-
dence   **40 Edward** i.e., my son, the former Prince of Wales   **41 Harry** i.e.,
my husband, King Henry VI   **42 Thou** i.e., Queen Elizabeth. **Edward**
i.e., Edward V   **43 Richard** i.e., the young Duke of York   **44 Richard** i.e.,
Duke of York, the Duchess's husband and father of Richard III, killed by
Margaret's army at the Battle of Wakefield in 1460   **45 Rutland** i.e.,
Edmund, son of the Duke of York, also killed at Wakefield   **49 teeth**
(Richard was supposedly born with teeth.)   **50 worry** tear to pieces
52 excellent unparalleled   **53 gallèd** sore with weeping

How do I thank thee that this carnal cur 56
Preys on the issue of his mother's body 57
And makes her pew-fellow with others' moan! 58

DUCHESS
O Harry's wife, triumph not in my woes!
God witness with me, I have wept for thine.

QUEEN MARGARET
Bear with me. I am hungry for revenge,
And now I cloy me with beholding it. 62
Thy Edward he is dead that killed my Edward; 63
Thy other Edward dead, to quit my Edward; 64
Young York he is but boot, because both they 65
Matched not the high perfection of my loss.
Thy Clarence he is dead that stabbed my Edward;
And the beholders of this frantic play, 68
Th' adulterate Hastings, Rivers, Vaughan, Grey, 69
Untimely smothered in their dusky graves.
Richard yet lives, hell's black intelligencer, 71
Only reserved their factor to buy souls 72
And send them thither; but at hand, at hand
Ensues his piteous and unpitied end. 74
Earth gapes, hell burns, fiends roar, saints pray,
To have him suddenly conveyed from hence.
Cancel his bond of life, dear God, I pray,
That I may live and say, "The dog is dead!"

QUEEN ELIZABETH
O, thou didst prophesy the time would come
That I should wish for thee to help me curse
That bottled spider, that foul bunch-backed toad! 81

QUEEN MARGARET
I called thee then vain flourish of my fortune; 82
I called thee then poor shadow, painted queen,
The presentation of but what I was, 84

56 carnal flesh-eating 57 issue offspring 58 pew-fellow i.e., intimate
associate 62 cloy me satiate myself 63 Thy Edward Edward IV. my
Edward the son of Henry VI 64 other Edward Edward V. quit requite 65 Young York Richard, Duke of York, the younger of the princes
murdered in the Tower. but boot merely into the bargain 68 frantic
insane 69 adulterate adulterous 71 intelligencer agent, go-between,
spy 72 Only . . . factor chosen above all others as their (hell's) agent
74 piteous deplorable 81 bottled bottle-shaped, swollen (as at
1.3.242). bunch-backed hunchbacked 82 flourish ornament, embel-
lishment 84 presentation representation

The flattering index of a direful pageant,   85
One heaved a-high to be hurled down below,
A mother only mocked with two fair babes,
A dream of what thou wast, a garish flag   88
To be the aim of every dangerous shot;   89
A sign of dignity, a breath, a bubble,   90
A queen in jest, only to fill the scene.
Where is thy husband now? Where be thy brothers?
Where be thy two sons? Wherein dost thou joy?
Who sues and kneels and says, "God save the Queen"?
Where be the bending peers that flattered thee?   95
Where be the thronging troops that followed thee?   96
Decline all this, and see what now thou art: 97
For happy wife, a most distressèd widow;
For joyful mother, one that wails the name;
For one being sued to, one that humbly sues;
For queen, a very caitiff crowned with care;   101
For she that scorned at me, now scorned of me;   102
For she being feared of all, now fearing one;   103
For she commanding all, obeyed of none.   104
Thus hath the course of justice whirled about
And left thee but a very prey to time,
Having no more but thought of what thou wast
To torture thee the more, being what thou art.
Thou didst usurp my place, and dost thou not
Usurp the just proportion of my sorrow?
Now thy proud neck bears half my burdened yoke,   111
From which even here I slip my weary head
And leave the burden of it all on thee.
Farewell, York's wife, and queen of sad mischance!
These English woes shall make me smile in France.
                              [*She starts to leave.*]

QUEEN ELIZABETH
O thou well skilled in curses, stay awhile,
And teach me how to curse mine enemies!

---

85 index argument, preface, prologue. **pageant** spectacular entertain-
ment **88–89 garish . . . shot** i.e., standard-bearer, conspicuous in appearance, and thus the target of enemy fire **90 sign** mere token
95 bending bowing **96 troops** supporters **97 Decline** go through in
order. (A grammatical metaphor.) **101 caitiff** wretch, slave **102, 103,
104 of** by **111 burdened** burdensome

QUEEN MARGARET
  Forbear to sleep the nights, and fast the days;
  Compare dead happiness with living woe;
  Think that thy babes were sweeter than they were
  And he that slew them fouler than he is.
  Bett'ring thy loss makes the bad causer worse;   122
  Revolving this will teach thee how to curse.   123

QUEEN ELIZABETH
  My words are dull. O, quicken them with thine!   124

QUEEN MARGARET
  Thy woes will make them sharp, and pierce like mine.
                            Exit Margaret.

DUCHESS
  Why should calamity be full of words?

QUEEN ELIZABETH
  Windy attorneys to their client's woes,   127
  Airy succeeders of intestate joys,   128
  Poor breathing orators of miseries,   129
  Let them have scope! Though what they will impart
  Help nothing else, yet do they ease the heart.

DUCHESS
  If so, then be not tongue-tied. Go with me,
  And in the breath of bitter words let's smother
  My damnèd son that thy two sweet sons smothered.
                        [Sound trumpet.]
  The trumpet sounds. Be copious in exclaims.   135

    Enter King Richard and his train [marching,
    with drums and trumpets].

KING RICHARD
  Who intercepts me in my expedition?   136

DUCHESS
  O, she that might have intercepted thee,
  By strangling thee in her accursèd womb,
  From all the slaughters, wretch, that thou hast done!

122 Bett'ring magnifying   **123 Revolving** meditating on   **124 quicken** put life into   **127 Windy . . . woes** i.e., words, which are airy pleaders in behalf of one who is suffering   **128 succeeders** heirs. **intestate** having died without anything to bequeath   **129 breathing** speaking **135 exclaims** exclamations   **136 expedition** (1) haste (2) military undertaking

QUEEN ELIZABETH
  Hid'st thou that forehead with a golden crown
  Where should be branded, if that right were right,
  The slaughter of the prince that owed that crown   142
  And the dire death of my poor sons and brothers?
  Tell me, thou villain slave, where are my children?

DUCHESS
  Thou toad, thou toad, where is thy brother Clarence?
  And little Ned Plantagenet, his son?   146

QUEEN ELIZABETH
  Where is the gentle Rivers, Vaughan, Grey?

DUCHESS   Where is kind Hastings?

KING RICHARD
  A flourish, trumpets! Strike alarum, drums!   149
  Let not the heavens hear these telltale women   150
  Rail on the Lord's anointed. Strike, I say!

                   Flourish. Alarums.
  Either be patient and entreat me fair,   152
  Or with the clamorous report of war   153
  Thus will I drown your exclamations.

DUCHESS   Art thou my son?

KING RICHARD
  Ay, I thank God, my father, and yourself.

DUCHESS
  Then patiently hear my impatience.

KING RICHARD
  Madam, I have a touch of your condition,   158
  That cannot brook the accent of reproof.

DUCHESS
  O, let me speak!

KING RICHARD   Do then, but I'll not hear.

DUCHESS
  I will be mild and gentle in my words.

KING RICHARD
  And brief, good Mother, for I am in haste.

---

142 owed owned   **146 Ned Plantagenet** (See 4.3.36.)   **149 alarum** the cry or signal "allarme" (to arms)   **150 telltale** tattling, gabbling **152 entreat me fair** treat me with courtesy   **153 report** noise **158 condition** disposition

DUCHESS
Art thou so hasty? I have stayed for thee,   163
God knows, in torment and in agony.

KING RICHARD
And came I not at last to comfort you?

DUCHESS
No, by the Holy Rood, thou know'st it well,   166
Thou cam'st on earth to make the earth my hell.
A grievous burden was thy birth to me;
Tetchy and wayward was thy infancy;   169
Thy schooldays frightful, desperate, wild, and furious;   170
Thy prime of manhood daring, bold, and venturous;
Thy age confirmed, proud, subtle, sly, and bloody,   172
More mild, but yet more harmful—kind in hatred.   173
What comfortable hour canst thou name
That ever graced me with thy company?

KING RICHARD
Faith, none, but Humphrey Hour, that called Your Grace   176
To breakfast once forth of my company.   177
If I be so disgracious in your eye,   178
Let me march on and not offend you madam.—
Strike up the drum.

DUCHESS   I prithee, hear me speak.

KING RICHARD
You speak too bitterly.

DUCHESS   Hear me a word,
For I shall never speak to thee again.

KING RICHARD   So.

DUCHESS
Either thou wilt die by God's just ordinance
Ere from this war thou turn a conqueror,   185
Or I with grief and extreme age shall perish
And nevermore behold thy face again.
Therefore take with thee my most grievous curse,
Which in the day of battle tire thee more

---

163 stayed waited   **166 Holy Rood** Christ's cross   **169 Tetchy** fretful, peevish   **170 frightful** frightening   **172 age confirmed** riper manhood **173 kind in hatred** concealing hatred under pretense of kindness **176 Humphrey Hour** (To "dine with Duke Humphrey" was to go hungry. The passage is obscure.)   **177 forth of** away from   **178 disgracious** unpleasing, disliked   **185 turn** return

Than all the complete armor that thou wear'st!
My prayers on the adverse party fight,   191
And there the little souls of Edward's children
Whisper the spirits of thine enemies   193
And promise them success and victory!
Bloody thou art, bloody will be thy end;
Shame serves thy life and doth thy death attend. *Exit.* 196

QUEEN ELIZABETH
Though far more cause, yet much less spirit to curse
Abides in me; I say amen to her.

KING RICHARD
Stay, madam, I must talk a word with you.

QUEEN ELIZABETH
I have no more sons of the royal blood
For thee to slaughter. For my daughters, Richard,
They shall be praying nuns, not weeping queens,
And therefore level not to hit their lives.   203

KING RICHARD
You have a daughter called Elizabeth,
Virtuous and fair, royal and gracious.

QUEEN ELIZABETH
And must she die for this? O, let her live,
And I'll corrupt her manners, stain her beauty,   207
Slander myself as false to Edward's bed,
Throw over her the veil of infamy;
So she may live unscarred of bleeding slaughter,   210
I will confess she was not Edward's daughter.

KING RICHARD
Wrong not her birth; she is a royal princess.

QUEEN ELIZABETH
To save her life, I'll say she is not so.

KING RICHARD
Her life is safest only in her birth.

QUEEN ELIZABETH
And only in that safety died her brothers.

KING RICHARD
Lo, at their birth good stars were opposite.   216

---

191 party side   **193 Whisper** whisper to   **196 serves** accompanies
203 level aim   **207 manners** morals   **210 So** provided   **216 opposite**
hostile, antagonistic

QUEEN ELIZABETH
  No, to their lives ill friends were contrary.   217

KING RICHARD
  All unavoided is the doom of destiny.   218

QUEEN ELIZABETH
  True, when avoided grace makes destiny.   219
  My babes were destined to a fairer death,
  If grace had blessed thee with a fairer life.

KING RICHARD
  You speak as if that I had slain my cousins.

QUEEN ELIZABETH
  Cousins, indeed, and by their uncle cozened   223
  Of comfort, kingdom, kindred, freedom, life.
  Whose hand soever lanced their tender hearts,   225
  Thy head, all indirectly, gave direction.   226
  No doubt the murderous knife was dull and blunt
  Till it was whetted on thy stone-hard heart,   228
  To revel in the entrails of my lambs.
  But that still use of grief makes wild grief tame,   230
  My tongue should to thy ears not name my boys
  Till that my nails were anchored in thine eyes;
  And I, in such a desperate bay of death,   233
  Like a poor bark of sails and tackling reft,   234
  Rush all to pieces on thy rocky bosom.

KING RICHARD
  Madam, so thrive I in my enterprise   236
  And dangerous success of bloody wars   237
  As I intend more good to you and yours
  Than ever you or yours by me were harmed!

QUEEN ELIZABETH
  What good is covered with the face of heaven,   240
  To be discovered, that can do me good?

KING RICHARD
  Th' advancement of your children, gentle lady.

---

217 contrary opposed   **218 unavoided** unavoidable   **219 avoided grace**
i.e., Richard, in whom grace is void or lacking   **223 cozened** cheated
225 Whose hand soever whoever it was whose hand   **226 all indirectly**
even if by indirect means   **228 whetted** sharpened   **230 But** except.
still continual   **233 bay** (1) inlet (2) position of a hunted animal turning
to face the hounds   **234 reft** bereft   **236 so thrive I** may I so thrive
237 success sequel, result   **240 covered with** hidden by (and therefore
not yet revealed to humanity)

QUEEN ELIZABETH
Up to some scaffold, there to lose their heads.

KING RICHARD
Unto the dignity and height of fortune,
The high imperial type of this earth's glory.   245

QUEEN ELIZABETH
Flatter my sorrow with report of it;
Tell me what state, what dignity, what honor,
Canst thou demise to any child of mine?   248

KING RICHARD
Even all I have—ay, and myself and all—
Will I withal endow a child of thine,
So in the Lethe of thy angry soul   251
Thou drown the sad remembrance of those wrongs
Which thou supposest I have done to thee.

QUEEN ELIZABETH
Be brief, lest that the process of thy kindness   254
Last longer telling than thy kindness' date.   255

KING RICHARD
Then know that from my soul I love thy daughter.   256

QUEEN ELIZABETH
My daughter's mother thinks it with her soul.

KING RICHARD   What do you think?

QUEEN ELIZABETH
That thou dost love my daughter from thy soul.
So from thy soul's love didst thou love her brothers,   260
And from my heart's love I do thank thee for it.

KING RICHARD
Be not so hasty to confound my meaning.
I mean that with my soul I love thy daughter
And do intend to make her Queen of England.

QUEEN ELIZABETH
Well then, who dost thou mean shall be her king?

KING RICHARD
Even he that makes her queen. Who else should be?

---

245 imperial type symbol of rule   **248 demise** convey, transmit, lease
251 So provided that.   **Lethe** river in the underworld, the waters of
which produce forgetfulness   **254 process** story   **255 date** term of
existence   **256 from** with. (But Queen Elizabeth, in the next lines,
sarcastically uses the word in the sense "apart from.")   **260 So** just so.
(Said ironically.)

QUEEN ELIZABETH
What, thou?

KING RICHARD   Even so. How think you of it?

QUEEN ELIZABETH
How canst thou woo her?

KING RICHARD   That would I learn of you,
As one being best acquainted with her humor.   269

QUEEN ELIZABETH
And wilt thou learn of me?

KING RICHARD   Madam, with all my heart.

QUEEN ELIZABETH
Send to her, by the man that slew her brothers,
A pair of bleeding hearts; thereon engrave
"Edward" and "York"; then haply will she weep.   273
Therefore present to her—as sometime Margaret   274
Did to thy father, steeped in Rutland's blood—   275
A handkerchief, which, say to her, did drain
The purple sap from her sweet brothers' body;
And bid her wipe her weeping eyes withal.
If this inducement move her not to love,
Send her a letter of thy noble deeds.
Tell her thou mad'st away her uncle Clarence,
Her uncle Rivers, ay, and for her sake
Mad'st quick conveyance with her good aunt Anne.   283

KING RICHARD
You mock me, madam. This is not the way
To win your daughter.

QUEEN ELIZABETH   There is no other way,
Unless thou couldst put on some other shape
And not be Richard that hath done all this.

KING RICHARD
Say that I did all this for love of her.

QUEEN ELIZABETH
Nay, then indeed she cannot choose but hate thee,
Having bought love with such a bloody spoil.   290

KING RICHARD
Look what is done cannot be now amended.   291

---

269 humor mood   **273 haply** perhaps   **274 sometime** once
275 Rutland's (See *3 Henry VI*, 1.4.79–83.)   **283 conveyance with** riddance
of   **290 spoil** slaughter. (A hunting term.)   **291 Look what** whatever

Men shall deal unadvisedly sometimes,   292
Which after-hours gives leisure to repent.
If I did take the kingdom from your sons,
To make amends I'll give it to your daughter.
If I have killed the issue of your womb,
To quicken your increase I will beget   297
Mine issue of your blood upon your daughter.
A grandam's name is little less in love
Than is the doting title of a mother;
They are as children but one step below,
Even of your metal, of your very blood,   302
Of all one pain, save for a night of groans
Endured of her for whom you bid like sorrow.   304
Your children were vexation to your youth,
But mine shall be a comfort to your age.
The loss you have is but a son being king,
And by that loss your daughter is made queen.
I cannot make you what amends I would;
Therefore accept such kindness as I can.   310
Dorset your son, that with a fearful soul
Leads discontented steps in foreign soil,
This fair alliance quickly shall call home
To high promotions and great dignity.
The king that calls your beauteous daughter wife
Familiarly shall call thy Dorset brother;   316
Again shall you be mother to a king,
And all the ruins of distressful times
Repaired with double riches of content.
What? We have many goodly days to see.
The liquid drops of tears that you have shed
Shall come again, transformed to orient pearl,   322
Advantaging their love with interest   323
Of ten times double gain of happiness.
Go then, my mother, to thy daughter go.
Make bold her bashful years with your experience;
Prepare her ears to hear a wooer's tale;

---

292 deal act   **297 quicken your increase** give new life to your (dead)
progeny   **302 metal** substance (with a suggestion also of *mettle*, spirit.
The Folio reads *mettall.*)   **304 of** by.   **bid** endured, bided   **310 can** am
able (to give)   **316 Familiarly** familially   **322 orient** bright, shining
323 Advantaging augmenting.   **their love** i.e., the love that prompted
tears

Put in her tender heart th' aspiring flame
Of golden sovereignty; acquaint the Princess
With the sweet silent hours of marriage joys.
And when this arm of mine hath chastisèd
The petty rebel, dull-brained Buckingham,
Bound with triumphant garlands will I come
And lead thy daughter to a conqueror's bed;
To whom I will retail my conquest won,   335
And she shall be sole victoress, Caesar's Caesar.

QUEEN ELIZABETH
What were I best to say? Her father's brother
Would be her lord? Or shall I say her uncle?
Or he that slew her brothers and her uncles?
Under what title shall I woo for thee
That God, the law, my honor, and her love
Can make seem pleasing to her tender years?

KING RICHARD
Infer fair England's peace by this alliance.   343

QUEEN ELIZABETH
Which she shall purchase with still lasting war.

KING RICHARD
Tell her the King, that may command, entreats.

QUEEN ELIZABETH
That at her hands which the King's King forbids.   346

KING RICHARD
Say she shall be a high and mighty queen.

QUEEN ELIZABETH
To vail the title, as her mother doth.   348

KING RICHARD
Say I will love her everlastingly.

QUEEN ELIZABETH
But how long shall that title "ever" last?

KING RICHARD
Sweetly in force unto her fair life's end.

QUEEN ELIZABETH
But how long fairly shall her sweet life last?

KING RICHARD
As long as heaven and nature lengthens it.

---

335 retail relate   **343 Infer** allege, adduce (as a reason)   **346 forbids**
(*The Book of Common Prayer,* echoing the injunctions of Leviticus 18,
prohibits the marriage of a man with his brother's daughter.)   **348 vail**
lower, abase as a sign of submission

QUEEN ELIZABETH
　As long as hell and Richard likes of it.
KING RICHARD
　Say I, her sovereign, am her subject low.
QUEEN ELIZABETH
　But she, your subject, loathes such sovereignty.
KING RICHARD
　Be eloquent in my behalf to her.
QUEEN ELIZABETH
　An honest tale speeds best being plainly told.   358
KING RICHARD
　Then plainly to her tell my loving tale.
QUEEN ELIZABETH
　Plain and not honest is too harsh a style.   360
KING RICHARD
　Your reasons are too shallow and too quick.   361
QUEEN ELIZABETH
　O, no, my reasons are too deep and dead—
　Too deep and dead, poor infants, in their graves.
KING RICHARD
　Harp not on that string, madam; that is past.
QUEEN ELIZABETH
　Harp on it still shall I till heartstrings break.
KING RICHARD
　Now, by my George, my Garter, and my crown—   366
QUEEN ELIZABETH
　Profaned, dishonored, and the third usurped.
KING RICHARD
　I swear—
QUEEN ELIZABETH　By nothing, for this is no oath.
　Thy George, profaned, hath lost his lordly honor;   369
　Thy Garter, blemished, pawned his knightly virtue;
　Thy crown, usurped, disgraced his kingly glory.
　If something thou wouldst swear to be believed,
　Swear then by something that thou hast not wronged.

---

358 speeds succeeds **360 too . . . style** i.e., a discordant combination
361 quick hasty (with a pun on the meaning "alive," contrasted with
dead in the next line, just as *shallow* is punningly contrasted with
deep) **366 George . . . Garter** (The George, a badge showing Saint
George slaying the dragon, was not added to the insignia of the Order
of the Garter until the reign of Henry VII or Henry VIII.) **369 his** its
(as also in ll. 370, 371)

KING RICHARD
  Then, by myself—
QUEEN ELIZABETH   Thyself is self-misused.
KING RICHARD
  Now, by the world—
QUEEN ELIZABETH   'Tis full of thy foul wrongs.
KING RICHARD
  My father's death—
QUEEN ELIZABETH   Thy life hath it dishonored.
KING RICHARD
  Why then, by God—
QUEEN ELIZABETH   God's wrong is most of all.
  If thou didst fear to break an oath with Him,
  The unity the King my husband made   379
  Thou hadst not broken, nor my brothers died.
  If thou hadst feared to break an oath by Him,
  Th' imperial metal circling now thy head
  Had graced the tender temples of my child,
  And both the princes had been breathing here,
  Which now, two tender bedfellows for dust,
  Thy broken faith hath made the prey for worms.
  What canst thou swear by now?
KING RICHARD   The time to come.
QUEEN ELIZABETH
  That thou hast wrongèd in the time o'erpast;
  For I myself have many tears to wash
  Hereafter time, for time past wronged by thee.   390
  The children live whose fathers thou hast slaughtered,
  Ungoverned youth, to wail it in their age;   392
  The parents live whose children thou hast butchered,
  Old barren plants, to wail it with their age.
  Swear not by time to come, for that thou hast
  Misused ere used, by times ill-used o'erpast.
KING RICHARD
  As I intend to prosper and repent,   397
  So thrive I in my dangerous affairs
  Of hostile arms! Myself myself confound!   399

379 unity i.e., the reconciliation between Queen Elizabeth and her enemies
390 Hereafter time the future   **392 Ungoverned** i.e., without a father's
guidance or rule   **397 As . . . repent** i.e., I swear that as I hope to thrive
and intend to repent   **399 Myself . . . confound** may I destroy myself

Heaven and fortune bar me happy hours!
Day, yield me not thy light, nor, night, thy rest!
Be opposite all planets of good luck   402
To my proceeding if, with dear heart's love,
Immaculate devotion, holy thoughts,
I tender not thy beauteous princely daughter!   405
In her consists my happiness and thine;
Without her, follows to myself and thee,
Herself, the land, and many a Christian soul,
Death, desolation, ruin, and decay.
It cannot be avoided but by this;
It will not be avoided but by this.
Therefore, dear Mother—I must call you so—
Be the attorney of my love to her.
Plead what I will be, not what I have been,
Not my deserts, but what I will deserve.
Urge the necessity and state of times,
And be not peevish-fond in great designs.   417

QUEEN ELIZABETH
Shall I be tempted of the devil thus?

KING RICHARD
Ay, if the devil tempt you to do good.

QUEEN ELIZABETH
Shall I forget myself to be myself?   420

KING RICHARD
Ay, if yourself's remembrance wrong yourself.   421

QUEEN ELIZABETH   Yet thou didst kill my children.

KING RICHARD
But in your daughter's womb I bury them,
Where in that nest of spicery they will breed   424
Selves of themselves, to your recomfort.   425

QUEEN ELIZABETH
Shall I go win my daughter to thy will?

KING RICHARD
And be a happy mother by the deed.

---

402 opposite opposed, adverse   **405 tender** have a tender regard for
417 peevish-fond childishly foolish   **420 Shall ... myself** i.e., shall I
forget who I am, the person wronged by Richard   **421 wrong yourself**
i.e., interfere with what is to your advantage   **424 nest of spicery** (The
fabled phoenix arose anew from the nest of spices, its funeral pyre.)
425 recomforture comfort, consolation

QUEEN ELIZABETH
I go. Write to me very shortly,
And you shall understand from me her mind.
KING RICHARD
Bear her my true love's kiss; and so, farewell.
                              Exit Queen [Elizabeth].
Relenting fool, and shallow, changing woman!

    Enter Ratcliffe; [Catesby following].

How now, what news?
RATCLIFFE
Most mighty sovereign, on the western coast
Rideth a puissant navy; to our shores   434
Throng many doubtful hollow-hearted friends,   435
Unarmed, and unresolved to beat them back.
'Tis thought that Richmond is their admiral;   437
And there they hull, expecting but the aid   438
Of Buckingham to welcome them ashore.
KING RICHARD
Some light-foot friend post to the Duke of Norfolk: 440
Ratcliffe, thyself, or Catesby. Where is he?
CATESBY
Here, my good lord.
KING RICHARD   Catesby, fly to the Duke.
CATESBY
I will, my lord, with all convenient haste.   443
KING RICHARD
Ratcliffe, come hither. Post to Salisbury.
When thou com'st thither—[*To Catesby.*] Dull,
    unmindful villain,
Why stay'st thou here, and go'st not to the Duke?
CATESBY
First, mighty liege, tell me Your Highness' pleasure,
What from Your Grace I shall deliver to him.
KING RICHARD
O, true, good Catesby. Bid him levy straight

---

434 puissant powerful **435 doubtful** apprehensive **437 their admiral**
i.e., of the *puissant navy* named three lines earlier **438 hull** drift with
the sails furled **440 light-foot** swift-footed **443 convenient** appropriate, suitable

The greatest strength and power that he can make,   450
And meet me suddenly at Salisbury.   451

CATESBY I go.   *Exit.*

RATCLIFFE
What, may it please you, shall I do at Salisbury?

KING RICHARD
Why, what wouldst thou do there before I go?

RATCLIFFE
Your Highness told me I should post before.   455

KING RICHARD
My mind is changed.

Enter Lord Stanley, [Earl of Derby].

                    Stanley, what news with you?

STANLEY
None good, my liege, to please you with the hearing,
Nor none so bad but well may be reported.

KING RICHARD
Heyday, a riddle! Neither good nor bad!
What need'st thou run so many miles about,
When thou mayst tell thy tale the nearest way?   461
Once more, what news?

STANLEY   Richmond is on the seas.

KING RICHARD
There let him sink, and be the seas on him!
White-livered runagate, what doth he there?   464

STANLEY
I know not, mighty sovereign, but by guess.

KING RICHARD Well, as you guess?

STANLEY
Stirred up by Dorset, Buckingham, and Morton,
He makes for England, here to claim the crown.

KING RICHARD
Is the chair empty? Is the sword unswayed?   469
Is the King dead? The empire unpossessed?   470
What heir of York is there alive but we?
And who is England's king but great York's heir?
Then tell me, what makes he upon the seas?   473

450 make raise **451 suddenly** swiftly **455 post** hasten **461 the near-est way** directly, simply **464 White-livered runagate** cowardly rene-gade, fugitive **469 chair** throne **470 empire** kingdom **473 makes he** is he doing

STANLEY
Unless for that, my liege, I cannot guess.

KING RICHARD
Unless for that he comes to be your liege,
You cannot guess wherefore the Welshman comes.   476
Thou wilt revolt and fly to him, I fear.

STANLEY
No, my good lord; therefore mistrust me not.

KING RICHARD
Where is thy power, then, to beat him back?   479
Where be thy tenants and thy followers?
Are they not now upon the western shore,
Safe-conducting the rebels from their ships?

STANLEY
No, my good lord, my friends are in the north.

KING RICHARD
Cold friends to me! What do they in the north
When they should serve their sovereign in the west?

STANLEY
They have not been commanded, mighty King.
Pleaseth Your Majesty to give me leave,   487
I'll muster up my friends and meet Your Grace
Where and what time Your Majesty shall please.

KING RICHARD
Ay, thou wouldst be gone to join with Richmond.
But I'll not trust thee.

STANLEY   Most mighty sovereign,
You have no cause to hold my friendship doubtful.
I never was nor never will be false.

KING RICHARD
Go then and muster men, but leave behind
Your son, George Stanley. Look your heart be firm,
Or else his head's assurance is but frail.   496

STANLEY
So deal with him as I prove true to you.
          Exit Stanley, [Earl of Derby].

   Enter a Messenger.

476 Welshman (Richmond was the grandson of Owen Tudor, a Welshman of Anglesea, who fathered three sons and a daughter by Katharine of Valois, widow of Henry V.)   **479 power** army
487 Pleaseth may it please   **496 assurance** safety

FIRST MESSENGER

My gracious sovereign, now in Devonshire,
As I by friends am well advertisèd,   499
Sir Edward Courtney and the haughty prelate,
Bishop of Exeter, his elder brother,
With many more confederates, are in arms.

Enter another Messenger.

SECOND MESSENGER

In Kent, my liege, the Guildfords are in arms,
And every hour more competitors   504
Flock to the rebels, and their power grows strong.

Enter another Messenger.

THIRD MESSENGER

My lord, the army of great Buckingham—

KING RICHARD

Out on you, owls! Nothing but songs of death?   507
        He striketh him.
There, take thou that, till thou bring better news.

THIRD MESSENGER

The news I have to tell Your Majesty
Is that by sudden floods and fall of waters
Buckingham's army is dispersed and scattered,
And he himself wandered away alone,
No man knows whither.

KING RICHARD   I cry thee mercy.
There is my purse to cure that blow of thine.

        [He gives money.]

Hath any well-advisèd friend proclaimed   515
Reward to him that brings the traitor in?

THIRD MESSENGER

Such proclamation hath been made, my lord.

Enter another Messenger.

FOURTH MESSENGER

Sir Thomas Lovell and Lord Marquess Dorset,   518

---

499 advertisèd informed   **504 competitors** confederates   **507 owls** (The cry of the owl was thought to portend death.)   **515 well-advisèd** prudent   **518 Sir Thomas Lovell** (Not the Lovell of 3.4 and 3.5, who was historically Sir Francis Lovell, Richard's Lord Chamberlain, but perhaps related to him.)

'Tis said, my liege, in Yorkshire are in arms.
But this good comfort bring I to Your Highness:
The Breton navy is dispersed by tempest.
Richmond, in Dorsetshire, sent out a boat
Unto the shore, to ask those on the banks
If they were his assistants, yea or no,
Who answered him they came from Buckingham
Upon his party. He, mistrusting them,
Hoised sail and made his course again for Brittany.   527

NG RICHARD
March on, march on, since we are up in arms,
If not to fight with foreign enemies,
Yet to beat down these rebels here at home.

     Enter Catesby.

ATESBY
My liege, the Duke of Buckingham is taken!
That is the best news. That the Earl of Richmond
Is with a mighty power landed at Milford   533
Is colder tidings, yet they must be told.

NG RICHARD
Away towards Salisbury! While we reason here,
A royal battle might be won and lost.
Someone take order Buckingham be brought
To Salisbury. The rest march on with me.

               Flourish. Exeunt.

❖

.5   *Enter [Lord Stanley, Earl of] Derby and Sir*
          Christopher [Urswick, a priest].

TANLEY
Sir Christopher, tell Richmond this from me:

---

27 Hoised hoisted   **533 Milford** i.e., Milford Haven on the coast of
ales in the county of Pembroke. (A gap of two years is bridged here.
ichmond's first fruitless expedition was in October 1483; his landing
Milford was in August 1485.)

5. Location: London. The house of Lord Stanley, Earl of Derby.
d. Sir (Honorific title for a clergyman.)

That in the sty of the most deadly boar
My son George Stanley is franked up in hold.   3
If I revolt, off goes young George's head;
The fear of that holds off my present aid.
So get thee gone; commend me to thy lord.
Withal say that the Queen hath heartily consented   7
He should espouse Elizabeth her daughter.   8
But tell me, where is princely Richmond now?

CHRISTOPHER
At Pembroke, or at Ha'rfordwest, in Wales.   10

STANLEY   What men of name resort to him?   11

CHRISTOPHER
Sir Walter Herbert, a renownèd soldier,
Sir Gilbert Talbot, Sir William Stanley,
Oxford, redoubted Pembroke, Sir James Blunt,   14
And Rice ap Thomas, with a valiant crew,
And many other of great name and worth;
And towards London do they bend their power,   17
If by the way they be not fought withal.

STANLEY
Well, hie thee to thy lord; I kiss his hand.   19
My letter will resolve him of my mind. [*He gives a letter.*] 20
Farewell.   *Exeunt.*

❖

---

3 franked up in hold shut up in custody, as in a pigpen   **7 Withal** in
addition   **8 espouse** marry   **10 Ha'rfordwest** Haverfordwest, in Wales
11 name rank   **14 redoubted** dreaded.   **Pembroke** i.e., Jasper Tudor,
Earl of Pembroke, uncle to Richmond   **17 bend their power** direct their
forces   **19 hie** hasten   **20 resolve him of** inform him concerning

5.1   *Enter Buckingham, with [Sheriff and]*
halberds, led to execution.

BUCKINGHAM
  Will not King Richard let me speak with him?
SHERIFF
  No, my good lord; therefore be patient.
BUCKINGHAM
  Hastings, and Edward's children, Grey, and Rivers,
  Holy King Henry, and thy fair son Edward,   4
  Vaughan, and all that have miscarrièd   5
  By underhand corrupted foul injustice,
  If that your moody discontented souls   7
  Do through the clouds behold this present hour,
  Even for revenge mock my destruction!
  This is All Souls' Day, fellow, is it not?   10
SHERIFF   It is, my lord.
BUCKINGHAM
  Why, then All Souls' Day is my body's doomsday.
  This is the day which, in King Edward's time,
  I wished might fall on me when I was found
  False to his children and his wife's allies;
  This is the day wherein I wished to fall
  By the false faith of him whom most I trusted;
  This, this All Souls' Day to my fearful soul
  Is the determined respite of my wrongs.   19
  That high All-Seer which I dallied with
  Hath turned my feignèd prayer on my head
  And given in earnest what I begged in jest.
  Thus doth he force the swords of wicked men
  To turn their own points in their masters' bosoms.
  Thus Margaret's curse falls heavy on my neck:
  "When he," quoth she, "shall split thy heart with
    sorrow,
  Remember Margaret was a prophetess."

5.1. Location: Salisbury. An open place.
4 thy i.e., Henry's   5 miscarrièd perished   7 moody angry.   discontented i.e., still seeking vengeance   10 All Souls' Day November 2, the day on which the Roman Catholic Church intercedes for all Christian souls   19 determined . . . wrongs i.e., the preordained date to which the punishment of my evil practices was respited or postponed

Come lead me, officers, to the block of shame.
Wrong hath but wrong, and blame the due of blame.
                    Exeunt Buckingham with officers.

❧

5.2   *Enter Richmond, Oxford, [Sir James] Blunt,*
        [Sir Walter] Herbert, and others, with drum
        and colors.

RICHMOND
    Fellows in arms, and my most loving friends
    Bruised underneath the yoke of tyranny,
    Thus far into the bowels of the land   3
    Have we marched on without impediment;
    And here receive we from our father Stanley   5
    Lines of fair comfort and encouragement.
    The wretched, bloody, and usurping boar,
    That spoiled your summer fields and fruitful vines,   8
    Swills your warm blood like wash, and makes his trough 9
    In your emboweled bosoms, this foul swine   10
    Is now even in the center of this isle,
    Near to the town of Leicester, as we learn.
    From Tamworth thither is but one day's march.
    In God's name, cheerly on, courageous friends,   14
    To reap the harvest of perpetual peace
    By this one bloody trial of sharp war.

OXFORD
    Every man's conscience is a thousand men,
    To fight against this guilty homicide.

HERBERT
    I doubt not but his friends will turn to us.

BLUNT
    He hath no friends but what are friends for fear,   20
    Which in his dearest need will fly from him.   21

RICHMOND
    All for our vantage. Then, in God's name, march!

5.2. Location: A camp near Tamworth.
3 bowels i.e., center   **5 father** i.e., stepfather, Lord Stanley, Earl of
Derby   **8 spoiled** despoiled   **9 Swills** gulps.   **wash** hog's wash, swill
10 emboweled disemboweled   **14 cheerly** cheerily, heartily   **20 for fear**
i.e., out of fearing Richard   **21 dearest** direst

True hope is swift and flies with swallow's wings;
Kings it makes gods and meaner creatures kings.   24

                           Exeunt omnes.

❖

5.3   *Enter King Richard in arms, with Norfolk,*
        Ratcliffe, and the Earl of Surrey [and others].

KING RICHARD
   Here pitch our tent, even here in Bosworth Field.
   My lord of Surrey, why look you so sad?
SURREY
   My heart is ten times lighter than my looks.
KING RICHARD
   My lord of Norfolk—
NORFOLK   Here, most gracious liege.
KING RICHARD
   Norfolk, we must have knocks; ha! Must we not?   5
NORFOLK
   We must both give and take, my loving lord.
KING RICHARD
   Up with my tent! Here will I lie tonight.
      [*Soldiers begin to set up King Richard's tent.*]
   But where tomorrow? Well, all's one for that.   8
   Who hath descried the number of the traitors?   9
NORFOLK
   Six or seven thousand is their utmost power.
KING RICHARD
   Why, our battalia trebles that account.   11
   Besides, the King's name is a tower of strength,
   Which they upon the adverse faction want.   13
   Up with the tent! Come, noble gentlemen,
   Let us survey the vantage of the ground.   15
   Call for some men of sound direction.   16
   Let's lack no discipline, make no delay,

---

24 meaner of lower degree   **s.d. omnes** all

5.3. Location: Bosworth Field.
5 knocks blows   **8 all's . . . that** be that as it may   **9 descried** discovered   **11 battalia** army   **13 want** lack   **15 vantage of the ground** i.e., way in which the field can best be used for tactical advantage
16 direction judgment, military skill

For, lords, tomorrow is a busy day.   *Exeunt.*

*Enter [on the other side of the stage] Richmond,
Sir William Brandon, Oxford, and Dorset, [Blunt,
Herbert, and others. Some of the soldiers pitch
Richmond's tent.]*

RICHMOND
The weary sun hath made a golden set,
And, by the bright track of his fiery car,   20
Gives token of a goodly day tomorrow.
Sir William Brandon, you shall bear my standard.
Give me some ink and paper in my tent.
I'll draw the form and model of our battle,   24
Limit each leader to his several charge,   25
And part in just proportion our small power.   26
My lord of Oxford, you, Sir William Brandon,
And you, Sir Walter Herbert, stay with me.
The Earl of Pembroke keeps his regiment;   29
Good Captain Blunt, bear my good-night to him,
And by the second hour in the morning
Desire the Earl to see me in my tent.
Yet one thing more, good Captain, do for me:
Where is Lord Stanley quartered, do you know?

BLUNT
Unless I have mista'en his colors much,
Which well I am assured I have not done,
His regiment lies half a mile at least
South from the mighty power of the King.

RICHMOND
If without peril it be possible,
Sweet Blunt, make some good means to speak with him,
And give him from me this most needful note.   41
                         [*He gives a letter.*]

BLUNT
Upon my life, my lord, I'll undertake it.
And so, God give you quiet rest tonight!

RICHMOND
Good night, good Captain Blunt. [*Exit Blunt.*] Come,
gentlemen,

---

20 car chariot (of Phoebus)   **24 form and model** formation and plan
25 Limit appoint.   **several charge** individual command   **26 power**
army   **29 keeps** i.e., is with   **41 needful** essential

Let us consult upon tomorrow's business.
Into my tent; the dew is raw and cold.

They withdraw into the tent.

Enter [to his tent, King] Richard, Ratcliffe,
Norfolk, and Catesby.

KING RICHARD
  What is 't o'clock?
CATESBY   It's suppertime, my lord;
  It's nine o'clock.
KING RICHARD   I will not sup tonight.
  Give me some ink and paper.
  What, is my beaver easier than it was,   50
  And all my armor laid into my tent?
CATESBY
  It is, my liege, and all things are in readiness.
KING RICHARD
  Good Norfolk, hie thee to thy charge.
  Use careful watch, choose trusty sentinels.
NORFOLK   I go, my lord.
KING RICHARD
  Stir with the lark tomorrow, gentle Norfolk.
NORFOLK   I warrant you, my lord.   [*Exit.*] 57
  KING RICHARD   Catesby!
CATESBY
  My lord?
KING RICHARD   Send out a pursuivant at arms   59
  To Stanley's regiment. Bid him bring his power   60
  Before sunrising, lest his son George fall
  Into the blind cave of eternal night.   [*Exit Catesby.*]
  Fill me a bowl of wine. Give me a watch.   63
  Saddle white Surrey for the field tomorrow.   64
  Look that my staves be sound and not too heavy.   65
  Ratcliffe!

---

50 beaver face-guard or visor of helmet.   **easier** more loosely fitting
57 warrant guarantee   **59 pursuivant at arms** junior officer attendant
on a herald   **60 power** forces   **63 watch** watch light, candle marked
into equal divisions to show time; or, perhaps, sentinel   **64 white**
Surrey (The name seems to be Shakespeare's invention. The chroniclers
say that Richard was mounted on a "great white courser.")   **65 staves**
lance shafts

RATCLIFFE   My lord?

KING RICHARD
  Sawst thou the melancholy Lord Northumberland?

RATCLIFFE
  Thomas the Earl of Surrey and himself,
  Much about cockshut time, from troop to troop   70
  Went through the army, cheering up the soldiers.

KING RICHARD
  So, I am satisfied. Give me a bowl of wine.
  I have not that alacrity of spirit,
  Nor cheer of mind, that I was wont to have.   74
                          [*Wine is brought.*]
  Set it down. Is ink and paper ready?

RATCLIFFE
  It is, my lord.

KING RICHARD   Bid my guard watch. Leave me.
  Ratcliffe, about the mid of night come to my tent
  And help to arm me. Leave me, I say.
                    Exit Ratcliffe. [*Richard sleeps.*]

  Enter [*Lord Stanley, Earl of*] *Derby, to Richmond*
  in his tent, [*lords and others attending*].

STANLEY
  Fortune and victory sit on thy helm!   79

RICHMOND
  All comfort that the dark night can afford
  Be to thy person, noble father-in-law!   81
  Tell me, how fares our loving mother?

STANLEY
  I, by attorney, bless thee from thy mother,   83
  Who prays continually for Richmond's good.
  So much for that. The silent hours steal on,
  And flaky darkness breaks within the east.   86
  In brief—for so the season bids us be—   87
  Prepare thy battle early in the morning,   88
  And put thy fortune to the arbitrament   89
  Of bloody strokes and mortal-staring war.   90

70 cockshut time evening twilight; possibly, the time at which the
poultry are shut up   **74 was wont** used   **79 helm** helmet   **81 father-in-
law** i.e., stepfather   **83 attorney** deputy   **86 flaky** streaked with light
87 season time of day   **88 battle** troops   **89 arbitrament** arbitration
90 mortal-staring fatal-visaged

I, as I may—that which I would I cannot—   91
With best advantage will deceive the time   92
And aid thee in this doubtful shock of arms.   93
But on thy side I may not be too forward,   94
Lest, being seen, thy brother, tender George,   95
Be executed in his father's sight.
Farewell. The leisure and the fearful time   97
Cuts off the ceremonious vows of love
And ample interchange of sweet discourse
Which so long sundered friends should dwell upon.
God give us leisure for these rites of love!
Once more, adieu. Be valiant, and speed well!   102

RICHMOND
Good lords, conduct him to his regiment.
I'll strive with troubled thoughts to take a nap,   104
Lest leaden slumber peise me down tomorrow,   105
When I should mount with wings of victory.
Once more, good night, kind lords and gentlemen.
             Exeunt. [Richmond remains.]
O Thou, whose captain I account myself,
Look on my forces with a gracious eye;
Put in their hands thy bruising irons of wrath,
That they may crush down with a heavy fall
The usurping helmets of our adversaries!
Make us thy ministers of chastisement,
That we may praise thee in the victory!
To thee I do commend my watchful soul
Ere I let fall the windows of mine eyes.   116
Sleeping and waking, O, defend me still!   [*He sleeps.*]

             Enter the Ghost of young Prince Edward, son [of]
             Harry the Sixth, to Richard.

GHOST (*To Richard*)
Let me sit heavy on thy soul tomorrow!   118
Think how thou stabbedst me in my prime of youth

---

91 that . . . cannot i.e., I cannot fight openly on your side, though I want
to   **92 With . . . time** i.e., as best I can will work for our side without
seeming to do so   **93 shock** encounter   **94 forward** zealous   **95 brother**
i.e., stepbrother.   **tender** young, of tender years   **97 leisure** i.e., brief
time allowed   **102 speed well** may you succeed   **104 with** i.e., in spite
of   **105 peise** weigh   **116 windows** i.e., eyelids   **118 sit heavy on** be
oppressive to

At Tewkesbury. Despair therefore and die!
(*To Richmond*.) Be cheerful, Richmond, for the wrongèd
  souls
Of butchered princes fight in thy behalf.
King Henry's issue, Richmond, comforts thee.   [*Exit*.]

  Enter the Ghost of Henry the Sixth.

GHOST (*To Richard*)
  When I was mortal, my anointed body
  By thee was punchèd full of deadly holes.
  Think on the Tower and me. Despair and die!   126
  Harry the Sixth bids thee despair and die!
  (*To Richmond*.) Virtuous and holy, be thou conqueror!
  Harry, that prophesied thou shouldst be king,   129
  Doth comfort thee in thy sleep. Live and flourish!
                                              [*Exit*.]

  Enter the Ghost of Clarence.

GHOST [*To Richard*]
  Let me sit heavy in thy soul tomorrow,
  I, that was washed to death with fulsome wine,   132
  Poor Clarence, by thy guile betrayed to death!
  Tomorrow in the battle think on me,
  And fall thy edgeless sword. Despair and die!   135
  (*To Richmond*.) Thou offspring of the house of
    Lancaster,
  The wrongèd heirs of York do pray for thee.
  Good angels guard thy battle! Live and flourish!   138
                                              [*Exit*.]

  Enter the Ghosts of Rivers, Grey, [*and*] *Vaughan*.

GHOST OF RIVERS [*To Richard*]
  Let me sit heavy in thy soul tomorrow,
  Rivers that died at Pomfret! Despair and die!
GHOST OF GREY [*To Richard*]
  Think upon Grey, and let thy soul despair!

---

126 Tower (Where Henry VI was supposed to have been murdered.)
129 prophesied (See *3 Henry VI*, 4.6.68 ff.)   **132 washed to death** i.e.,
drowned in a butt of malmsey.   **fulsome** cloying   **135 fall** may it fall.
edgeless blunt, useless   **138 battle** troops

GHOST OF VAUGHAN [*To Richard*]
Think upon Vaughan, and, with guilty fear,
Let fall thy lance. Despair and die!
ALL (*To Richmond*)
Awake, and think our wrongs in Richard's bosom
Will conquer him! Awake, and win the day!

[*Exeunt Ghosts.*]

　　Enter the Ghost of Hastings.

GHOST [*To Richard*]
Bloody and guilty, guiltily awake
And in a bloody battle end thy days!
Think on Lord Hastings. Despair and die!
(*To Richmond.*) Quiet untroubled soul, awake, awake!
Arm, fight, and conquer for fair England's sake!

[*Exit.*]

　　Enter the Ghosts of the two young Princes.

GHOSTS (*To Richard*)
Dream on thy cousins smothered in the Tower.　151
Let us be lead within thy bosom, Richard,
And weigh thee down to ruin, shame, and death!
Thy nephews' souls bid thee despair and die!
(*To Richmond.*) Sleep, Richmond, sleep in peace and
　　wake in joy.
Good angels guard thee from the boar's annoy!　156
Live, and beget a happy race of kings!
Edward's unhappy sons do bid thee flourish.

[*Exeunt Ghosts.*]

　　Enter the Ghost of Lady Anne, his wife.

GHOST [*To Richard*]
Richard, thy wife, that wretched Anne thy wife,
That never slept a quiet hour with thee,
Now fills thy sleep with perturbations.
Tomorrow in the battle think on me,
And fall thy edgeless sword. Despair and die!
(*To Richmond.*) Thou quiet soul, sleep thou a quiet sleep;
Dream of success and happy victory!
Thy adversary's wife doth pray for thee.　　[*Exit.*]

---

151 cousins i.e., nephews　　**156 the boar's annoy** i.e., Richard's attack

Enter the Ghost of Buckingham.

GHOST [*To Richard*]
The first was I that helped thee to the crown;
The last was I that felt thy tyranny.
O, in the battle think on Buckingham,
And die in terror of thy guiltiness!
Dream on, dream on of bloody deeds and death;
Fainting, despair; despairing, yield thy breath!   172
(*To Richmond.*) I died for hope ere I could lend thee aid;   173
But cheer thy heart and be thou not dismayed.
God and good angels fight on Richmond's side,
And Richard fall in height of all his pride!   [*Exit.*]   176
                    Richard starteth up out of a dream.

KING RICHARD
Give me another horse! Bind up my wounds!
Have mercy, Jesu!—Soft, I did but dream.
O coward conscience, how dost thou afflict me!
The lights burn blue. It is now dead midnight.   180
Cold fearful drops stand on my trembling flesh.
What do I fear? Myself? There's none else by.
Richard loves Richard; that is, I am I.
Is there a murderer here? No. Yes, I am.
Then fly. What, from myself? Great reason why: 185
Lest I revenge. What, myself upon myself?
Alack, I love myself. Wherefore? For any good   187
That I myself have done unto myself?
O, no! Alas, I rather hate myself
For hateful deeds committed by myself!
I am a villain. Yet I lie, I am not.
Fool, of thyself speak well. Fool, do not flatter.
My conscience hath a thousand several tongues,   193
And every tongue brings in a several tale,
And every tale condemns me for a villain.
Perjury, perjury, in the highest degree,
Murder, stern murder, in the direst degree,
All several sins, all used in each degree,   198

172 Fainting losing heart   **173 for hope** i.e., for want of hope, hoping in
vain to help   **176 Richard fall** may Richard fall   **180 lights burn blue**
(Superstitiously regarded as evidence of the presence of ghosts.)
185 fly flee   **187 Wherefore** why   **193 several** different, separate
198 used committed.   **degree** i.e., of infamy, from bad to worst

Throng to the bar, crying all, "Guilty! Guilty!"   199
I shall despair. There is no creature loves me,
And if I die no soul will pity me.
And wherefore should they, since that I myself
Find in myself no pity to myself?
Methought the souls of all that I had murdered
Came to my tent, and every one did threat
Tomorrow's vengeance on the head of Richard.

    Enter Ratcliffe.

RATCLIFFE My lord!
KING RICHARD Zounds! Who is there?
RATCLIFFE
Ratcliffe, my lord, 'tis I. The early village cock
Hath twice done salutation to the morn.
Your friends are up and buckle on their armor.
KING RICHARD
O Ratcliffe, I have dreamed a fearful dream!
What think'st thou, will our friends prove all true?
RATCLIFFE
No doubt, my lord.
KING RICHARD   O Ratcliffe, I fear, I fear!
RATCLIFFE
Nay, good my lord, be not afraid of shadows.
KING RICHARD
By the apostle Paul, shadows tonight
Have struck more terror to the soul of Richard
Than can the substance of ten thousand soldiers
Armèd in proof and led by shallow Richmond.   219
'Tis not yet near day. Come, go with me;
Under our tents I'll play the eavesdropper,
To see if any mean to shrink from me.
                Exeunt [*Richard and Ratcliffe*].

    Enter the Lords to Richmond, [*sitting in his tent*].

LORDS Good morrow, Richmond!
RICHMOND
Cry mercy, lords and watchful gentlemen,   224
That you have ta'en a tardy sluggard here.

---

199 bar i.e., bar of justice **219 proof** armor that is proof against weap-
ons **224 Cry mercy** I beg your pardon

A LORD   How have you slept, my lord?

RICHMOND
  The sweetest sleep and fairest-boding dreams
  That ever entered in a drowsy head
  Have I since your departure had, my lords.
  Methought their souls whose bodies Richard murdered
  Came to my tent and cried on victory.   231
  I promise you, my soul is very jocund   232
  In the remembrance of so fair a dream.
  How far into the morning is it, lords?

A LORD   Upon the stroke of four.

RICHMOND
  Why, then 'tis time to arm and give direction.

        His oration to his soldiers.

  More than I have said, loving countrymen,
  The leisure and enforcement of the time   238
  Forbids to dwell upon. Yet remember this:
  God and our good cause fight upon our side.
  The prayers of holy saints and wrongèd souls,
  Like high-reared bulwarks, stand before our faces.
  Richard except, those whom we fight against   243
  Had rather have us win than him they follow.
  For what is he they follow? Truly, gentlemen,
  A bloody tyrant and a homicide;
  One raised in blood, and one in blood established;   247
  One that made means to come by what he hath,   248
  And slaughtered those that were the means to help him;
  A base foul stone, made precious by the foil   250
  Of England's chair, where he is falsely set;   251
  One that hath ever been God's enemy.
  Then if you fight against God's enemy,
  God will in justice ward you as his soldiers;   254
  If you do sweat to put a tyrant down,
  You sleep in peace, the tyrant being slain;
  If you do fight against your country's foes,

---

231 cried on uttered the cry of. (A hunting term; i.e., "urged on to.")
232 jocund cheerful   **238 leisure** i.e., brief time allowed   **243 except**
excepted   **247 in blood** by bloodshed   **248 made means** i.e., has taken
advantage, created opportunity   **250 foil** a thin leaf of metal placed under
a gem to set it off to advantage   **251 chair** throne   **254 ward** protect

Your country's fat shall pay your pains the hire;   258
If you do fight in safeguard of your wives,
Your wives shall welcome home the conquerors;
If you do free your children from the sword,
Your children's children quits it in your age.   262
Then, in the name of God and all these rights,
Advance your standards, draw your willing swords.   264
For me, the ransom of my bold attempt   265
Shall be this cold corpse on the earth's cold face;   266
But if I thrive, the gain of my attempt
The least of you shall share his part thereof.
Sound drums and trumpets boldly and cheerfully;
God and Saint George! Richmond and victory!

                                 [Exeunt.]

    Enter King Richard, Ratcliffe, [attendants and
    forces].

KING RICHARD
What said Northumberland as touching Richmond?
RATCLIFFE
That he was never trainèd up in arms.
KING RICHARD
He said the truth. And what said Surrey then?
RATCLIFFE
He smiled and said, "The better for our purpose."
KING RICHARD
He was in the right, and so indeed it is.
                          The clock striketh.
Tell the clock there. Give me a calendar.   276
Who saw the sun today?   *[He takes an almanac.]*
RATCLIFFE   Not I, my lord.
KING RICHARD
Then he disdains to shine, for by the book   278
He should have braved the east an hour ago.   279
A black day will it be to somebody.
Ratcliffe!

---

258 fat prosperity, wealth. **pains** efforts. **hire** reward **262 quits**
requites **264 Advance** raise **265–266 the ransom . . . face** i.e., if I fail,
there will be no question of ransom, but only death **276 Tell** count the
strokes of. **calendar** almanac **278 the book** i.e., the almanac
279 braved made splendid

RATCLIFFE
  My lord?
KING RICHARD   The sun will not be seen today;
    The sky doth frown and lour upon our army.   283
    I would these dewy tears were from the ground.
    Not shine today? Why, what is that to me
    More than to Richmond? For the selfsame heaven
    That frowns on me looks sadly upon him.

        Enter Norfolk.

NORFOLK
  Arm, arm, my lord, the foe vaunts in the field!   288
KING RICHARD
  Come, bustle, bustle! Caparison my horse.   289
  Call up Lord Stanley; bid him bring his power.
  I will lead forth my soldiers to the plain,
  And thus my battle shall be ordered: 292
  My foreward shall be drawn out all in length,   293
  Consisting equally of horse and foot;
  Our archers shall be placèd in the midst.
  John, Duke of Norfolk, Thomas, Earl of Surrey,
  Shall have the leading of this foot and horse.
  They thus directed, we will follow   298
  In the main battle, whose puissance on either side   299
  Shall be well wingèd with our chiefest horse.   300
  This, and Saint George to boot! What think'st thou,
    Norfolk?   301
NORFOLK
  A good direction, warlike sovereign.
  This found I on my tent this morning.
                    He showeth him a paper.
KING RICHARD [*Reads*]
    "Jockey of Norfolk, be not so bold,   304
    For Dickon thy master is bought and sold."   305
  A thing devisèd by the enemy.
  Go, gentlemen, every man unto his charge.

283 lour look threateningly **288 vaunts** boasts his strength
289 Caparison put on the battle trappings of **292 battle** troops
293 foreward vanguard **298 directed** deployed **299 main battle** main
body of troops **300 wingèd** flanked. **horse** cavalry **301 to boot** i.e., to
give us aid in addition **304 Jockey** i.e., Jack, John **305 Dickon** i.e., Dick,
Richard. **bought and sold** i.e., betrayed for a bribe, brought to confusion

Let not our babbling dreams affright our souls;
Conscience is but a word that cowards use,
Devised at first to keep the strong in awe.
Our strong arms be our conscience, swords our law!
March on, join bravely, let us to it pell-mell;   312
If not to heaven, then hand in hand to hell.

     His oration to his army.

What shall I say more than I have inferred?   314
Remember whom you are to cope withal:
A sort of vagabonds, rascals, and runaways,   316
A scum of Bretons and base lackey peasants,   317
Whom their o'ercloyèd country vomits forth   318
To desperate adventures and assured destruction.
You sleeping safe, they bring to you unrest;
You having lands, and blessed with beauteous wives,
They would restrain the one, distain the other.   322
And who doth lead them but a paltry fellow,
Long kept in Brittany at our mother's cost?   324
A milksop, one that never in his life
Felt so much cold as over shoes in snow?   326
Let's whip these stragglers o'er the seas again.
Lash hence these overweening rags of France,
These famished beggars, weary of their lives,
Who, but for dreaming on this fond exploit,   330
For want of means, poor rats, had hanged themselves.   331
If we be conquered, let men conquer us,
And not these bastard Bretons, whom our fathers
Have in their own land beaten, bobbed, and thumped,   334
And in record left them the heirs of shame.   335
Shall these enjoy our lands? Lie with our wives?
Ravish our daughters? [*Drum afar off.*] Hark! I hear
    their drum.

312 pell-mell in confused haste   **314 inferred** stated   **316 sort** gang
317 lackey servile   **318 o'ercloyèd** satiated, glutted   **322 restrain** de-
prive you of.   **distain** defile, sully   **324 our mother's** (Richmond's
mother was not Richard's. This error occurs in the second edition of
Holinshed's *Chronicles*. The first edition reads "brothers," the reference being to the fact that Richmond had been supported at the court
of the Duke of Brittany at the cost of Charles, Duke of Burgundy,
Richard's brother-in-law.)   **326 over shoes** i.e., over his shoe-tops
330 fond foolish   **331 want of means** poverty   **334 bobbed** thrashed
335 record history

Fight, gentlemen of England! Fight, bold yeomen!
Draw, archers, draw your arrows to the head!
Spur your proud horses hard, and ride in blood;
Amaze the welkin with your broken staves!   341

[*Enter a Messenger.*]

What says Lord Stanley? Will he bring his power?
MESSENGER   My lord, he doth deny to come.   343
KING RICHARD   Off with his son George's head!
NORFOLK
My lord, the enemy is past the marsh.
After the battle let George Stanley die.
KING RICHARD
A thousand hearts are great within my bosom.
Advance our standards, set upon our foes;
Our ancient word of courage, fair Saint George,   349
Inspire us with the spleen of fiery dragons!
Upon them! Victory sits on our helms.   *Exeunt.*

5.4   *Alarum. Excursions. Enter [Norfolk and forces
           fighting; to him] Catesby.*

CATESBY
Rescue, my lord of Norfolk, rescue, rescue!
The King enacts more wonders than a man,   2
Daring an opposite to every danger.   3
His horse is slain, and all on foot he fights,
Seeking for Richmond in the throat of death.
Rescue, fair lord, or else the day is lost!

[*Alarums.*] *Enter [King] Richard.*

KING RICHARD
A horse! A horse! My kingdom for a horse!
CATESBY
Withdraw, my lord. I'll help you to a horse.

341 Amaze the welkin fright the skies   **343 deny** refuse   **349 word of
courage** battle cry

5.4. Location: Bosworth Field, as before; the action is continuous.
s.d. **Excursions** sorties   **2 than a man** than seems possible for a human
being   **3 Daring . . . danger** boldly facing every danger in battle

KING RICHARD

Slave, I have set my life upon a cast,   9
And I will stand the hazard of the die.   10
I think there be six Richmonds in the field;   11
Five have I slain today instead of him.
A horse! A horse! My kingdom for a horse!   [*Exeunt.*]

5.5   *Alarum. Enter Richard and Richmond; they*
fight. Richard is slain. Then, retreat being
sounded, [flourish, and] enter Richmond, [Lord
Stanley, Earl of] Derby bearing the crown, with
other lords, etc.

RICHMOND

God and your arms be praised, victorious friends!
The day is ours; the bloody dog is dead.

STANLEY [*Offering him the crown*]

Courageous Richmond, well hast thou acquit thee.
Lo, here this long-usurpèd royalty
From the dead temples of this bloody wretch
Have I plucked off, to grace thy brows withal.   6
Wear it, enjoy it, and make much of it.

RICHMOND

Great God of heaven, say amen to all!
But, tell me, is young George Stanley living?

STANLEY

He is, my lord, and safe in Leicester town,
Whither, if it please you, we may now withdraw us.

RICHMOND

What men of name are slain on either side?

STANLEY

John, Duke of Norfolk, Walter, Lord Ferrers,
Sir Robert Brackenbury, and Sir William Brandon.

RICHMOND

Inter their bodies as becomes their births.
Proclaim a pardon to the soldiers fled

---

9 cast throw of the dice   **10 die** (Singular of *dice*.)   **11 six Richmonds** i.e., Richmond himself and five men dressed like him as a safety precaution

5.5. Location: Action continues at Bosworth Field.
s.d. retreat trumpet signal to withdraw, cease the attack   **6 withal** with

That in submission will return to us,
And then, as we have ta'en the Sacrament,   18
We will unite the white rose and the red.
Smile heaven upon this fair conjunction,   20
That long have frowned upon their enmity!
What traitor hears me and says not amen?
England hath long been mad, and scarred herself;
The brother blindly shed the brother's blood,
The father rashly slaughtered his own son,
The son, compelled, been butcher to the sire.
All this divided York and Lancaster,
Divided in their dire division.
O, now let Richmond and Elizabeth,
The true succeeders of each royal house,
By God's fair ordinance conjoin together!   31
And let their heirs, God, if thy will be so,
Enrich the time to come with smooth-faced peace,
With smiling plenty, and fair prosperous days!
Abate the edge of traitors, gracious Lord,   35
That would reduce these bloody days again   36
And make poor England weep in streams of blood!
Let them not live to taste this land's increase
That would with treason wound this fair land's peace!
Now civil wounds are stopped, peace lives again.   40
That she may long live here, God say amen!   *Exeunt*.

18 ta'en the Sacrament sworn a sacred oath on the Sacrament (to marry Princess Elizabeth, daughter of Edward IV, thereby uniting the houses of York and of Lancaster, white rose and red)   **20 conjunction** union. (An astrological metaphor.)   **31 ordinance** decree   **35 Abate** blunt, render ineffective   **36 reduce** bring back   **40 stopped** closed up

Date and Text

A quarto edition of *Richard III*, registered by Andrew Wise on October 20, 1597, appeared later that same year with the following title:

> THE TRAGEDY OF King Richard the third. Containing, His treacherous Plots against his brother Clarence: the pittiefull murther of his iunocent nephewes: his tyrannicall vsurpation: with the whole course of his detested life, and most deserued death. As it hath beene lately Acted by the Right honourable the Lord Chamberlaine his seruants. AT LONDON Printed by Valentine Sims, for Andrew Wise, dwelling in Paules Chu[r]ch-yard, at the Signe of the Angell. 1597.

This text, one of the most perplexing in all Shakespeare, is generally regarded as a memorial reconstruction of a peculiar kind, one in which the acting company banded together to reconstruct a play of which the copy was missing. The reconstructed version may later have been cut, perhaps for provincial performance. This defective text was the basis of the 1597 quarto, which was reprinted in 1598, 1602, 1605, 1612, 1622, 1629, and 1634, each reprint successively more error-laden than the previous one. The First Folio text of 1623 seems to have been set mainly from copies of the third and sixth quartos (1602, 1622) which had been sporadically but heavily corrected against an independent manuscript—possibly Shakespeare's own manuscript or a copy of it. Parts of the Folio text, however, were set from an uncorrected copy of the third quarto (1602), and for those passages (3.1.1–158 and 5.3.48 to end of play) the first quarto, from which the third was derived, must serve as copy text. Otherwise, the Folio text is the most authoritative, though it must be approached with caution.

The situation is indeed fraught with unusual uncertainty, since there are many opportunities for F to have perpetuated errors of the earlier quartos; moreover, its "improvements" over the readings of those quartos could in some instances be editorial sophistications. Q1, because it may sometimes be closer to Shakespeare's original, offers some readings that demand serious attention. Especially when

F's reading differs from Q1 and is instead derived from
Q2–6, Q1 should be preferred unless it is manifestly wrong.
At the same time, however, since Q1 may reflect adaptation
of the original acting text, its changes may not represent
Shakespeare's artistic intention either. For these reasons,
one must be wary of Q1's assignment of speeches when
they vary from F's assignments, and also of Q1's cuts, some
of them substantial.

The play is mentioned by Francis Meres in 1598 in his *Palladis Tamia: Wit's Treasury* (a slender volume on contemporary literature and art; valuable because it lists most of the
plays of Shakespeare that existed at that time). John Weever
names a *"Richard"* in his *Epigrams*, published in 1599.
Most scholars date *Richard III* 1592–1594, on the basis of
its style and its close affinity to the *Henry VI* series (completed probably in 1591). The play may have been influenced by the anonymous *The True Tragedy of Richard III*,
registered in June 1594, but probably written in 1590–1592
or even earlier. Shakespeare's play may also have been influenced by Thomas Kyd's *The Spanish Tragedy* (c. 1587)
and by Christopher Marlowe's dramas (he died in 1593).

Textual Notes

These textual notes are not a historical collation, either of the early quartos and folios or of more recent editions; they are simply a record of departures in this edition from the copy text. The reading adopted in this edition appears in boldface, followed by the rejected reading from the copy text, i.e., the First Folio. Only major alterations in punctuation are noted. Changes in lineation are not indicated, nor are some minor and obvious typographical errors.

Abbreviations used:
F the First Folio
Q quarto
s.d. stage direction
s.p. speech prefix

Copy text: the First Folio, except for two passages, 3.1.1–158 and 5.3.48 to end of play, for which Q1 is copy text. Unless otherwise indicated, the adopted readings are from the first quarto of 1597 [Q1].

1.1. 1 s.p. Richard [not in F] **41 s.d. Enter . . . Brackenbury** [eds.] Enter Clarence, and Brakenbury guarded **45 the th'** **52 for** but **65 tempers him to this** tempts him to this harsh **75 to her for his** for her **103 I** I do **124 the** this **133 prey** play

1.2. 27 life [eds.] death **38 s.p. Halberdier** [eds.] Gen **39 stand** Stand'st **78 of a** of **80 t' accuse** [eds.] to curse **94 hand** hands **141 thee** the **171 words** word **198 was man** Man was **204 s.p. Richard** [not in F] **205** [not in F] **227 s.d. Exeunt** [eds.] Exit [also at l. 229] **228 Richard Sirs . . . corpse** [not in F] **238 at all** withall

1.3. 17 come comes **lords** Lord **19 s.p. [and elsewhere] Stanley** Der **54 whom** who **63 of** on **70** [not in F] **109 s.d.** [at l. 110 in F] **114** [not in F] **155 Ah, little** A little **160 of** off **309 s.p. Queen Elizabeth** Mar **342 s.p. First Murderer** Vil [also at ll. 350 and 355]

1.4. 9 Methought [Q4] Me thoughts **13 Thence** There **22 waters** water **22, 23 my** mine **25 Ten** A **39 seek** find **41 Which** Who **64 my lord** Lord **86 s.p. First Murderer** [eds.] 2. Mur **89 s.p. Second Murderer** [eds.] 1 **99 s.d. Exit** [at l. 97 in F] **100 I** we **122 Faith** [not in F] **126 Zounds** come **147 Zounds** [not in F] **152 Tut** [not in F] **192 to have redemption** for any goodnesse **193** [not in F] **240** [not in F] **242 of** on **269** [in F, printed after l. 263]

2.1. s.d. Buckingham [eds.] Buckingham, Wooduill **5 in** to **7 Rivers and Hastings** Dorset and Riuers **39 God** heauen **57 unwittingly** vnwillingly **59 By** To **68** [F follows with a line: "Of you Lord *Wooduill*, and Lord *Scales* of you"] **93 but** and **108 at** and

2.2. 1 s.p. Boy Edw 3 s.p. [and throughout scene] Girl [eds.] Daugh **3 do you** do **47 have I** haue **83 weep** weepes **84–85 Clarence . . . they** Clarence weep, so do not they **87 Pour** Power **142 Ludlow** London [also at l. 154] **145** [not in F] **145 s.d. Manent** [eds.] Manet

2.3. 44 Ensuing Pursuing [but the catchword on p. 184 in F is "Ensuing"]

2.4. 1 hear heard   **21 s.p. Archbishop** Car [Q1] Yor [F]   **65 death** earth

3.1. 1–158 [based on Q1 as copy text]   **2 s.p. [and elsewhere] Richard** Glo
60 [bracketed s.d. from F]   **150 s.d. [A sennet]** [from F]   **Hastings** Hast.
Dors   **Manent** [F2] Manet

3.2. 78 as you do as

3.3. 1 [not in F]

3.4. 58 [not in F]   **79 s.d. Manent** manet   **82 raze** rowse

3.5. 4 wert were   **20 innocence** innocencie   **34 Look . . . Mayor** [not in F;
after l. 26 in Q1]   **66 cause** case   **74 meet'st advantage** meetest vantage
104 Penker [eds.] Peuker   **105 s.d. Exeunt** [eds.] Exit   **109 s.d. Exit** Exeunt

3.6. 12 who's who

3.7. 20 mine my   **33 spake** spoke   **40 wisdoms** wisdome [not in F]
44 s.p. Richard [not in F]   **54 we'll** we   **83 My lord** [not in F]   **125 her** his
[also in ll. 126 and 127]   **219 Zounds! I'll** we will   **220** [not in F]
240 Richard King Richard   **241 s.p. Mayor and Citizens** All   **247 cousin**
Cousins

4.1. s.d. [F: Enter the Queene, Anne Duchesse of Gloucester, the Duchesse of
Yorke, and Marquesse Dorset]   **15 s.p. Brackenbury** Lieu [and at ll. 18 and
26]

4.2. 36 My lord [not in F]   **72 there** then   **90 Hereford** Hertford
99–118 [not in F]

4.3. 5 ruthless ruthfull   **13 Which** And   **15 once** one   **31 at** and   **33 thee**
the   **53 leads** leds

4.4. 10 unblown vnblowed   **39** [not in F]   **o'er** over [Q1]   **41 Harry** [eds.]
Husband   **45 holp'st** hop'st   **52–53** [lines reversed in F]   **64 Thy** The
112 weary wearied   **118 nights . . . days** night . . . day   **128 intestate** intes-
tine   **141 Where** Where't   **225 lanced** [eds.] lanch'd   **239 or** and
268 would I I would   **284 This is** this   **324 Of ten** [eds.] Often
364–365 [lines reversed in F, and the s.p. Queen Elizabeth is missing]
366 s.p. King Richard [not in F]   **377 God** Heauen   **God's Heanens**   **392 in**
with   **396 o'erpast** repast   **417 fond** found   **430 s.d. Exit Queen** [at l. 429 in
F]   **431 s.d. Enter Ratcliffe** [at l. 432 in F]   **444 Ratcliffe** [eds.] Catesby
498 s.p. First Messenger Mess   **503 s.p. Second Messenger** Mess
506 s.p. Third Messenger Mess [also at ll. 509 and 517]   **507 you** ye
518 s.p. Fourth Messenger Mess   **534 tidings** Newes, but

5.1. 11 is, my lord is

5.2. 11 center Centry   **12 Near** Ne're

5.3. 20 track tract   **28 you** [eds.] your   **48 ff. [to the end of the play]** [copy
text is Q1]   **54 sentinels** [F] centinell [Q1]   **59 s.p. Catesby** [eds.] Rat   **79 sit**
[F] set [Q1; also at l. 131]   **85 that. The** that the [Q1]   **100 sundered** sun-
dried [Q1]   **107 s.d. [Richmond remains]** [substantially from F]
139 s.p. Ghost of Rivers King [Q1]   **141 s.p. Ghost of Grey** Gray
142 s.p. Ghost of Vaughan Vaugh   **145 Will** Wel [Q1]   **146–150** [after line

158 in Q1]   **151 s.p. Ghosts** [F] Ghost [Q1]   **159 s.p. Ghost** [not in Q1]
167 s.p. Ghost [not in Q1]   **176 fall** [F] falls [Q1]   **183 am** and [Q1]
223 s.p. Lords Lo [Q1]   **226, 235 s.p. A Lord** Lo [Q1]   **270 s.d. Ratcliffe** Rat.
& c.   **299 main** [F] matne [Q1]   **301 boot** bootes [Q1]   **304 s.p. King Richard**
[at l. 306 ("King") in Q1]   **351 them! Victory** them victorie [Q1]

5.5. 13 s.p. Stanley [not in Q1]   **13 Ferrers** Ferri [Q1]   **15 becomes** become
[Q1]   **41 s.d. Exeunt** [F; not in Q1]

Shakespeare's Sources

Richard III, like the *Henry VI* series, is based on Edward Hall's *The Union of the Noble and Illustre Families of Lancaster and York* (1548) and on the 1587 edition of Raphael Holinshed's *The Chronicles of England, Scotland, and Ireland*. (A selection from the third volume of Holinshed follows.) Both of these historical compilations were deeply indebted for their hostile view of Richard III to Polydore Vergil and Thomas More. Vergil, a papal tax collector who came to England in 1501, spent many years under the patronage of Henry VII writing in Latin his *Anglica Historia* (first published in Basel, 1534). This work portrayed Richard negatively in order to glorify the claim of the Tudor monarch who had deposed Richard in 1485. Vergil argued that England's suffering was a divinely sent scourge, intended to cleanse England of rebelliousness and prepare the English people for the providential reward of Tudor rule.

Thomas More's *The History of King Richard III*, left unfinished in 1513, was published in two slightly differing versions, one in English (1557) and one in Latin (1566). Thomas More obtained much information and possibly an early draft of his narrative from Cardinal Morton, in whose household More lived as a youth. Morton had figured in the struggles of Richard III's reign—he was the Bishop of Ely from whom Richard requested the strawberries (3.4.32–33)—and had become a bitter enemy of the Yorkist king. Thomas More's own purpose in writing the life of Richard III was surely not to glorify Henry VII, with whom More had a strained relationship, but to characterize the evil of political opportunism. His portrait of Richard becomes that of the generic tyrant, behaving as such tyrants behaved in the various literary models from Renaissance Italy with which More was doubtless familiar. The result was, in any case, one-sided. The historical Richard seems to have been no worse than many another late medieval ruler and had indeed some admirable ideas on efficiency in government. More's blackened portrait, because it served the purposes of the Tudor state, became part of the legend and was available to Shakespeare in many versions. Holinshed incorporated verbatim a good deal of More's account.

Apart from Hall's and Holinshed's chronicles, those of Robert Fabyan (first published in 1516) and the *Annals* of John Stow (1580, 1592) may have provided Shakespeare with further details. Another possible source is *A Mirror for Magistrates* (first published in 1559), where, for example, in "The Complaint of George, Duke of Clarence," we find the riddling prophecy about the letter G (see 1.1.39). A second edition of the *Mirror* (1563) contains the Complaints of Edward IV, Anthony Woodville (Lord Rivers), Hastings, Buckingham, Shore's wife, and others. Shakespeare's particular indebtedness to the *Mirror* is not great, though he certainly was familiar with it. The same is probably true of the Latin tragedy *Richardus Tertius* by Thomas Legge (1579) at Cambridge, which contains an interesting scene of Richard's wooing of the Lady Anne not reported in the chronicles. The anonymous *The True Tragedy of Richard III* (published 1594, written c. 1590–1592) may have been useful in its fusing of Senecan revenge motifs with English history, and in its focus on the single figure of Richard. The Richard of this anonymous play is an overreacher, a worshiper of Fortune who meets his nemesis in the devoutly Christian Earl of Richmond. Opinion is divided as to whether Shakespeare actually used the play, chiefly because by 1590 he could have found the legend of Richard III set forth in so many works.

The Third Volume of Chronicles (1587 edition)
Compiled by Raphael Holinshed

EDWARD THE FOURTH

[Holinshed describes the funeral of King Henry VI (1471) in which the dead King, carried in an open coffin, bleeds in the presence of beholders. It is carried to Blackfriars and thence to the monastery at Chertsey.

Dissension between King Edward and his younger brother Clarence continues to be the subject of talk, especially about a prophecy that King Edward should be succeeded by a ruler whose name begins with G. Clarence is imprisoned and secretly drowned in a butt (a large cask) of malmsey in 1478. King Edward, although consenting to his death, publicly laments his loss. Edward dies in April 1483, leaving the throne nominally occupied by Prince Edward, aged thirteen. The Duke of York, his younger brother, is eleven.]

[THE REIGN OF] EDWARD THE FIFTH

Richard, the third son [of Richard, Duke of York], of whom we now entreat,[1] was in wit[1] and courage equal with either of them, in body and prowess far under them both; little of stature, ill-featured of limbs, crookbacked, his left shoulder much higher than his right; hard-favored of visage, and such as is in states called warly,[2] in other men otherwise. He was malicious, wrathful, envious, and from afore his birth ever froward.[3] It is for truth reported that the Duchess his mother had so much ado in her travail[4] that she could not be delivered of him uncut, and that he came into the world with the feet forward, as men be borne outward,[5] and (as the fame runneth[6] also) not untoothed—whether men of hatred report above the truth or else that Nature changed her course in his beginning which in the course of his life many things unnaturally committed. So that the full confluence of these qualities, with the defects of favor and amiable proportion, gave proof to this rule of physiognomy:

> *Distortum vultum*
> *sequitur distorsio morum.*[7]

None evil captain was he[8] in the war, as to which his disposition was more meetly[9] than for peace. Sundry victories had he, and sometimes overthrows; but never on default as for his own person, either of hardiness or politic order.[10] Free was he called of dispense,[11] and somewhat above his

---

1 entreat . . . wit treat, was in intelligence   **2 in states called warly** in noblemen called warlike, bellicose   **3 froward** evilly-disposed, refractory   **4 travail** labor   **5 be borne outward** i.e., are carried away on the funeral bier when they die   **6 as the fame runneth** as rumor has it   **7 Distortum . . . morum** a warped visage follows from a warped moral sense   **8 None evil captain was he** he was by no means a bad military commander   **9 meetly** suited   **10 and sometimes . . . politic order** and sometimes he suffered defeat, though never through his own fault either in bravery or in skillful ordering of his troops   **11 Free . . . dispense** he was reputed generous

power liberal;[12] with large gifts he gat him unsteadfast friendship for which he was fain to pill and spoil[13] in other places, and got him steadfast hatred. He was close and secret, a deep dissembler, lowly of countenance,[14] arrogant of heart, outwardly companionable where he inwardly hated, not letting[15] to kiss whom he thought to kill; despiteous[16] and cruel, not for evil will alway, but ofter for ambition, and either for the surety or increase of his estate.

Friend and foe was much what indifferent[17] where his advantage grew; he spared no man's death whose life withstood his purpose. He slew with his own hands King Henry the Sixth, being prisoner in the Tower, as men constantly said, and that without commandment or knowledge of the King, which[18] would undoubtedly, if he had intended that thing, have appointed that butcherly office to some other than his own born brother. Some wise men also ween that his drift,[19] covertly conveyed, lacked not in helping forth his brother of Clarence to his death, which he resisted[20] openly, howbeit somewhat (as men deemed) more faintly than he that were heartily minded to his wealth.[21]

And they that thus deem think that he long time in King Edward's life forethought[22] to be king in case that the King his brother (whose life he looked that evil diet should shorten) should happen to decease (as indeed he did) while his children were young. And they deem that for this intent he was glad of his brother's death the Duke of Clarence, whose life must needs have hindered him so intending, whether the same Duke of Clarence had kept him[23] true to his nephew the young King or enterprised to be king himself. But of all this point is there no certainty, and whoso divineth[24] upon conjectures may as well shoot too far as too short. . . .

But now to return to the course of this history. Were it

12 **above his power liberal** generous above his ability to pay for it
13 **fain to pill and spoil** obliged to plunder and despoil   14 **lowly of**
countenance outwardly humble of expression   15 **letting** hesitating,
scrupling   16 **despiteous** full of despite, haughty, contemptuous
17 **was much what indifferent** was a matter of indifference   18 **which**
who   19 **ween that his drift** conjecture that Richard's plotting
20 **resisted** denied   21 **than he that . . . wealth** than one thinking whole-
heartedly of his (Clarence's) well-being   22 **forethought** planned, intended   23 **him** himself   24 **divineth** speculates

that the Duke of Gloucester had of old foreminded this conclusion or was now at erst[25] thereunto moved and put in
hope by the occasion of the tender age of the young princes
his nephews, as opportunity and likelihood of speed[26] put-
teth a man in courage of that[27] he never intended, certain it
is that he contrived their destruction, with the usurpation
of the regal dignity upon himself. And forsomuch as he well
wist and holp[28] to maintain a long-continued grudge and
heartburning between the Queen's kindred and the King's
blood,[29] either party envying other's[30] authority, he now
thought that their division should be (as it was indeed) a
furtherly[31] beginning to the pursuit of his intent.

Nay, he was resolved that the same was a sure ground for
the foundation of all his building, if he might first, under
the pretext of revenging of old displeasure, abuse the anger
and ignorance of the t'one party to the destruction of the
tother, and then win to his purpose as many as he could;
and those that could not be won might be lost ere they
looked therefor. For of one thing was he certain, that if his
intent were perceived he should soon have made peace between both the parties with his own blood.[32] King Edward
in his life,[33] albeit that this dissension between his friends
somewhat irked him, yet in his good health he somewhat
the less regarded it[34] because he thought, whatsoever business[35] should fall between them, himself should alway be
able to rule both the parties.

But in his last sickness, when he perceived his natural
strength so sore enfeebled that he despaired all recovery,
then he, considering the youth of his children, albeit he
nothing less mistrusted than that that happened,[36] yet well
foreseeing that many harms might grow by their debate
while the youth of his children should lack discretion of
themselves and good counsel of their friends (of which either party should counsel for their own commodity,[37] and

---

25 at erst at first   26 speed success   27 that what   28 wist and holp
knew about and helped   29 blood kindred   30 other's the other's
31 furtherly favorable   32 he should . . . blood i.e., his enemies would
have joined together to destroy him   33 in his life as long as he continued to live   34 he somewhat . . . it he did not worry about it too
much   35 business i.e., quarrel   36 albeit . . . happened i.e., although
he could not imagine anything so bad as what actually happened
37 commodity benefit, self-interest

rather by pleasant[38] advice to win themselves favor than by profitable advertisement[39] to do the children good), he called some of them before him that were at variance, and in especial the Lord Marquess Dorset, the Queen's son by her first husband.

So did he also William, the Lord Hastings, a nobleman, then Lord Chamberlain, against whom the Queen specially grudged for the great favor the King bare[40] him, and also for that[41] she thought him secretly familiar with the King in wanton company. Her kindred also bare him sore,[42] as well for that the King had made him Captain of Calais (which office the Lord Rivers, brother to the Queen, claimed of the King's former promise) as for divers other great gifts which he received that they looked for. When these lords, with divers other of both the parties, were come in presence,[43] the King, lifting up himself, and underset with pillows, as it is reported, on[44] this wise said unto them:

[Holinshed reports the oration of King Edward on his deathbed.]

But the lords, recomforting[45] him with as good words as they could, and answering for the time as they thought to stand with his pleasure, there in his presence, as by their words appeared, each forgave other and joined their hands together, when, as it after appeared by their deeds, their hearts were far asunder. As soon as the King was departed the noble Prince his son drew toward London, which at the time of his decease kept his household at Ludlow in Wales. . . .

To the governance and ordering of this young prince, at his sending thither, was there appointed Sir Anthony Woodville, Lord Rivers and brother unto the Queen, a right honorable man, as valiant of hand as politic in counsel. Adjoined were there unto him other of the same party; and in effect, everyone, as he was nearest of kin unto the Queen, so was he planted next about[46] the Prince. That drift by the Queen not unwisely devised, whereby her blood might of

---

38 pleasant flattering **39 advertisement** instruction, admonition **40 bare** bore **41 for that** because **42 bare him sore** bore him a grudge **43 in presence** into the royal presence **44 on** in **45 recomforting** comforting **46 next about** nearest to

youth be rooted into the Prince's favor, the Duke of Gloucester turned unto their destruction, and upon that ground set the foundation of all his unhappy building.

[Richard soon wins the support of Lord Hastings and the Duke of Buckingham by exploiting their resentment of the Queen and her powerful kindred. Together they resolve to remove those persons from their positions of influence around the young Prince. Richard does so by tricking the Queen into believing it necessary that the Prince be escorted to London by a large force—one so large that it causes alarm for the Prince's safety and gives Richard excuse to order the arrests of Lord Richard Grey, Sir Thomas Vaughan, and Lord Rivers. (These three are later beheaded at Pomfret.) The Queen, dismayed at these arrests and separated from her son Edward, takes refuge in sanctuary at Westminster, bringing her youngest son Richard with her. Thomas Rotherham, the Archbishop of York and Lord Chancellor, brings the Great Seal to her there and offers what comfort he can.

Prince Edward is thereupon escorted from Stony Stratford to London by those who are loyal to Richard of Gloucester.]

When the King approached near to the city, Edmund Shaw, goldsmith, then mayor, with William White and John Matthew, sheriffs, and all the other aldermen, in scarlet, with five hundred horse of the citizens, in violet, received him reverently at Hornsea and, riding from thence, accompanied him into the city, which he entered the fourth day of May, the first and last year of his reign. But the Duke of Gloucester bare him[47] in open sight so reverently to the Prince, with all semblance of lowliness, that, from the great obloquy in which he was so late[48] before, he was suddenly fallen in so great trust that at the Council next assembled he was made the only man chosen and thought most meet to be Protector of the King and his realm; so that, were it destiny or were it folly, the lamb was betaken to the wolf to keep.

47 bare him bore himself, conducted himself   **48 obloquy . . . late** disgrace in which he was so recently

[Other appointments to the Privy Council are made.]

Now, all were it so[49] that the Protector so sore thirsted for
the finishing of that he had begun that thought every day a
year till it were achieved, yet durst he no further attempt as
long as he had but half his prey in his hand.[50]

And why? Well did he wit[51] that if he deposed the one
brother, all the realm would fall to the other, if he either
remained in sanctuary or should haply be shortly conveyed
to his father's liberty.[52] Wherefore incontinent[53] at the next
meeting of the lords at the Council he proposed to them
that it was a heinous deed of the Queen, and proceeding
of great malice toward the King's councillors, that she
should keep in sanctuary the King's brother from him,
whose special pleasure and comfort were to have his
brother with him.

[Holinshed reports Richard's subtle oration to the Council,
urging that the Archbishop of York be sent to the Queen
with the request that she surrender custody of her younger
son; if she refuse, young Richard ought to be brought
against her will. The Council agrees, and when the Archbishop expresses reservations about violating sanctuary,
Buckingham argues that sanctuary is not available to children: "And verily, I have often heard of sanctuary men, but I
never heard erst of sanctuary children." At length the Archbishop prevails upon the Queen by offering his own guaran-
tees of protection, and brings young Richard to his uncle of
Gloucester at the Council meeting.]

When the Lord Cardinal, and these other lords with him,
had received this young duke,[54] they brought him into the
Star Chamber,[55] where the Protector took him in his arms

---

49 all were it so albeit   **50 but half . . . hand** i.e., Prince Edward in his
custody but not Edward's younger brother Richard   **51 wit** know
52 his father's liberty i.e., his father's domain or property, where
Richard of Gloucester would not be able to touch him   **53 incontinent**
immediately   **54 this young duke** i.e., Richard, Duke of York   **55 the
Star Chamber** (In the fourteenth and fifteenth centuries, this room in
the royal palace at Westminster was used by the King's Council as it sat
to exercise jurisdiction; by the end of the fifteenth century it had become a court of criminal jurisdiction, and was infamous under the
Stuart kings as the place from which they exercised their arbitrary use
of royal power.)

and kissed him with these words: "Now welcome, my lord, even with all my very heart!" And he said in that of likelihood as he thought.[56] Thereupon, forthwith they brought him unto the King his brother into the Bishop's palace at Paul's, and from thence through the city honorably into the Tower, out of the which after that day they never came abroad.[57] When the Protector had both the children in his hands, he opened himself[58] more boldly, both to certain other men and also chiefly to the Duke of Buckingham—although I know that many thought that this Duke was privy to all the Protector's counsel even from the beginning; and some of the Protector's friends said that the Duke was the first mover of the Protector to this matter, sending a privy messenger unto him straight after King Edward's death.

But others again, which knew better the subtle wit of the Protector, deny that he ever opened his enterprise to the Duke until he had brought to pass the things before rehearsed.[59] But when he had imprisoned the Queen's kinsfolks and gotten both her sons into his own hands, then he opened the rest of his purpose with less fear to them whom he thought meet for the matter, and specially to the Duke, who, being won to his purpose, he thought his strength more than half increased.

[Buckingham is persuaded to join Richard's wicked enterprise only when he sees that it cannot be avoided in any case and that it can be turned to Buckingham's own advantage.]

Then it was agreed that the Protector should have the Duke's aid to make him king, and that the Protector's only lawful son should marry the Duke's daughter, and that the Protector should grant him the quiet possession of the earldom of Hereford, which he claimed as his inheritance and could never obtain it in King Edward's time.

Besides these requests of the Duke, the Protector, of his own mind, promised him a great quantity of the King's trea-

---

56 And he . . . thought i.e., he probably meant what he said; he *was* glad to see the young Prince   **57 abroad** out in the open air   **58 opened himself** revealed his intention   **59 rehearsed** recited, recounted

sure and of his household stuff. And when they were thus at a point[60] between themselves, they went about to prepare for the coronation of the young King, as they would have it seem. And that they might turn both the eyes and minds of men from perceiving of their drifts otherwhere, the lords, being sent for from all parts of the realm, came thick to that solemnity. But the Protector and the Duke, after that they had sent the Lord Cardinal, the Archbishop of York (then Lord Chancellor), the Bishop of Ely, the Lord Stanley, and the Lord Hastings (then Lord Chamberlain), with many other noblemen, to commune[61] and devise about the coronation in one place, as fast were they in another place contriving the contrary, and to make the Protector king.

To which Council, albeit there were adhibited[62] very few, and they were secret,[63] yet began there, here and thereabouts, some manner of muttering among the people, as though all should not long be well, though they neither wist[64] what they feared nor wherefore—were it that before such great things, men's hearts of a secret instinct of nature misgive them, as the sea without wind swelleth of himself[65] sometimes before a tempest, or were it that some one man, haply somewhat perceiving,[66] filled many men with suspicion, though he showed few men what he knew. Howbeit, somewhat[67] the dealing itself made men to muse on the matter, though the Council were close.[68] For little by little all folk withdrew from the Tower and drew unto Crosby's in Bishopsgate's Street where the Protector kept his household. The Protector had the resort, the King in manner desolate.[69]

While some, for their business, made suit to them that had the doing,[70] some were by their friends secretly warned that it might haply turn them to no good to be too much attendant about the King without the Protector's appointment,[71] which removed also divers of the Prince's old ser-

---

60 at a point agreed upon terms   **61 commune** confer   **62 adhibited** admitted   **63 secret** closemouthed   **64 wist** knew   **65 himself** itself   **66 haply somewhat perceiving** perhaps perceiving something   **67 somewhat** to some extent   **68 close** reticent, secretive   **69 The Protector . . . desolate** i.e., everyone flocked to the Protector Richard, leaving the young King friendless   **70 made suit . . . doing** brought their petitions to those persons constitutionally authorized to deal with them, i.e., the young King's representatives   **71 appointment** agreement

vants from him and set new about him. Thus many things coming together, partly by chance, partly of purpose, caused at length not common people only, that wonde[72] with the wind, but wise men also, and some lords eke,[73] to mark the matter and muse thereon, so far forth that the Lord Stanley (that was after[74] Earl of Derby) wisely mistrusted it and said unto the Lord Hastings that he much misliked these two several councils. "For while we," quoth he, "talk of one matter in the t'one place, little wot[75] we whereof they talk in the tother place."

"My lord," quoth the Lord Hastings, "on my life, never doubt you,[76] for while one man is there which is never thence, never can there be thing once moved[77] that should sound amiss toward me but it should be in mine ears ere it were well out of their mouths." This meant he by Catesby,[78] which was of his near secret counsel and whom he very familiarly used,[79] and in his most weighty matters put no man in so special trust, reckoning himself to no man so lief, sith[80] he well wist there was no man so much to him beholden as was this Catesby, which was a man well learned in the laws of this land and, by the special favor of the Lord Chamberlain, in good authority; and much rule bare[81] in all the county of Leicester, where the Lord Chamberlain's power chiefly lay.

But surely great pity was it that he had not had either more truth or less wit,[82] for his dissimulation only[83] kept all that mischief up. In whom if the Lord Hastings had not put so special trust, the Lord Stanley and he had departed with divers other lords and broken all the dance[84] for[85] many ill signs that he saw which he now construes all to the best. So surely thought he that there could be none harm toward him in that Council intended where Catesby was. And of truth the Protector and the Duke of Buckingham made very

---

72 wonde flinch, wind, turn   **73 eke** also   **74 that was after** who was afterward   **75 wot** know   **76 doubt you** fear   **77 moved** proposed, urged   **78 This meant ... Catesby** by this he meant (William) Catesby   **79 which was ... used** who was in his confidence and with whom he was on very familiar terms   **80 lief, sith** beloved, since   **81 much rule bare** bore much authority   **82 that he ... wit** i.e., that Catesby was not either more truthful or less clever   **83 for his dissimulation only** for it was his (Catesby's) dissimulation alone that   **84 broken all the dance** i.e., would have broken up Richard's carefully orchestrated plan   **85 for** on account of

good semblance unto the Lord Hastings, and kept him much in company.[86] And undoubtedly the Protector loved him well and loath was to have lost him, saving for fear lest his life should have quailed[87] their purpose.

For which cause he moved Catesby to prove with some words cast out afar off[88] whether he could think it possible to win the Lord Hastings unto their part. But Catesby, whether he assayed[89] him or assayed him not, reported unto them that he found him so fast,[90] and heard him speak so terrible words,[91] that he durst no further break.[92] And of truth the Lord Chamberlain of very trust[93] showed unto Catesby the distrust that others began to have in the matter. And therefore he, fearing lest their motion might with the Lord Hastings minish his credence,[94] whereunto only all the matter leaned, procured[95] the Protector hastily to rid him. And much the rather for that[96] he trusted by his death to obtain much of the rule that the Lord Hastings bare in his country, the only desire whereof was the allective[97] that induced him to be partner and one special contriver of all this horrible treason.

Whereupon soon after, that is to wit[98] on the Friday being the thirteenth of June, many lords assembled in the Tower and there sat in Council, devising the honorable solemnity of the King's coronation, of which the time appointed then so near approached that the pageants and subtleties were in making[99] day and night at Westminster, and much victuals killed therefor that afterward was cast away. These lords so sitting together communing[100] of this matter, the Protector came in amongst them first about nine of the clock, saluting them courteously and excusing himself that

---

86 made ... company looked with favor on the Lord Hastings and saw a good deal of him   **87 saving ... quailed** were it not for fear that he (Hastings), if he remained alive, would have spoiled   **88 he moved ... off** he induced Catesby to ascertain by indirect questioning   **89 assayed** examined   **90 fast** i.e., loyal to young King Edward   **91 so terrible words** i.e., words so threatening to Richard's cause   **92 break** disclose his purpose   **93 of very trust** trustingly   **94 lest their ... credence** i.e., lest what others were muttering cause Catesby to lose his credit with the Lord Hastings   **95 procured** induced, caused   **96 the rather for that** the sooner because   **97 the only desire ... allective** the desire of which was the sole allure   **98 to wit** i.e., to say   **99 subtleties were in making** ingenious contrivances were being made   **100 communing** consulting

he had been from them so long, saying merrily that he had been a sleeper that day.

After a little talking with them, he said unto the Bishop of Ely: "My lord, you have very good strawberries at your garden in Holborn. I require[101] you let us have a mess[102] of them." "Gladly, my lord," quoth he, "would God I had some better thing as ready to your pleasure as that!" And therewithal in all the haste he sent his servant for a mess of strawberries. The Protector set the lords fast in communing and, thereupon praying them to spare him for a little while, departed thence. And soon after one hour, between ten and eleven, he returned into the chamber amongst them, all changed, with a wonderful sour angry countenance, knitting the brows, frowning, and fretting and gnawing on his lips, and so sat him down in his place.

All the lords were much dismayed and sore marveled at this manner of sudden change and what thing should him ail. Then, when he had sitten still awhile, thus he began: "What were they worthy to have that compass and imagine[103] the destruction of me, being so near of blood unto the King and Protector of his royal person and his realm?" At this question all the lords sat sore astonied,[104] musing much by whom this question should be meant,[105] of which every man wist himself clear. Then the Lord Chamberlain, as he that for the love between them[106] thought he might be boldest with him, answered and said that they were worthy to be punished as heinous traitors, whatsoever they were. And all the other[107] affirmed the same. "That is," quoth he,[108] "yonder sorceress my brother's wife and other with her" (meaning the Queen).

At these words many of the other lords were greatly abashed that favored her. But the Lord Hastings was in his mind better content that it was moved by her[109] than by any other whom he loved better; albeit his heart somewhat grudged that he was not afore made of counsel in this mat-

---

101 require beg **102 mess** portion, serving **103 that compass and imagine** who contrive and plot **104 sore astonied** greatly astonished **105 musing much . . . meant** wondering a good deal whom the question was directed against **106 them** i.e., Hastings and Richard **107 other** others **108 he** i.e., Richard **109 moved by her** i.e., urged against the Queen

ter, as he was of the taking of her kindred[110] and of their putting to death, which were by his assent before devised to be beheaded at Pomfret this selfsame day; in which he was not ware that it was by other devised that he himself should be beheaded the same day at London. Then said the Protector: "Ye shall all see in what wise that sorceress, and that other witch of her counsel, Shore's wife, with their affinity,[111] have by their sorcery and witchcraft wasted my body." And therewith he plucked up his doublet sleeve to his elbow, upon his left arm, where he showed a wearish withered arm and small, as it was never other.[112]

Hereupon every man's mind sore misgave them, well perceiving that this matter was but a quarrel.[113] For they well wist that the Queen was too wise to go about any such folly. And also, if she would,[114] yet would she, of all folk least, make Shore's wife of her counsel whom of all women she most hated as that concubine whom the King her husband had most loved. And also no man was there present but well knew that his arm was ever such since his birth. Natheless,[115] the Lord Chamberlain (which from the death of King Edward kept Shore's wife, on whom he somewhat doted in the King's life, saving as it is said he that while forbare her of reverence toward the King or else of a certain kind of fidelity to his friend)[116] answered and said: "Certainly, my lord, if they have so heinously done, they be worthy heinous punishment."

"What?" quoth the Protector. "Thou servest me, I ween, with if's and with and's. I tell thee they have so done, and that I will make good on thy body, traitor!" And therewith, as in a great anger, he clapped his fist upon the board a great rap. At which token one cried "Treason!" without[117]

---

110 **taking of her kindred** arresting of her, the Queen's, kindred
111 **affinity** family ties through marriage   112 **a wearish . . . other** a small, shriveled, withered arm, no different from what it had always been   113 **quarrel** ground for complaint, excuse for quarreling   114 **if she would** even if she wanted to   115 **Natheless** nevertheless   116 **in the King's life . . . to his friend** i.e., while King Edward was still alive, except that it is said he did not keep her as his mistress during that time out of a sense of reverent duty toward the King or else out of a sense of personal loyalty to the King, who was his friend. (Hastings had too much delicacy to take Shore's wife away from King Edward.)
117 **without** outside of

the chamber. Therewith a door clapped,[118] and in come[119] there rushing men in harness,[120] as many as the chamber might hold. And anon the Protector said to the Lord Hastings: "I arrest thee, traitor!" "What, me, my lord?" quoth he. "Yea, thee, traitor!" quoth the Protector. And another let fly at the Lord Stanley, which shrunk at the stroke and fell under the table or else his head had been cleft to the teeth, for as shortly as he shrank yet ran the blood about his ears.

Then were they all quickly bestowed in divers chambers, except the Lord Chamberlain, whom the Protector bade speed and shrive him apace.[121] "For, by Saint Paul," quoth he, "I will not to dinner till I see thy head off!" It booted him[122] not to ask why, but heavily took a priest at adventure[123] and made a short shrift,[124] for a longer would not be suffered, the Protector made so much haste to dinner, which he might not go to until this were done for saving of his oath. So was he brought forth to the green beside the chapel within the Tower, and his head laid down upon a long log of timber and there stricken off. . . .

A marvelous case is it to hear either the warnings of that he should have voided or the tokens[125] of that he could not void. For the self[126] night next before his death, the Lord Stanley sent a trusty messenger unto him at midnight in all the haste, requiring him to rise and ride away with him, for he was disposed utterly no longer to bide, he had so fearful a dream; in which him thought that a boar with his tusks so razed[127] them both by the heads that the blood ran about both their shoulders. And forsomuch as the Protector gave the boar for his cognizance,[128] this dream made so fearful an impression in his heart that he was throughly determined no longer to tarry, but had his horse ready, if the Lord Hastings would go with him, to ride yet so far the same night that they should be out of danger ere day.

"Ha, good lord," quoth the Lord Hastings to this messen-

---

118 clapped briskly opened with a bang   **119 come** came   **120 harness** armor   **121 speed and shrive him apace** hurry up and make his confession quickly   **122 booted him** availed him   **123 heavily . . . at adventure** sadly he chose a priest at random   **124 shrift** confession   **125 tokens** signs, prophecies   **126 self** very   **127 razed** cut, wounded   **128 gave the boar for his cognizance** displayed the boar as his badge on his coat of arms

ger, "leaneth my lord thy master so much to such trifles
and hath such faith in dreams, which either his own fear
fantasieth or do rise in the night's rest by reason of his
day's thought? Tell him it is plain witchcraft to believe in
such dreams, which if they were tokens of things to come,
why thinketh he not that we might be as likely to make them
true by our going, if we were caught and brought back, as
friends fail fliers;[129] for then had the boar a cause likely to
raze us with his tusks, as folk that fled for some falsehood.
Wherefore, either is there peril, or none there is indeed; or,
if any be, it is rather in going than biding.[130] And in case we
should needs fall in peril one way or other, yet had I rather
that men should see that it were by other men's falsehood
than think it were either by our own fault or faint heart.
And therefore go to thy master, man, and commend me to
him, and pray him be merry and have no fear, for I ensure
him I am as sure of the man that he wotteth of as I am of
mine own hand." "God send grace, sir," quoth the messenger, and went his way.

Certain is it also that, in riding towards the Tower the
same morning in which he was beheaded, his horse twice or
thrice stumbled with him, almost to the falling. Which
thing, albeit each man wot well daily happeneth to them to
whom no such mischance is toward,[131] yet hath it been of an
old rite and custom observed as a token oftentimes notably
foregoing some great misfortune. Now this that followeth
was no warning but an envious scorn.[132] The same morning,
ere he was up, came a knight unto him, as it were of courtesy, to accompany him to the Council, but of truth sent by
the Protector to haste him thitherwards, with whom he was
of secret confederacy in that purpose—a mean[133] man at
that time, and now of great authority.

This knight, I say, when it happened the Lord Chamberlain by the way to stay[134] his horse and commune awhile
with a priest whom he met in the Tower Street, brake his
tale[135] and said merrily to him: "What, my lord, I pray you,
come on. Whereto talk you so long with that priest? You

---

129 friends fail fliers friends desert those who flee   **130 biding** staying   **131 toward** impending   **132 envious scorn** malicious mockery
133 mean of low station   **134 stay** stop   **135 brake his tale** interrupted

have no need of a priest yet." And therewith he laughed upon him, as though he would say, "Ye shall have soon." But so little wist the tother what he meant, and so little mistrusted, that he was never merrier nor never so full of good hope in his life. . . .

Upon the very Tower Wharf, so near the place where his head was off soon after, there met he with one Hastings, a pursuivant[136] of his own name. And at their meeting in that place, he was put in remembrance of another time in which it had happened them before to meet in like manner together in the same place. At which other time the Lord Chamberlain had been accused unto King Edward by the Lord Rivers, the Queen's brother, in such wise as he was for the while (but it lasted not long) far fallen into the King's indignation[137] and stood in great fear of himself.[138] And forsomuch as he now met this pursuivant in the same place, that jeopardy so well passed, it gave him great pleasure to talk with him thereof, with whom he had before talked thereof in the same place, while he was therein.[139]

And therefore he said: "Ha, Hastings, art thou remembered when I met thee here once with an heavy heart?" "Yea, my lord," quoth he, "that remember I well, and thanked be God they gat no good nor you no harm thereby." "Thou wouldst say so," quoth he, "if thou knewest as much as I know, which few know else as yet, and more shall shortly." That meant he by[140] the lords of the Queen's kindred, that were taken before and should that day be beheaded at Pomfret, which he well wist but nothing ware[141] that the ax hung over his own head. "In faith, man," quoth he, "I was never so sorry, nor never stood in so great dread in my life, as I did when thou and I met here. And lo, how the world is turned! Now stand mine enemies in the danger, as thou mayst hap to hear more hereafter, and I never in my life so merry nor never in so great surety."

O good God, the blindness of our mortal nature! When he most feared, he was in good surety; when he reckoned himself surest, he lost his life, and that within two hours after.

---

136 **pursuivant** royal messenger with power to serve summonses
137 **indignation** displeasure   138 **of himself** for his life   139 **therein** i.e., in that jeopardy   140 **That meant he by** by that he meant   141 **nothing ware** was not at all aware

Thus ended this honorable man, a good knight and a gentle, of great authority with his prince, of living somewhat dissolute, plain and open to his enemy and secret to his friend, easy to beguile, as he that of good heart and courage forestudied no perils, a loving man and passing well[142] beloved, very faithful and trusty enough, trusting too much. Now flew the fame[143] of this lord's death swiftly through the city, and so forth further about, like a wind in every man's ear. But the Protector, immediately after dinner, intending to set some color[144] upon the matter, sent in all the haste for many substantial men[145] out of the city into the Tower.

Now, at their coming, himself with the Duke of Buckingham stood harnessed in old ill-faring briganders,[146] such as no man should ween that they would vouchsafe[147] to have put upon their backs except that some sudden necessity had constrained them. And then the Protector showed them that the Lord Chamberlain, and other of his conspiracy,[148] had contrived to have suddenly destroyed him and the Duke, there the same day in the Council. And what they intended further was as yet not well known. Of which their treason he never had knowledge before ten of the clock the same forenoon, which sudden fear drave them to put on for their defense such harness[149] as came next to hand. And so had God holpen them that the mischief turned upon them that would have done it. And this he required[150] them to report.

Every man answered him fair, as though no man mistrusted the matter, which of truth no man believed. Yet for the further appeasing of the people's minds, he sent immediately after dinner in all the haste one herald-of-arms with a proclamation to be made through the city in the King's name containing that the Lord Hastings, with divers other of his traitorous purpose, had before conspired the same day to have slain the Lord Protector and the Duke of Buckingham sitting in the Council and after to have taken upon them to rule the King and the realm at their pleasure. . . .

---

142 passing well surpassingly   **143 fame** rumor   **144 color** excuse, pretense of legitimacy   **145 substantial men** men of property   **146 ill-faring briganders** armor in bad condition   **147 vouchsafe** consent, deign   **148 other of his conspiracy** others in conspiracy with him   **149 harness** armor   **150 required** asked, urged

The means whereby: namely, his evil company, sinister procuring, and ungracious example, as well in many other things as in the vicious living and inordinate abusion of his body, both with many other and also specially with Shore's wife, which was one also of his most secret counsel in this most heinous treason, with whom he lay nightly and namely[151] the night last past next before his death. So that it was the less marvel if ungracious living brought him to an unhappy ending. . . .

Now was this proclamation made within two hours after that he was beheaded, and it was so curiously indited[152] and so fair written in parchment, in so well a set hand and therewith of itself so long a process,[153] that every child might well perceive that it was prepared before. For all the time between his death and the proclaiming could scant have sufficed unto the bare writing alone, all had it been but in paper[154] and scribbled forth in haste at adventure.[155]

[Shore's wife is forced to do public penance. The Queen's kindred are beheaded at Pomfret by order of Sir Richard Ratcliffe, declaring their innocence before dying. Richard's next project is to cast doubt on the legitimacy of the young King and his brother.]

But certain it is that Doctor Shaw was of counsel in the beginning, so far forth that they determined that he should first break[156] the matter in a sermon at Paul's Cross in which he should, by the authority of his preaching, incline the people to the Protector's ghostly[157] purpose. But now was all the labor and study in the device of some convenient pretext for which the people should be content to depose the Prince and accept the Protector for King. In which, divers things they devised. But the chief thing and the weightiest of all that invention rested in this: that they should allege bastardy, either in King Edward[158] himself or in his children or both, so that he[159] should seem disabled to

---

151 **namely** specifically   152 **curiously indited** skillfully inscribed
153 **process** narrative, discourse   154 **all had it been but in paper** even
if it had been written on paper (rather than parchment)   155 **at adventure** at random, recklessly   156 **break** divulge   157 **ghostly** spiritual,
i.e., diabolical   158 **Edward** i.e., Edward IV   159 **he** i.e., Edward IV

inherit the crown by[160] the Duke of York, and the Prince by him.

To lay[161] bastardy in King Edward sounded openly to the rebuke of the Protector's own mother, which was mother to them both, for in that point could be no other color but to pretend[162] that his own mother was an adulteress; which notwithstanding, to further this purpose he letted not.[163] But nevertheless he would that point should be less and more favorably handled,[164] not even fully plain and directly, but that the matter should be touched aslope,[165] craftily, as though men spared in that point to speak all the truth for fear of his displeasure. But the other point, concerning the bastardy that they devised to surmise[166] in King Edward's children, that would he should be openly declared and enforced to the uttermost.

[Holinshed provides some background on Edward IV's marriage relating to this issue of legitimacy, especially about his contract with Elizabeth Lucy. Doctor Shaw declares Edward's marriage with the Queen to have been unlawful because of this precontract. Besides, neither Edward IV nor Clarence is thought to bear any family resemblance to their father, the Duke of York, unlike Richard, who resembles his father closely.

At the Guildhall, on the following Tuesday, Buckingham addresses the Mayor, aldermen, and commoners on the subject of Edward IV's insatiable lust.]

"For no woman was there anywhere, young or old, rich or poor, whom he set his eye upon, in whom he anything liked, either person or favor, speech, pace, or countenance, but, without any fear of God or respect of his honor, murmur or grudge of the world, he would importunely pursue his appetite and have her, to the great destruction of many a good woman and great dolor to their husbands and their other friends, which, being honest people of themselves, so much regard the cleanness of their house, the chastity of their

---

160 by from **161 lay** allege **162 could be . . . pretend** there was nothing else for it but to allege **163 letted not** did not hesitate **164 he would . . . handled** wished that that point should be less plainly and more discreetly handled **165 aslope** i.e., indirectly, gingerly **166 devised to surmise** undertook to allege

wives and their children, that them were liefer to leese[167] all that they had besides than to have such a villainy done them. And all were it that,[168] with this and other importable[169] dealing, the realm was in every part annoyed, yet specially ye here, the citizens of this noble city, as well for that amongst you is most plenty of all such things as minister matter to such injuries, as for that you were nearest at hand, sith that near hereabouts was commonly his most abiding."[170]

[Buckingham dwells on the precontract to Elizabeth Lucy and on Richard's reluctance to have the matter of Edward IV's bastardy discussed openly because of Richard's "filial reverence to the Duchess his mother."]

When the Duke had said,[171] and looked[172] that the people, whom he hoped that the Mayor had framed[173] before, should, after this proposition made, have cried "King Richard, King Richard!" all was hushed and mute and not one word answered thereunto.

[By way of explanation, the Mayor offers the excuse that the people "had not been accustomed there to be spoken unto but by the Recorder." When the Recorder speaks to them, showing "everything as the Duke's words and no part his own," the people remain silent still.]

At these words the people began to whisper among themselves secretly, that the voice was neither loud nor distinct but, as it were, the sound of a swarm of bees; till, at the last, in the nether end of the hall, an ambushment[174] of the Duke's servants and Nesfield's,* and other belonging to the Protector, with some prentices and lads that thrust into the hall amongst the press,[175] began suddenly at men's

---

167 them were liefer to leese they would rather lose   **168 all were it that** while it is certainly true that   **169 importable** unbearable, intolerable   **170 as well for . . . abiding** as much because among you are plentiful means to redress such injuries as because you have been especially vulnerable, living as you do in this area where he was usually dwelling close at hand   **171 said** finished talking   **172 looked** expected **173 framed** prepared, fashioned to his purpose   **174 ambushment** surprise party, concealed group   **175 press** crowd, throng

backs to cry out as loud as their throats would give, "King Richard, King Richard!" and threw up their caps in token of joy. And they that stood before cast back their heads,[176] marveling thereof, but nothing they said. Now when the Duke and the Mayor saw this manner, they wisely turned it to their purpose and said it was a goodly cry and a joyful to hear every man with one voice, no man saying nay.

"Wherefore, friends," quoth the Duke, "sith we perceive it is all your whole minds to have this noble man for your king (whereof we shall make His Grace so effectual report that we doubt not but it shall redound unto your great weal and commodity),[177] we require ye that ye tomorrow go with us, and we with you, unto His Noble Grace to make our humble request unto him in manner before remembered." And therewith the lords came down,[178] and the company dissolved and departed, the more part all sad—some with glad semblance that were not very merry; and some of those that came thither with the Duke, not able to dissemble their sorrow, were fain[179] at his back to turn their face to the wall while the dolor of their hearts burst out of their eyes.

Then, on the morrow after, the Mayor, with all the aldermen and chief commoners of the city, in their best manner appareled, assembling themselves together, resorted unto Baynard's Castle, where the Protector lay.[180] To which place repaired also, according to their appointment,[181] the Duke of Buckingham and divers noblemen with him, besides many knights and other gentlemen. And thereupon the Duke sent word unto the Lord Protector of the being there of a great and honorable company to move[182] a great matter unto His Grace. Whereupon the Protector made difficulty[183] to come out unto them but if[184] he first knew some part of their errand, as though he doubted[185] and partly mistrusted the coming of such a number unto him so suddenly without any warning or knowledge whether they came for good or harm.

Then the Duke, when he had showed[186] this to the Mayor

---

176 cast back their heads turned their heads around   **177 weal and commodity** welfare and benefit   **178 came down** i.e., descended from the dais   **179 fain** obliged   **180 lay** resided   **181 appointment** agreement, purpose   **182 move** urge   **183 made difficulty** appeared to be reluctant, played hard to get   **184 but if** unless   **185 doubted** feared **186 showed** revealed

and other that they might thereby see how little the Protector looked for this matter, they sent unto him by the messenger such loving message again and therewith so humbly besought him to vouchsafe that they might resort to his presence to propose[187] their intent, of which they would unto none other person any part disclose; that at the last he came forth of his chamber, and yet not down unto them, but stood above in a gallery over them, where they might see him and speak to him, as though he would not yet come too near them till he wist what they meant. And thereupon the Duke of Buckingham first made humble petition unto him, on the behalf of them all, that His Grace would pardon them and license them to propose unto His Grace the intent of their coming, without his displeasure, without which pardon obtained they durst not be bold to move him of that matter.[188]

In which, albeit they meant as much honor to His Grace as wealth to all the realm besides, yet were they not sure how His Grace would take it, whom they would in no wise offend. Then the Protector, as he was very gentle of himself,[189] and also longed sore to wit[190] what they meant, gave him leave to propose what him liked, verily trusting, for the good mind that he bare them all, none of them anything would intend unto himward wherewith[191] he ought to be grieved. When the Duke had this leave and pardon to speak, then waxed he bold to show him their intent and purpose, with all the causes moving them thereunto (as ye before have heard), and finally to beseech His Grace that it would like him, of his[192] accustomed goodness and zeal unto the realm, now with his eye of pity to behold the long-continued distress and decay of the same, and to set his gracious hands to redress and amendment thereof.

All which he might well do by taking upon him the crown and governance of this realm according to his right and title lawfully descended unto him; and, to the laud[193] of God,

---

187 propose put forward, propound   **188 move . . . matter** urge that matter to him   **189 very gentle of himself** i.e., graceful and yielding by nature. (This is, in indirect quotation, what Richard says of himself to Buckingham and the others.)   **190 longed sore to wit** longed greatly to know   **191 none . . . wherewith** none of them would have any intentions toward him with which   **192 that it . . . of his** that he would be pleased, out of his   **193 laud** praise

profit of the land, and unto His Noble Grace so much the more honor and less pain, in that never prince reigned upon any people that were so glad to live under his obeisance[194] as the people of this realm under his. When the Protector had heard the proposition he looked very strangely[195] thereat, and answered that all were it[196] that he partly knew the things by them alleged to be true, yet such entire love he bare unto King Edward and his children, and* so much more regarded his honor in other realms about[197] than the crown of any one (of which he was never desirous), that he could not find in his heart in this point to incline to their desire. For in all other nations, where the truth were not well known, it should peradventure be thought that it were his own ambitious mind and device to depose the Prince and take himself the crown. . . .

Upon this answer given, the Duke, by the Protector's license, a little round[198] as well with other noblemen about him as with the Mayor and Recorder of London. And after that, upon like pardon desired and obtained, he showed[199] aloud unto the Protector,* for a final conclusion, that the realm was appointed[200] King Edward's line should not any longer reign upon them, both for that[201] they had so far gone that it was now no surety to retreat as for that[202] they thought it for the weal universal to take that way, although[203] they had not yet begun it. Wherefore, if it would like His Grace to take the crown upon him, they would humbly beseech him thereunto. If he would give them a resolute answer to the contrary, which they would be loath to hear, then must they needs seek and should not fail to find some other nobleman that would. These words much moved the Protector, which else (as every man may wit)[204] would never of likelihood have inclined thereunto.

But when he saw there was none other way but that either

---

194 obeisance command, authority   **195 looked very strangely** i.e., acted coy, standoffish   **196 all were it** granted   **197 regarded . . . about** was concerned for his reputation in other neighboring countries   **198 a little round** whispered a little   **199 showed** demonstrated in speech   **200 appointed** resolved, determined (that)   **201 for that** because   **202 as for that** and also because   **203 for the weal . . . although** i.e., for the benefit of all to take the alternative of naming Richard, even if   **204 wit** know. (Said as indirect quotation of what Richard says about himself.)

he must take it or else he and his both go from it, he said
unto the lords and commons: "Sith we perceive well that all
the realm is so set . . . we be content and agree favorably to
incline to your petition and request, and according to the
same, here we take upon us the royal estate, preeminence,
and kingdom of the two noble realms, England and
France. . . ."

With this there was a great shout, crying "King Richard,
King Richard!" And then the lords went up to the King (for
so he was from that time called) and the people departed.

[THE REIGN OF] RICHARD THE THIRD

[Richard comes to the Great Hall at Westminster on July 6,
1483, with his wife, Queen Anne, whom he married in 1472,
and is crowned.]

King Richard, after his coronation, taking his way to Gloucester to visit in his new honor the town of which he bare
the name of old,* devised as he rode to fulfill the thing
which he before had intended. And forsomuch as his mind
gave him[205] that, his nephews living, men would not reckon
that he could have right to the realm, he thought therefore
without delay to rid them, as though the killing of his kinsmen could amend his cause and make him a kindly[206] king.
Whereupon he sent one John Greene, whom he specially
trusted, unto Sir Robert Brackenbury, constable of the
Tower, with a letter and credence[207] also that the same Sir
Robert should in any wise put the two children to death.

This John Greene did his errand unto Brackenbury,
kneeling before[208] Our Lady in the Tower, who plainly answered that he would never put them to death to die therefor. With which answer John Greene, returning, recounted
the same to King Richard at Warwick, yet in his way.[209]
Wherewith he took such displeasure and thought[210] that the

---

205 forsomuch . . . gave him forasmuch as he feared   206 kindly right-
ful   207 letter and credence letter of authorization   208 kneeling
before i.e., kneeling before and praying to an image of   209 yet in his
way still on his journey   210 thought vexation

same night he said unto a secret page of his: "Ah, whom shall a man trust? Those that I have brought up myself, those that I had weened would most surely serve me, even those fail me and at my commandment will do nothing for me." "Sir," quoth his page, "there lieth one on your pallet without[211] that, I dare well say, to do Your Grace pleasure the thing were right hard that he would refuse." Meaning this by[212] Sir James Tyrrel, which was a man of right goodly personage, and for nature's gifts worthy to have served a much better prince if he had well served God and by grace obtained as much truth and good will as he had strength and wit.

The man had an high heart[213] and sore longed upward,[214] not rising yet so fast as he had hoped, being hindered and kept under by the means of Sir Richard Ratcliffe and Sir William Catesby, which, longing for no more partners of the prince's favor and namely[215] not for him whose pride they wist would bear no peer,[216] kept him by secret drifts[217] out of all secret trust; which thing this page well had marked and known. Wherefore, this occasion offered, of very special friendship he took his time to put him forward[218] and by such wise do him good that all the enemies he had (except the devil) could never have done him so much hurt. For upon this page's words King Richard arose (for this communication had he sitting at the draft,[219] a convenient carpet for such a counsel) and came out into the pallet chamber,[220] on which he found in bed Sir James and Sir Thomas Tyrrel,* of person like and brethren of blood but nothing of kin in conditions.[221]

Then said the King merrily to them: "What, sirs, be ye in bed so soon?" And calling up Sir James brake to him secretly his mind in this mischievous matter, in which he found him nothing strange.[222] Wherefore on the morrow he

---

211 there lieth ... without there is one of your followers lying outside the room on his straw bed **212 this by** by this **213 an high heart** an ambitious spirit **214 sore longed upward** longed greatly for promotion **215 namely** especially **216 bear no peer** tolerate no equal **217 drifts** devices, schemes **218 of very ... forward** out of special friendship (for Tyrrel) the page took the opportunity to put forward Tyrrel's name **219 draft** privy **220 pallet chamber** anteroom in which attendants slept on straw beds, keeping guard **221 conditions** personal qualities **222 nothing strange** not at all reluctant

sent him to Brackenbury with a letter by which he was commanded to deliver Sir James all the keys of the Tower for one night, to the end he might there accomplish the King's pleasure in such things as he had given him commandment. After which letter delivered and the keys received, Sir James appointed the night next ensuing to destroy them,[223] devising before and preparing the means. The Prince, as soon as the Protector left that name and took himself as King, had it showed unto him that he should not reign but his uncle should have the crown. At which word the Prince, sore abashed, began to sigh, and said, "Alas, I would my uncle would let me have my life yet, though I leese my kingdom."

Then he that told him the tale[224] used him with good words and put him in the best comfort he could. But forthwith was the Prince and his brother both shut up and all other removed from them, only one (called Black Will or William Slaughter) excepted, set to serve them and see them sure.[225] After which time the Prince never tied his points[226] nor aught raught of[227] himself; but, with that young babe his brother, lingered with thought[228] and heaviness until this traitorous death delivered them of that wretchedness. For Sir James Tyrrel devised that they should be murdered in their beds, to the execution whereof he appointed Miles Forrest, one of the four that kept[229] them, a fellow fleshed in murder before time.[230] To him he joined one John Dighton, his own horsekeeper, a big, broad, square, and strong knave.

Then, all the other being removed from them, this Miles Forrest and John Dighton, about midnight, the silly[231] children lying in their beds, came into the chamber and, suddenly lapping them up among the clothes,[232] so to-bewrapped them[233] and entangled them, keeping down by force the featherbed and pillows hard unto their mouths, that, within

223 them i.e., the two young princes   224 the tale i.e., the news that Richard had assumed the kingship   225 see them sure make sure they didn't escape   226 points laces for fastening clothing. (The Prince neglected his appearance.)   227 aught raught of took any care of 228 thought grief   229 kept guarded   230 fleshed . . . time initiated into murder already   231 silly innocent   232 clothes bedclothes 233 to-bewrapped them wrapped them entirely

a while, smothered and stifled, their breath failing, they gave up to God their innocent souls into the joys of heaven, leaving to the tormentors[234] their bodies dead in the bed. Which after that the wretches perceived, first by the struggling with the pains of death and after long lying still, to be thoroughly dead, they laid their bodies naked out upon the bed and fetched Sir James to see them; which, upon the sight of them caused those murderers to bury them at the stair foot, meetly[235] deep in the ground under a great heap of stones.

Then rode Sir James in great haste to King Richard and showed him all the manner of the murder; who gave him great thanks and (as some say) there made him knight. But he allowed not[236] (as I have heard) the burying in so vile a corner, saying that he would have them buried in a better place because they were a king's sons. Lo, the honorable courage[237] of a king! Whereupon they say that a priest of Sir Robert Brackenbury's took up the bodies again and secretly interred them in such place as, by the occasion of his death which only knew it, could never since come to light. Very truth is it, and well known, that at such time as Sir James Tyrrel was in the Tower, for treason committed against the most famous prince King Henry the Seventh, both Dighton and he were examined and confessed the murder in manner above written; but whither the bodies were removed they could nothing tell.

[Richard never has a quiet moment, haunted by his nephews' murder, suspecting enemies everywhere. He is troubled by fearful dreams. And indeed the Duke of Buckingham conspires against him, having been disappointed of his hopes of receiving the Earl of Hereford's lands and now repenting his part in Richard's evil schemes.

The Bishop of Ely, John Morton, goes to join the Earl of Richmond in Flanders. The Countess of Richmond, the Earl's mother, and Queen Elizabeth, widow of Edward IV, are urged to endorse a plan to unite the houses of Lancaster and York by marrying the young Earl to Elizabeth's daughter (also named Elizabeth). The Countess com-

---

234 tormentors executioners   **235 meetly** suitably   **236 allowed not** did not approve   **237 courage** spirit. (Said ironically.)

missions Sir Christopher Urswick, a priest, to go to the
Earl of Richmond (now in Brittany) with this same pro-
posal. Richmond, thus fortified by alliance, prepares for
war against Richard. Forces loyal to him gather strength in
England. Richard meanwhile marches against Buckingham, who is taken and beheaded on All Souls' Day, 1483.
Richmond sails in October, landing in Dorset, but returns
to Brittany. Richard is troubled by a prophecy that he will
not live long once he has seen Rougemont (punning on Richmond), and by Lord Stanley's presumed loyalty to Richmond since his wife is Richmond's mother. Richard takes
vengeance on the deviser of a rhyme: "The Cat, the Rat, and
Lovell our dog / Rule all England under an hog." Richard
makes an attempt to be reconciled to Queen Elizabeth so
that he may marry her daughter (his niece) if his present
queen, Anne, were to die. Queen Elizabeth accedes to his
messengers' persuasions and urges her son the Marquess
to leave Richmond—such is "the inconstancy of this
woman." Richard spreads a rumor that Anne his queen is
dead, and she does in fact die in 1485.

Richmond returns to England again in August 1485 from
Harfleur, landing at Milford Haven in Wales and marching
toward Shrewsbury. Richard takes Lord Stanley's son
George into custody as a pledge of his father's loyalty. The
climactic battle takes place at Bosworth Field. The night before the battle is a terrifying one for Richard.]

The fame[238] went that he had the same night a dreadful and
terrible dream, for it seemed to him, being asleep, that he did
see divers images like terrible devils which pulled and
haled[239] him, not suffering him to take any quiet or rest. The
which strange vision not so suddenly strake[240] his heart with
a sudden fear but it stuffed his head and troubled his mind
with many busy and dreadful imaginations. For incontinent[241] after, his heart being almost damped, he prognosticated before the doubtful chance[242] of the battle to come, not
using the alacrity and mirth of mind and countenance as he

---

238 fame rumor   **239 haled** tugged   **240 strake** struck   **241 incontinent**
immediately   **242 prognosticated . . . chance** predicted the uncertain
outcome

was accustomed to do before he came toward the battle. And lest that it might be suspected that he was abashed for fear of his enemies, and for that cause looked so piteously, he recited and declared to his familiar friends in the morning his wonderful vision and fearful dream.

But I think this was no dream but a punction[243] and prick of his sinful conscience; for the conscience is so much more charged and aggrieved as the offense is greater and more heinous in degree.

[Richard, on the day of battle itself, orders the disposition of his troops. His army is more than twice the size of Richmond's. In his oration to his troops, Richard confesses his wickedness in obtaining the throne but stresses his penitence therefor. The enemy, he says, are "a company of traitors, thieves, outlaws, and runagates"[244] who will "destroy us, our wives, and children," and who are led by a "Welsh milksop." Richard's followers profess to be encouraged, but in fact their loyalty is only superficial. The Earl of Richmond, meanwhile, comforts his men with his graciousness and courage. His yellow hair is "like the burnished gold," his eyes, "gray, shining, and quick," his answers to questions ready and prompt. He bids his men to fight in God's cause against soldiers who obey only out of fear.

The climax of the battle itself centers on the fight between the two leaders.]

While the two forewards[245] thus mortally fought, each intending to vanquish and convince[246] the other, King Richard was admonished by his explorators and espials[247] that the Earl of Richmond, accompanied with a small number of men-of-arms, was not far off. And as he approached and marched toward him, he perfectly knew his personage by certain demonstrations and tokens which he had learned and known of others that were able to give him full information. Now, being inflamed with ire and vexed with outrageous malice, he put his spurs to his horse and rode out

---

243 punction puncturing **244 runagates** fugitives **245 forewards** vanguards **246 convince** overthrow **247 admonished . . . espials** warned by his scouts

of the side of the range of his battle,[248] leaving the vanguard fighting, and like a hungry lion ran with spear in rest[249] toward him. The Earl of Richmond perceived well the King furiously coming toward him, and because the whole hope of his wealth and purpose was to be determined by battle, he gladly proffered to encounter with him body to body and man to man.

King Richard set on so sharply at the first brunt[250] that he overthrew the Earl's standard and slew Sir William Brandon, his standard-bearer (which was father to Sir Charles Brandon, by King Henry the Eighth created Duke of Suffolk), and matched hand to hand with Sir John Cheyney, a man of great force and strength, which would have resisted him, but the said John was by him manfully overthrown. And so, he making open passage by dint of sword as he went forward, the Earl of Richmond withstood his violence and kept him at the sword's point, without advantage, longer than his companions either thought or judged;[251] which,[252] being almost in despair of victory, were suddenly recomforted by Sir William Stanley, which came to his succors with three thousand tall[253] men. At which very instant, King Richard's men were driven back and fled, and he himself, manfully fighting in the middle of his enemies, was slain; and, as he worthily had deserved, came to a bloody death as he had led a bloody life.

[The casualties in the battle include John, Duke of Norfolk, who had been warned from taking Richard's side in the battle by this rhyme written upon his gate: "Jack of Norfolk, be not too bold, / For Diccon thy master is bought and sold." Also dead are Walter, Lord Ferrers of Chartley, Sir Richard Ratcliffe, and Robert Brackenbury. Sir William Catesby is beheaded afterward. The story goes about that Richard might have escaped the battle, being provided with a swift horse, as the battle started to turn against him, but that he chose instead to stake everything on his chance of success.

Richmond gives thanks to God for a great victory and is

---

248 battle battalion   **249 with spear in rest** with his spear's base resting in its support, in the attack position   **250 brunt** attack   **251 judged** i.e., judged possible   **252 which** who, i.e., Richmond's troops   **253 tall** valiant

crowned by Lord Stanley with the crown that is found "amongst the spoil in the field." On January 18, 1486, Richmond, now King Henry VII, marries Elizabeth of York.]

———————

The second edition of Raphael Holinshed's *Chronicles* was published in 1587. This selection is based on that edition, Volume 3, folios 712–760.

In the following, the departures from the original text appear in boldface; the original readings are in roman.

p. 173 *Nesfield's Nathfields   **p. 176 *and that** that   ***Protector** protector, that
p. 177 *of old of his old   **p. 178 *Tyrrel** Tirrels

Further Reading

Brooke, Nicholas. *"Richard III." Shakespeare's Early Tragedies.* London: Methuen, 1968. Brooke argues that Shakespeare explores the contradiction between Richard's tragic assertion of his individual will and history's providential pattern. For Brooke, Richard becomes a character of some sympathy: less a monster than an emblem, however distorted, of human limitation and desire.

Campbell, Lily B. "The Tragical Doings of King Richard III." *Shakespeare's "Histories": Mirrors of Elizabethan Policy.* San Marino, Calif.: Huntington Library, 1947. Campbell argues that *Richard III* blurs conventional distinctions between tragedy and the history play, emphasizing both Richard's moral sins and his "offenses against the common weal." Richard III was used in Elizabethan political controversy as "the archetype of Machiavellianism, his activities being made the pattern by which to interpret the doings of political aspirants," and this becomes for Campbell the key to the play's meaning.

Clemen, Wolfgang. *A Commentary on Shakespeare's "Richard III,"* trans., Jean Bonheim. London: Methuen, 1968. Clemen provides a detailed scene-by-scene commentary on *Richard III*, integrating studies of style, character, conventions, staging, and influence in explicating the play.

Heilman, Robert B. "Satiety and Conscience: Aspects of *Richard III.*" *Antioch Review* 24 (1964): 57–73. Rpt. in *Essays in Shakespearean Criticism*, ed. James L. Calderwood and Harold E. Toliver. Englewood Cliffs, N.J.: Prentice-Hall, 1970. Richard, according to Heilman, is an individual suffering from "a distemper of success," a "singular malaise of the summit." Richard is quickly sated with his successes, a satiety that "begets contempt" for his victims. While Shakespeare in his portrayal of Richard falls short of the complex psychological realism of the later tragedies, he nonetheless succeeds in "giving a new hue to melodrama."

Hunter, Robert Grams. *"Richard III." Shakespeare and the Mystery of God's Judgments.* Athens, Ga.: Univ. of Georgia

Press, 1976. In *Richard III* Hunter finds Shakespeare first exploring "the tragic implications of a belief in providence." Is Richard's evil the result of divine permission? Is Richard, like Richmond, God's agent? Is there for Richard the possibility of attaining grace? Shakespeare does not attempt to resolve the theological issues he raises; indeed, Hunter argues, the play's power derives from the sustained mystery of God's judgment.

Jones, Emrys. "*Richard III*: A Tudor Climax." *The Origins of Shakespeare*. Oxford: Oxford Univ. Press, 1977. Jones explores Shakespeare's "inventiveness" in absorbing and combining classical, historical, and native literary models. The play, which begins as a conventional tragedy of fortune, gives way to an ending that prefigures and celebrates Elizabeth's reign, as Shakespeare "creates an occasion for national thanksgiving and communal prayer."

Krieger, Murray. "The Dark Generations of *Richard III*." *The Play and Place of Criticism*. Baltimore: The Johns Hopkins Press, 1967. Krieger finds *Richard III* to be a world of "unrelieved ugliness." Richard is but "a fox among foxes," pretending to be a hypocrite as the others pretend to be decent. Richmond's triumph, however, transforms the world, purging it of the "spirit of usurpation and chaos" that Richard represents.

Miner, Madonne M. " 'Neither Mother, Wife, nor England's Queen.': The Roles of Women in *Richard III*." In *The Woman's Part: Feminist Criticism of Shakespeare*, ed. Carolyn Ruth Swift Lenz, Gayle Greene, and Carol Thomas Neely. Urbana, Ill.: Univ. of Illinois Press, 1980. Though the women's roles in *Richard III* have generally not been considered by critics, Miner finds the importance of women to be signaled by the play's frequent metaphors of birth and pregnancy. The women, she finds, are not allowed to play effective, autonomous roles but function as a "currency of exchange between men." Nonetheless, she sees that the play traces the women's understanding of their situation as they move from strife to solidarity.

Neill, Michael. "Shakespeare's Halle of Mirrors: Play, Politics, and Psychology in *Richard III*." *Shakespeare Studies* 8 (1975): 99–129. In the "ostentatious theatricality" of the play, Neill finds a political and psychological complexity that denies the neat providential design of Shakespeare's sources. England is seen as a "kingdom of mirror-plays and actor-shadows," and Richard's psyche as "at best a hall of mirrors, reflecting endlessly the insubstantial shadows of the lost self."

Ornstein, Robert. *"Richard III." A Kingdom for a Stage: The Achievement of Shakespeare's History Plays.* Cambridge: Harvard Univ. Press, 1972. Ornstein focuses on an audience's pleasure in Richard's confident plotting. Though the play finally balances Richard's consummate control in gaining the throne with his subsequent loss of nerve, it does not dramatize the providential victory of virtue over vice because the play is concerned with Richard's failure rather than Richmond's success.

Ribner, Irving. *The English History Play in the Age of Shakespeare,* 1957. Rev. ed., enl., New York: Barnes and Noble, 1965, pp. 112–119. Ribner finds in *Richard III*'s structural indebtedness to the morality play evidence of Shakespeare's insistence on the role of providence in history. England becomes itself a morality hero torn between the forces of good and evil, and it ultimately "wins salvation" as Richmond achieves the throne.

Rossiter, A. P. "Angel with Horns: The Unity of *Richard III.*" *Angel with Horns and Other Shakespeare Lectures,* ed. Graham Storey. London: Longmans, Green; New York: Theatre Arts Books, 1961. Denying that the play is an orthodox demonstration of providential history, Rossiter argues that Shakespeare adopted a dialectical method of presentation, emphasizing ambiguity, irony, and above all, paradox. The play, he finds, is not a "moral history" presenting the certainties of the Tudor myth but a "comic history" reveling in the ambivalence and contradictions of history as it is lived.

Saccio, Peter. "Richard III: The Last Plantagenet." *Shakespeare's English Kings: History, Chronicle, and Drama.* New York: Oxford Univ. Press, 1977. Saccio examines the largely self-serving Tudor accounts of Richard's personality and reign that served as Shakespeare's sources as well as the evidence of modern historical research to provide a fascinating account both of the King and of the process of writing history.

Sher, Antony. *Year of the King: An Actor's Diary and Sketch-*

book. London: Chatto and Windus, 1985. Sher, who played the title role in the acclaimed Royal Shakespeare Company's production of 1984, provides an engaging account of an actor's struggle to come to terms with the part of Richard. The diary also provides insight into the process of creative interchange between director, designers, and actors as the production took shape.

Spivack, Bernard. *Shakespeare and the Allegory of Evil*, pp. 386–407. New York: Columbia Univ. Press, 1958. Richard's character is, for Spivack, a hybrid of naturalistic and allegorical elements. When Richard invokes his similarity to "the formal Vice, Iniquity," he signals his relation to the popular villain of the morality drama and establishes the moral universe of the play.

Wheeler, Richard. "History, Character, and Conscience in *Richard III*." *Comparative Drama* 5 (1971–1972): 302–321. Wheeler argues that Shakespeare presents Richard both as a scourge of God serving a divine purpose and as a highly self-conscious actor "who imposes the conditions of the stage on the real world." The providential structure of the play becomes an effort to contain the terror and fascination of the self-assertive Richard within a historical model that Shakespeare "can no longer quite believe and not yet afford to abandon."

Memorable Lines

Now is the winter of our discontent
Made glorious summer by this sun of York.

(RICHARD   1.1.1–2)

Was ever woman in this humor wooed?
Was ever woman in this humor won?

(RICHARD   1.2.230–231)

          The world is grown so bad
That wrens make prey where eagles dare not perch.

(RICHARD   1.3.70–71)

And thus I clothe my naked villainy
With odd old ends stol'n forth of Holy Writ,
And seem a saint when most I play the devil.

(RICHARD   1.3.336–338)

So wise so young, they say, do never live long.

(RICHARD   3.1.79)

Short summers lightly have a forward spring.

(RICHARD   3.1.94)

If? Thou protector of this damnèd strumpet,
Talk'st thou to me of "ifs"? Thou art a traitor.
Off with his head! Now, by Saint Paul I swear,
I will not dine until I see the same.   (RICHARD   3.4.74–77)

          I am in
So far in blood that sin will pluck on sin.

(RICHARD   4.2.63–64)

I am not in the giving vein today.   (RICHARD   4.2.118)

So now prosperity begins to mellow
And drop into the rotten mouth of death.

(QUEEN MARGARET   4.4.1–2)

Harp not on that string.   (RICHARD   4.4.364)

Why, then All Souls' Day is my body's doomsday.
                              (BUCKINGHAM   5.1.12)

Wrong hath but wrong, and blame the due of blame.
                              (BUCKINGHAM   5.1.29)

True hope is swift and flies with swallow's wings;
Kings it makes gods and meaner creatures kings.
                              (RICHMOND   5.2.23–24)

The King's name is a tower of strength.   (RICHARD   5.3.12)

Tomorrow in the battle think on me,
And fall thy edgeless sword. Despair and die!
                    (GHOST OF CLARENCE   5.3.134–135)

O coward conscience, how dost thou afflict me!
                              (RICHARD   5.3.179)

A horse! A horse! My kingdom for a horse!   (RICHARD   5.4.7)

I have set my life upon a cast,
And I will stand the hazard of the die.   (RICHARD   5.4.9–10)

Contributors

DAVID BEVINGTON, Phyllis Fay Horton Professor of Humanities at the University of Chicago, is editor of *The Complete Works of Shakespeare* (Scott, Foresman, 1980) and of *Medieval Drama* (Houghton Mifflin, 1975). His latest critical study is *Action Is Eloquence: Shakespeare's Language of Gesture* (Harvard University Press, 1984).

DAVID SCOTT KASTAN, Professor of English and Comparative Literature at Columbia University, is the author of *Shakespeare and the Shapes of Time* (University Press of New England, 1982).

JAMES HAMMERSMITH, Associate Professor of English at Auburn University, has published essays on various facets of Renaissance drama, including literary criticism, textual criticism, and printing history.

ROBERT KEAN TURNER, Professor of English at the University of Wisconsin–Milwaukee, is a general editor of the New Variorum Shakespeare (Modern Language Association of America) and a contributing editor to *The Dramatic Works in the Beaumont and Fletcher Canon* (Cambridge University Press, 1966–).

JAMES SHAPIRO, who coedited the bibliographies with David Scott Kastan, is Assistant Professor of English at Columbia University.

❖

JOSEPH PAPP, one of the most important forces in theater today, is the founder and producer of the New York Shakespeare Festival, America's largest and most prolific theatrical institution. Since 1954 Mr. Papp has produced or directed all but one of Shakespeare's plays—in Central Park, in schools, off and on Broadway, and at the Festival's permanent home, The Public Theater. He has also produced such award-winning plays and musical works as *Hair*, *A Chorus Line*, *Plenty*, and *The Mystery of Edwin Drood*, among many others.

Shakespeare
ALIVE!

☐ 27081-8 $4.50/$5.50 in Canada

From Joseph Papp, America's foremost theater producer, and writer Elizabeth Kirkland: a captivating tour through the world of William Shakespeare.

Discover the London of Shakespeare's time, a fascinating place to be—full of mayhem and magic, exploration and exploitation, courtiers and foreigners. Stroll through narrow, winding streets crowded with merchants and minstrels, hoist a pint in a rowdy alehouse, and hurry across the river to the open-air Globe Theatre to the latest play written by a young man named Will Shakespeare.

SHAKESPEARE ALIVE! spirits you back to the very heart of that London—as everyday people might have experienced it. Find out how young people fell in love, how workers and artists made ends meet, what people found funny and what they feared most. Go on location with an Elizabethan theater company, learn how plays were produced, where Shakespeare's plots came from and how he transformed them. Hear the music of Shakespeare's language and the words we still use today that were first spoken in his time.

Open this book and elbow your way into the Globe with the groundlings. You'll be joining one of the most democratic audiences the theater has ever known—alewives, apprentices, shoemakers and nobles—in applauding the dazzling wordplay and swordplay brought to you by William Shakespeare.

Look for **SHAKESPEARE ALIVE!** at your local bookstore or use the coupon below:

Bantam is proud to announce an important new
edition of:

The Complete Works Of
William Shakespeare

Featuring:

*The complete texts with modern spelling and
punctuation

*Vivid, readable introductions by noted Shakespearean
  scholar David Bevington
*New forewords by Joseph Papp, renowned producer,
  director, and founder of the New York Shakespeare
  Festival
*Stunning, original cover art by Mark English, the
  most awarded illustrator in the history of the Society
  of Illustrators
*Photographs from some of the most celebrated
  performances by the New York Shakespeare Festival
*Complete source materials, notes, and annotated
  bibliographies based on the latest scholarships
*Stage histories for each play

ACCESSIBLE * AUTHORITATIVE * COMPLETE

SHAKESPEARE
The Complete works in 29 Volumes

Bantam Drama Classics

☐	21279	Sophocles: Complete Plays	$3.25
☐	21219	Euripides: Ten Plays	$3.50
☐	21261	Aristophanes: Complete Plays	$3.95
☐	21280	Henrik Ibsen: Four Great Plays	$2.95
☐	21118	Rostand: Cyrano De Bergerac	$1.75
☐	21211	Anton Chekhov: Five Major Plays	$2.95

Buy them at your local bookstore or use this handy coupon for ordering:

Bantam Books, Dept. CL5, 414 East Golf Road,
Des Plaines, IL 60016

Please send me the books I have checked above. I am enclosing
$_____ (Please add $1.50 to cover postage and handling.)
Send check or money order—no cash or C.O.D.s please.

Mr/Ms _____

Address _____

City/State _____ Zip _____

CL5—2/88

Please allow four to six weeks for delivery. This offer expires
8/88. Prices and availability subject to change without notice.

BANTAM
SHOP-AT-HOME
C·A·T·A·L·O·G

Special Offer
Buy a Bantam Book
for only 50¢.

Now you can have Bantam's catalog filled with hundreds of titles plus take advantage of our unique and exciting bonus book offer. A special offer which gives you the opportunity to purchase a Bantam book for only 50¢. Here's how!

By ordering any five books at the regular price per order, you can also choose any other single book listed (up to a $5.95 value) for just 50¢. Some restrictions do apply, but for further details why not send for Bantam's catalog of titles today!

Just send us your name and address and we will send you a catalog!

BANTAM BOOKS, INC.
P.O. Box 1006, South Holland, Ill. 60473

Mr./Mrs./Ms. _____
(please print)

Address _____

City _____ State _____ Zip _____
FC(A)—10/87

Please allow four to six weeks for delivery.